Hugo's Simplified System

Scottish Gaelic
in Three Months

Roibeard Ó Maolalaigh
with
Iain MacAonghuis (Consultant)

Hugo's Language Books
www.dk.com

A DORLING KINDERSLEY BOOK

www.dk.com

This new and enlarged edition published in Great Britain
in 1998 by Hugo's Language Books,
an imprint of Dorling Kindersley Limited,
9 Henrietta Street, London WC2E 8PS

Copyright 1998, 1999 © Dorling Kindersley Ltd
4 6 8 10 9 7 5 3

A CIP catalogue record is available from the British Library.

ISBN 0 85285 369 6

Scottish Gaelic in Three Months is also available in
a pack with two cassettes, ISBN 0 85285 370 X

Written by
Roibeard Ó Maolalaigh B.A., M.A., Ph.D.
Lecturer, Department of Celtic and
Director, Centre for Irish Studies
University of Edinburgh

with
Iain MacAonghuis M.A., Ph.D. (Consultant)
Honorary Fellow (formerly Senior Lecturer)
University of Edinburgh

Edited by
Jenny Yoboué

Set in 10/12pt Plantin by
Keyset Composition, Colchester
Printed and bound by LegoPrint, Italy

Contents

Abbreviations used in this book

adj	adjective	*irreg*	irregular
adv	adverb	*lit*	literally
attr	attributive	*m*	masculine
cjn	conjunction	*obj*	object
DEP	dependent	*p*	prepositional
f	feminine	*pl*	plural
fam	familiar	*pred*	predicate
INDEP	independent	*sing*	singular
IPA	International Phonetic	*subj*	subject
	Association	*vb*	verb

Preface

Scottish Gaelic in Three Months has been written both as a
self-tuition course for beginners and also for use within the
classroom. You may want to learn Gaelic because of a general
interest in Celtic or Scottish history and culture, or because it was
the everyday language of your ancestors before they emigrated –
perhaps to Nova Scotia, where, on Cape Breton Island, Gaelic
speakers may still be found. The cynical observer may wonder if
the exercise is worthwhile, when only one and a half per cent of
Scotland's population speak the language. However, Gaelic is far
from being dead; in some parts of the Highlands and Western Isles
it is the everyday language, and it represents an important part of
the United Kingdom's cultural 'mix'. There are Gaelic-learning
classes in almost every area of Scotland.

Roibeard Ó Maolalaigh organises Beginners' Gaelic Courses at the
University of Edinburgh, where he lectures in the Department of
Celtic and is Director of the Centre for Irish Studies. His
consultant Iain MacAonghuis is a native speaker of Scottish Gaelic
who was born and brought up in the Western Isles. He lectured for
many years at the School of Scottish Studies, University of
Edinburgh (where he is now an Honorary Fellow), and has written
and broadcast on a range of Gaelic subjects.

Each lesson in *Scottish Gaelic in Three Months* contains some
essential points of grammar explained and illustrated, exercises, a
list of new vocabulary (with a guide to pronunciation, in
International Phonetics notation), and an item of conversation.
Ideally, you should spend about an hour a day on the course,
although this is by no means a firm rule. Do as much as you feel
capable of doing at a particular time; it is much better to learn a
little at a time, and to learn that thoroughly, than to force yourself
beyond your daily capacity to absorb new material. Spend the first
ten minutes of a daily session revising what you learned the day
before.

When you have completed our course on modern, everyday Gaelic,
you should have a good understanding of this wonderful language.

Gaelic: an introductory note

Scottish Gaelic has a standard orthography but otherwise tolerates quite a wide diversity. Local pronunciation and inflection are perfectly acceptable though often with the qualification that the native speaker tends to regard the speech of his or her own area as the most pleasing. Syntactical variation is minimal among the dialects of the language with phonological variation showing the greatest divergence.

Learners sometimes find this flexibility confusing at the start but soon realise it is essentially no different from the acceptance, say, of American, Australian or West Indian varieties of English as having equal status in pronunciation, syntax and idiom.

Unlike Welsh, Gaelic has no official status in the United Kingdom. This situation reflects the history of the language first within Scotland and later in the United Kingdom. In particular throughout the last few centuries, when western European languages in general achieved their standard form, Gaelic has lacked the social institutions – centrally either a state-based or an independent educational system – which shape a register of the language common to all educated speakers. It is true that the Presbyterian churches and their associated schools made a signal contribution in this respect, but even that fell far short of what is normally provided by a system of secular education. Gaelic has had simply no place in the centres of political power since the high Middle Ages.

To understand all this, it is necessary to see the language in an historical perspective. Gaelic was brought to Scotland by colonists from Ireland towards the end of the Roman Empire in Britain. By 500 AD these Gaels had established their Kingdom of Dàl Riada, centred on what is now Argyll in south-west Scotland; in Gaelic, Arra (or Earra) Ghàidheal, 'the coastland of the Gael'. To Roman writers they were Scotti – Scotia at this time denoted Ireland – although these names cannot be traced with certainty to an origin in Gaelic itself. But from these Latin forms came the name Scotland. In Gaelic, however, the country is Alba, as in Irish Gaelic and Alban in Welsh.

By the eleventh century, Gaelic was at its highest point in Scotland and known to some degree virtually throughout the country. A Gaelic-speaking court, supported by the Columban church, gave patronage to makers of literature at the highest levels of society.

With the Anglicisation of the dynasty late in that century, what has been described as a shift to an English way of life was deliberately planned and, as far as possible, implemented. The court itself became English and Norman-French in speech and the northern English dialect (Inglis) was fostered as the official language. The loss of status that these changes entailed for Gaelic had a profound and permanent effect.

In the mid-twelfth century the Lordship of the Isles, founded in part on the Norse kingdom of the Western and Southern Isles, but drawing also on the traditions of a former, wider Gaelic territory, emerged as a quasi-independent state. Until the Lordship was destroyed by the central authorities of Scotland in the late fifteenth century, Gaelic culture and learning continued to flourish. In the same twelfth century a reorganised literary order, whose main centres were in Ireland, was codifying Gaelic to produce an elegant formal register of the language, which we call Classical Gaelic. It was common to the learned classes of Ireland and Scotland and taught to the children of the aristocracy. It lasted in Scotland until the eighteenth century.

We can see this in religious prose (Bishop John Carswell's translation of the Book of Common Order in 1567 was the first Gaelic printed book and the first in any Celtic language), culminating in the translation of the scriptures in various phases until 1801. These literary activities involve a remarkably skilful transition from classical to vernacular Gaelic writing. On that basis, but drawing also on colloquial speech, Gaelic prose-writers developed a formal standard register whose strength is most evident in expository writings. Only in the twentieth century, however, and particularly with the founding of the periodical *Gairm* (1952–), and with new opportunities afforded by radio for short-story and other creative writing, was Gaelic freed from the rigidities of its older conventions. Verse too displays similar modulations from classical to vernacular Gaelic, although a tradition of oral vernacular song-poetry predominates. The renaissance of poetry in the twentieth century draws, with a variety of personal combinations, upon these resources.

Modern Gaelic offers the learner a wide spectrum of styles, ranging from formal registers, still in some degree associated with the church, to rich vivid idiomatic speech. Gaelic as a living language is now largely confined to north-western and island communities. But Gaelic speakers of local dialects are still to be found here and there throughout the Highlands. There are, besides, sizeable communities in the cities, particularly in Glasgow. A number of organisations are active in promoting the language. The oldest is An Comann Gaidhealach, founded at the end of the nineteenth century. In the last few years, the Gaelic College in Skye (at Sabhal Mór Ostaig), Comunn na Gàidhlig (CNAG) and Comann Luchd Ionnsachaidh (CLI) have all been established with the purpose of reviving the fortunes of the language.

While it is true that the history of the language is largely one of resistance to ethnocidal policies that sought to exclude the Gaels from the world of post-Renaissance Europe, contemporary developments in education, radio and television, and in literature generally, aim to redress the balance. And it should be noted that some of the most interesting writers now active on the literary scene are not native speakers but learners of Gaelic.

Glossary of grammatical terms

Fronting
This occurs when a word is moved from its usual position in a sentence to nearer the beginning of the sentence, for special emphasis.

Helping (Epenthetic) vowels
A vowel inserted between two consonants in certain words (usually containing l, r or n, e.g.: **Alba** 'Scotland' is pronounced as if it were 'Alaba'.

Lenition
Lenition (softening) is a process whereby certain consonants at the beginning of words are made 'softer'. This is indicated in writing by adding an 'h' to the consonant. Lenition changes **beag** ('small') to **bheag**, pronounced 'veg'.

Slenderisation/palatalisation
A process which makes consonants at the end of words sound slender. A sound is made slender by adding a 'y' sound, as in English 'yes' to its pronunciation. A 'g' sound, for example, is slenderised by pronouncing it like the 'g' in 'argue'.

Pronunciation and Lenition

The pronunciation of Scottish Gaelic is somewhat different to English in certain respects; not all letters have an equivalent sound in English, and some consonants change their sound according to their position in the word. This being so, please bear in mind that some of the following guidelines may only be approximate. The vocabulary lists in each lesson show the pronunciation of every word in International Phonetics Association (IPA) notation; the fact that you might not have a 'standard English' accent renders our customary form of imitated pronunciation untrustworthy.

Naturally, if you wish to hear and acquire perfect pronunciation, you should use the two cassette recordings which we have produced as an optional 'extra' to this Course. These tapes will allow you to hear the Gaelic words and phrases as you follow them in the book.

Whether you use the recordings or not, you should nevertheless read through the following notes on Scottish Gaelic pronunciation. There is no need to learn the rules by heart at this point. They should be referred to at frequent intervals, and soon you will become familiar with them. The same applies to the paragraphs dealing with lenition (a form of mutation, or change of consonant at the beginning of a word); this is a feature of the language which you cannot ignore but shouldn't get stuck on. In the meantime, you can start at Lesson 1.

Stress

Unlike English, the stress in Scottish Gaelic always falls on the first syllable of a word. Compare the word for 'police(man)' in English and Gaelic, where capital letters indicate the main stress:

English:	po**LICE**	/pə lis/
Scottish Gaelic:	**POIL**ios	/pɔləs/

There are some exceptions however, which are stressed on the second syllable. This is generally indicated by means of a hyphen in written and printed Gaelic, e.g.: **an-sin, a-rithist, a-staigh**.

1

Spelling, Alphabet

Although Scottish Gaelic spelling may seem complicated at first sight, it is in fact more regular than English, so that you can generally tell from the written form of a word how it is to be pronounced once you have become familiar with the spelling system. There are eighteen letters in the Gaelic alphabet; the letters j, k, q, v, w, x, y, z are not used, except in some recent loan-words. Despite having a slightly smaller alphabet, Scottish Gaelic has far more individual sounds than English. These are represented by various combinations of the eighteen letters, as we will see below.

Vowels

Accents

In Gaelic there are both short and long vowels. Long vowels are indicated by means of accents. There are two accents used in Scottish Gaelic:

the acute (´), found only on the letters e and o
the grave (`), found on a, o, u, i, e

The difference in pronunciation between a, o, u, i, e and à, ò, ù, ì, è respectively is one of pure length. The difference on the other hand between è, ò and é, ó respectively is one of quality. The grave è sounds like the 'ai' in 'fair'; the acute é sounds like the 'ay' in 'say'. Compare the French 'è' and 'é'.

The acute accent is occasionally also used to differentiate between unclear and clear vowels, e.g.:

as (unclear)   ás (clear)

Note: there has been a recent move to abandon the use of acute accents in Gaelic and many people prefer to use only the grave accent. However, both accents will be used for the purposes of this Course.

Pronunciation of Vowels

Gaelic letter	IPA symbol	
a	/a/	like 'a' in 'hat'
à	/aː/	like 'a' in 'halve'
o	/o,ɔ,ɤ/	like 'o' in 'coat', like 'o' in 'cot' and like 'u' in 'cut'

ò	/ɔ:/	like 'au' in 'caught'
ó	/o:/	like 'o' in 'owe'; the lips are more rounded for ó than for ò
u	/u,ɯ/	like 'oo' in 'took'
ù	/u:/	like 'oo' in 'cool'
i	/i/	like 'ee' in 'deep'
ì	/i:/	like 'ea' in 'bean'
e	/e,ɛ/	like 'a' in 'gate' and 'e' in 'get'
è	/ɛ:/	like 'ai' in 'fair'
é	/e:/	like 'ay' in 'say'

When **i** is added to any of these vowels, there is usually no change in pronunciation. The vowels appearing in the following rows are pronounced similarly:

Vowel	*Add i*	*Other vowels* (in this case a change in pronunciation is indicated)
a	ai	ea
à	ài	
o	oi	eo
ò	òi	eò, eòi
ó	ói	
u	ui†	iu, iui
i		io
ì		ìo
e	ei	ea
è	èi	
é	éi	

†Note that **ui** may be pronounced /u/ or /ɯ/.

The following vowel sounds should also be noted:

eu	/ia,e:/	like 'ia' in 'Maria' and 'ay' in 'say'
ao	/ɯ:/	has no equivalent in English. It is similar to 'oo' in 'cool' but with unrounded lips
aoi	/ɤi/	has no equivalent in English; it is similar to 'oy' in 'boy' but with unrounded 'o'
ia(i)	/iə/	like 'ea' in 'ear'
ua(i)	/uə/	like 'oo' in 'poor'
ea	/ɛ,a/	like 'e' in 'get' and 'a' in 'hat'
io	/i,u/	like 'ee' in 'deep' and 'oo' in 'took'
ìo	/iə/	like 'ea' in 'ear'

Diphthongs

We have met the diphthongs **ia, ua, aoi, eu**. There are five others. These diphthongs are not represented by a combination of vowel sounds but must be inferred from the following consonant(s). Short (stressed) vowels preceding **ll, nn, m** and **bh, mh, dh, gh** are frequently modified and pronounced as diphthongs, as follows:

Gaelic spelling	IPA	
all, ann, am	/au/	like 'ow' in 'how'
oll, onn, om	/ou/	like 'o' in standard English 'no'
aill, ainn, aim, aibh, aimh	/ai/	like 'y' in 'my'
einn, eim	/ei/	like 'ay' in 'say'
oill, oinn, oim, aidh, aigh, oidh, oigh	/ɤi/	has no equivalent in English; it is similar to 'y' in 'my' but the first part of the diphthong is like the 'u' in 'cut'. It is somewhere between 'y' in 'my' and 'oy' in 'boy'
uill, uinn, uim	/ui, ɯi/	has no equivalent in English; it is similar to the previous diphthong, but the first part of the diphthong is like an unrounded form of 'oo' in 'cool'

The above rules only hold when the consonants **ll, nn, m** are not followed by vowels, in which case the vowels are pronounced as normal. Compare:

ann /auɲ/ **Anna** /aɲə/
donn /d̥ouɲ/ **donna** /d̥oɲə/

Helping (Epenthetic) Vowels

A vowel is inserted between two consonants in certain words (usually containing **l, r** or **n**). This vowel is called a helping or epenthetic vowel; it is present in sound only, and is usually an exact copy of the preceding stressed vowel. (Think of someone with a good Scots accent saying 'harm' or 'film'; the 'r' and the 'l' are rolled, and the vowel is virtually repeated – 'harram', 'fillim'.) Here are some examples – the square brackets show that an epenthetic syllable is pronounced differently to ordinary disyllables:

Alba /[ala]bə/ Scotland

marbh /m[ara]v/   dead
arm   /[ara]m/   army

The realisation of these 'helping' syllables varies a great deal in Gaelic dialects; don't worry too much about them at this stage.

Consonants

In Gaelic the consonants may be divided into two groups, the 'broad' consonants and the 'slender' consonants. For every broad consonant, there is a corresponding slender consonant; so we may speak of a broad and slender **k** or **g** or **d** and so on.

A consonant is broad if it is preceded or followed by any of the broad vowels **a, o, u**; it is slender if preceded or followed by any of the slender vowels **i, e**. Preceding or following **a, o, u** indicate that a consonant is broad; preceding or following **i, e** indicate that a consonant is slender. Since a consonant cannot be both broad and slender, vowels on both sides of a consonant must agree according to 'colour' (broad or slender). This is sometimes stated as a rule:

     caol ri caol is leathann ri leathann

i.e. *slender with slender and broad with broad*

Consider the following examples:

caileag, balla, gille, daoine, baga, pàipear, Seumas, Màiri, brògan.

As is the case with most rules, there are some exceptions, e.g.: **dèante, esan**, etc.

Broad Consonants

The pronunciation of the broad consonants is in most cases similar to their English counterparts. But some essential differences will be observed.

Gaelic letter	*IPA*	
b	/b, p/	like 'b' in 'bad' at the beginning of a word; otherwise it is pronounced like 'p' in 'cap'
p	/p/	like 'p' in 'pad'
g	/g, k/	like 'g' in 'good' at the beginning of a word; otherwise it is pronounced like 'k' in 'cook'

k	/k/	like 'c' in 'cat'
d	/d̪, t̪/	like 'd' in dog at the beginning of a word; otherwise it is pronounced like 't' in cat. Tongue touches upper teeth
t	/t̪/	like 't' in tap. Tongue touches upper teeth.
l, ll	/l̪/	like a hollow 'l' as in 'full' with the tongue touching the upper teeth
n	/n̪, n/	is pronounced in a similar fashion to the hollow 'l' described above when it appears initially; otherwise broad 'n' is pronounced as in English
nn	/n̪/	is pronounced in a similar fashion to the hollow 'l' described above
r	/ɾ, r/	has no equivalent in English but is similar to a rolled 'r'; this sound appears for 'r' initially; otherwise broad 'r' is pronounced like 'r' in 'read'
rr	/ɾ/	has no equivalent in English but is similar to a rolled 'r'
ng	/ŋ/	like 'ng' in 'kong'

Broad **f, h, m, s** are pronounced like their English counterparts.

Slender Consonants

Gaelic letter	*IPA*	
b	/bʲ, pʲ/	like 'b' in 'bee' or like 'b' in 'beauty' at the beginning of a word; otherwise it is pronounced like 'p' in 'loop'
p	/pʲ/	like 'p' in 'pea' or like 'p' in 'pew'
g	/gʲ, kʲ/	like 'g' in 'argue' at the beginning of a word; otherwise it is pronounced like 'c' in 'cue'
k	/kʲ/	like 'c' in 'cue'
d	/dʲ, tʲ/	like 'j' in 'judge' at the beginning of a word; otherwise it is pronounced like 'ch' in 'chew'
t	/tʲ/	like 'ch' in 'chew'
l	/ʎ, l/	like 'll' in 'million' when it appears initially; otherwise slender 'l' is pronounced like 'l' in 'silly'
ll	/ʎ/	like 'll' in 'million'
n	/ɲ, n/	like the first 'n' in 'onion' when it appears initially; otherwise slender 'n' is pronounced like n in 'neat' and in some instances like the first 'n' in 'onion'

nn	/ɲ/	like the first 'n' in 'onion'
r	/rʲ/	has no equivalent in English and varies considerably from dialect to dialect; it is in some dialects similar to 'r' in 'tree'
ng	/ŋʲ/	like 'ng' in 'king'
f	/fʲ/	like 'f' in 'few'
h	/h, ç/	like 'h' in 'happy' and 'h' in 'hue'
m	/m, mʲ/	is pronounced like 'm' in 'meal' or like 'm' in 'mule'
s	/ʃ/	is pronounced like 'sh' in 'shoe'

Recent loan-words with 't' or 'd' from English are pronounced as in English, e.g:

| tì | /tiː/ | tea |
| dola | /dɔlə/ | doll |

Preaspiration

'Preaspiration' means the placing of an h-like sound before certain consonants.

The voiceless consonants **t, c, p** following a stressed vowel are usually preaspirated in Gaelic. The preaspiration takes the form of voiceless breathing /h/ before each of the consonants. The preaspiration may be realised as a 'ch' especially before **c**. Preaspiration is not so noticeable in some dialects, particularly in some north-western dialects. Here are some examples:

Gaelic spelling	*IPA*	
cat	cat	/kaht̪/
cait	cats	/kahtʲ/
mac	son	/mahkʲ/, /maxk/
mic	sons	/mihkʲ/, /miçkʲ/
map	map	/mahp/

Rt, rd groups

Related to preaspiration is the insertion of 's' between **r** and a following **t** and **d** in stressed syllables, e.g:

| ceart | /kʲarsd̪/ | right |
| àrd | /aːrsd̪/ | high |

Not all dialects insert 's' in these groups.

Hiatus

When two adjacent vowels are not joined together as one vowel, we say that there is hiatus (a gap) between them. In many words **bh**, **mh**, **dh**, **gh** are mute when they appear between vowels. The preceding and following syllables are generally not coalesced (i.e. joined together); there is a gap between such syllables. This hiatus will be denoted by a hyphen (the symbol /-/) in the IPA transcription. Here are some examples:

laghach	/ɫɣ-əx/	kind
saoghal	/sɯː-əɫ/	world
cladhach	/kɫɣ-əx/	digging
abhainn	/ã-iɲ/	river

-th-, which is usually pronounced as /h/, is used only in a small number of words to indicate hiatus, e.g.:

latha	/ɫa-ə/	day
fhathast	/ha-əsd̪/	yet
rathad	/ɾa-əd̪/	road

More consonants

In English when we write 'h' after 't', 'd', 'c', 'g', 'p', 's', 'w', we form new sounds 'th', 'dh', 'ch', 'gh', 'ph', 'sh', 'wh'. The letter **h** is used far more frequently in this way in Scottish Gaelic than in English. It is important to note that when **h** is added to a consonant in Scottish Gaelic, the resulting consonant is *never* pronounced as in English. Once again we must distinguish between broad and slender. Here is a list of the consonants which may be written with **h** to form new sounds:

Broad before / after a, o, u

Gaelic letter	IPA	
ph	/f/	like 'f' in 'fish'
bh	/v/	like 'v' in 'very'
ch	/x/	like 'ch' in Scottish 'loch' and German 'ch' in 'Bach'
gh	/ɣ/	the voiced version of 'ch'; like 'r' in French 'rire'
th	/h/	like 'h' in 'hat'; it is never pronounced like 'th' in 'think'

dh	/ɣ/	like broad 'gh' (i.e. like 'r' in French 'rire')
mh	/v/	like broad 'bh' (i.e. like 'v' in 'very')
sh	/h/	like broad 'th' (i.e. like 'h' in 'hat')
fh	–	is not pronounced (except in **fhathast** 'yet', **fhuair** 'got' and **fhalbh** 'go', in which case it is pronounced as **h**).

Slender *before/ after* ⎿ , e

Gaelic *IPA*
letter

ph	/f, fʲ/	like 'f' in 'fast' and 'f' in 'few'
bh	/v, vʲ/	like 'v' in 'very' and 'v' in 'view'
ch	/ç/	like 'h' in 'hue' or 'ch' in German 'ich'
gh	/j/	like 'y' in 'yes'
th	/h, ç/	like broad **th** or slender· **ch**
dh	/j/	like slender **gh**
mh	/v, vʲ/	like slender **bh**
sh	/h, ç/	like broad **sh** or like slender **ch**
fh	–	is not pronounced except in **fhéin** 'self', in which case it is pronounced as **h**

Initial Mutations

A characteristic which is common to all Celtic languages, including Irish, Manx, Welsh, Cornish and Breton, is the change of certain consonants at the beginning of words. These changes, sometimes called mutations, appear according to grammatical context. In Scottish Gaelic, there are two initial mutations, **lenition** and **nasalisation**. Lenition is very important and will be dealt with presently. Nasalisation, which varies according to dialect, is perhaps not as important for learners as lenition and is discussed in Appendix 4.

Lenition

Lenition (softening) is a process whereby certain consonants which appear at the beginning of words are made 'softer'. This is indicated in writing by adding an **h** to the consonant. For example lenition changes **p** to an 'f' sound which is spelled **ph**. Lenition changes an initial **b** to **bh**, **g** to **gh**, **c** to **ch**, **d** to **dh**, **t** to **th**, **m** to **mh**, **s** to **sh**, **f** to **fh**. See above for the pronunciation of these lenitions.

The **h** form of a consonant, when it appears at the beginning of words, is referred to as the lenited form of the consonant. Those consonants which can 'add' **h** are called lenitable consonants; there are only nine of them. Lenition is usually but not always caused by a preceding word. Consider the following example:

a cat	her cat
a chat	his cat

You will see that the word for 'her' and 'his' is **a**, the only difference between them being that the word for 'his' lenites a following (lenitable) consonant whereas the word for 'her' does not. We say that **a** 'his' is a leniting word and that it lenites a following word. We will distinguish between leniting and non-leniting words by placing the symbol * after those words which cause lenition. Lenition is extremely common in Scottish Gaelic and we will meet many more leniting words and particles in the lessons below. Here are some more examples of the words for 'his' and 'her':

bàta	boat	**a bàta**	her boat	**a bhàta**	his boat
piuthar	sister	**a piuthar**	her sister	**a phiuthar**	his sister
geansaidh	jumper	**a geansaidh**	her jumper	**a gheansaidh**	his jumper
cù	dog	**a cù**	her dog	**a chù**	his dog
dealbh	picture	**a dealbh**	her picture	**a dhealbh**	his picture
taigh	house	**a taigh**	her house	**a thaigh**	his house
mac	son	**a mac**	her son	**a mhac**	his son
sùil	eye	**a sùil**	her eye	**a shùil**	his eye
falt	hair	**a falt**	her hair	**a fhalt**	his hair

Slenderisation/palatalisation

We have seen above that for most consonants, there is a broad and a slender (palatalised) form, each one representing a separate sound in the language. For any consonant, broad and slender forms frequently alternate at the end of words, e.g.: **cat** 'a cat' and **cait** 'cats'. We say that **cait** is the slenderised form of **cat**. A word is slenderised by inserting an 'i' before the last consonant or group of consonants. The i before a final consonant tells us that the letter is to be pronounced differently, i.e. as a slender consonant. The change of broad **t** to slender **t** is called slenderisation. It is important to note that slenderisation only occurs at the end of words. Slenderisation is used to form the plural form of some nouns. Here are some examples:

cat	cat	**cait**	cats
dùn	fort	**dùin**	forts
balach	boy	**balaich**	boys
boireannach	woman	**boireannaich**	women
òran	song	**òrain**	songs

Slenderisation of a final consonant can in some cases cause the preceding vowel to change form. A list of the common changes will be found in Appendix 1. Here are a few examples where the preceding vowel is affected by the process of slenderisation:

mac	son	**mic**	sons
fear	man	**fir**	men
cnoc	hill	**cnuic**	hills
bòrd	table	**bùird**	tables
fiadh	deer	**féidh**	deer (*plural*)

Slenderisation is extremely important in Scottish Gaelic and we will meet many further instances of it in the lessons which follow.

Lenition and slenderisation

Lenition and slenderisation can operate simultaneously on a word. When we address a person in Gaelic, the name is preceded by **a**, which lenites the initial consonant, e.g.:

NORMAL FORM	ADDRESS FORM	
Mórag	**a Mhórag**	Morag
Màiri	**a Mhàiri**	Mary
Catrìona	**a Chatrìona**	Catherine

However, when we address a male, the name is also slenderised, e.g.:

NORMAL FORM	ADDRESS FORM	
Seumas	**a Sheumais**	James
Domhnall	**a Dhomhnaill**	Donald
Tormod	**a Thormoid**	Norman

Note: the sequence **chd** is usually pronounced **chg** in Scottish Gaelic.

Lesson 1

1 Pronouns

mi	*nree*	I
thu	*h oo*	you
e	*long a*	he/it
i	*ee*	she/it
sinn	*sh/ee/nnn*	we
sibh	*sh/ee/v*	you (*pl*)
iad	*e/at*	they

In Gaelic there are two words used for 'you', **thu** and **sibh**. **Sibh** is used to refer to (a) 'you' plural and (b) 'you' in formal or polite contexts, usually when addressing one's elders or superiors. **Thu** is used otherwise, generally in familiar contexts.

2 The verb *'tha'* ('to be') — *ha*

In sentences like 'John is young', 'Ann is small', 'James is tired' we use the verb **tha**. In Gaelic the order of words in such sentences is the same as English except that the verb comes first in the sentence. Consider the following examples:

Tha Iain òg.	John is young. *aw/K*
Tha Anna beag.	Ann is small. *by/e/k*
Tha Seumas sgìth.	James is tired. *st/gee/ch*
Tha Màiri toilichte.	Mary is happy. *t/u/lee/khg/ch/*
Tha Domhnall an-seo.	Donald is here. *an sho*
Tha Uilleam an-sin.	William is there. *an shin*
Tha Raghnall an-siud.	Ronald is yonder. *an shï/ut*
Tha Iain math.	John is good. *m a*
Tha Anna gu math.	Ann is well. *ga ma*
Tha mi sgìth.	I am tired.	
Tha thu làidir.	You are strong. *llaachee r*
Tha e fuar.	He/it is cold.	
Tha sinn blàth.	We are warm. *bl aah*
Tha sibh fliuch.	You are wet. *fl oo h*
Tha iad an-seo.	They are here.	

12 (* when a hyphen stress 2nd syllable)

3 Indefinite nouns

There is no indefinite article in Gaelic. **Cat** (*sing*) may be translated as 'cat' or 'a cat'. Likewise **cait** (*pl*) means 'cats' or 'some cats'.

cù	/ku:/	(a) dog
càr	/ka:r/	(a) car
deoch	/dʲɔx/	(a) drink
balach	/baɫəx/	(a) boy
caileag	/kalag/	(a) girl
rùm	/ɾu:m/	(a) room
taigh	/ʈɤj/	(a) house
airgead	/[ɛrʲɛ]gʲəd̪/	money

3a 'There is/are'

A noun not preceded by the definite article is referred to as an indefinite noun. When the subject of **tha** is an indefinite noun, we can translate 'there is' or 'there are':

Tha cat an-seo.	There is a cat here.
	(*lit* 'a cat is here')
Tha craobh an-sin.	There is a tree there.
	(*lit* 'a tree is there')
Tha caistealan an Glaschu.	There are castles in Glasgow.
	(*lit* 'castles are in Glasgow')

4 'To have'

Gaelic has no verb 'to have'. Instead a periphrastic (or 'long') construction involving the verb **tha** and the preposition **aig** 'at' is used. 'John has a cat' becomes:

Tha cat aig Iain	(*lit* 'a cat is at John')

Similarly:

Tha cù aig Màiri.	Mary has a dog.
Tha leabhar aig Anna.	Ann has a book.
Tha taigh aig Seumas.	James has a house.
Tha airgead aig Iain.	John has money.

14

4a Prepositional pronouns

Prepositions normally combine with pronouns to give prepositional pronouns, e.g.:

aig	+	mi	=	agam	at me
aig	+	thu	=	agad	at you
aig	+	e	=	aige	at him
aig	+	i	=	aice	at her
aig	+	sinn	=	againn	at us
aig	+	sibh	=	agaibh	at you
aig	+	iad	=	aca	at them

Tha càr agam. (NOT aig mi)   I have a car.
Tha leabhar agad.   You have a book.
Tha taigh aige.   He has a house.
Tha airgead aca.   They have money.

Exercise 1

Translate

1 Mary is happy.
2 John is strong.
3 I am warm.
4 They are cold.
5 We are here.
6 Ann has a book.
7 James has a car.
8 I have a drink.
9 We have a house.
10 She has a boy.

4b 'To know'

A periphrastic construction involving the verb **tha**, the noun **fios** 'knowledge' and the preposition **aig** 'at' is used to translate 'know' in Gaelic as follows:

tha f(h)ios aig Iain   John knows
tha f(h)ios agam   I know

This is generally used for 'know' in the sense of knowing facts as opposed to knowing a person. We will learn a different idiom for 'knowing people' in Lesson 4.

5 Negative and interrogative forms of 'tha'

To negate **tha**, simply replace **tha** with **chan eil**:

Chan eil Iain mór.	John is not big.
Chan eil Anna toilichte.	Ann is not happy.
Chan eil mi sgìth.	I am not tired.
Chan eil iad an-seo.	They are not here.
Chan eil cat aig Màiri.	Mary doesn't have a cat/ has no cat.
Chan eil deoch aig Domhnall.	Donald doesn't have a drink/ has no drink.
Chan eil airgead agam.	I don't have (any) money/ I have no money.

To form the interrogative (positive), replace **tha** with **am bheil**:

Am bheil Seumas sgìth?	Is James tired?
Am bheil Màiri fuar?	Is Mary cold?
Am bheil Iain an-seo?	Is John here?
Am bheil cat aig Anna?	Does Ann have a cat?
Am bheil airgead agad?	Do you have (any) money?

To form the interrogative (negative), replace **tha** with **nach eil**:

Nach eil Anna toilichte?	Isn't Ann happy?
Nach eil iad math?	Aren't they good?
Nach eil cù aig Domhnall?	Doesn't Donald have a dog?
Nach eil taigh aice?	Doesn't she have a house?

6 Answering questions

There is no single word for 'yes' or 'no' in Scottish Gaelic. A question is always answered by repeating or echoing the main verb of the question. There is no need to repeat the subject of the sentence. Consider the following examples:

Am bheil thu gu math?	Are you well?
Tha.	Yes.
Chan eil.	No.
Nach eil i an-sin?	Is she not there?
Tha.	Yes.
Chan eil.	No.

Where are you from?

Study the following phrases:

Có ás a tha thu?	Where are you from?
tha á Glaschu	from Glasgow
tha á Dùn Éideann	from Edinburgh
tha á Alba	from Scotland
tha á Éirinn	from Ireland
tha á Sasainn	from England

7 'I only have'

Consider the following examples:

Chan eil not agam.	I haven't got a pound.
Chan eil agam ach not.	I only have a pound.
Chan eil sgilling aig Seumas.	James hasn't got a penny.
Chan eil aig Seumas ach sgilling.	James only has a penny.

Ach normally means 'but'. **Chan eil aig Seumas ach sgilling** translates literally as 'James hasn't but a penny'.

Exercise 2

Translate

1 Ann is not tired.
2 James is not there.
3 Mary doesn't have a dog.
4 We have no money.
5 Is John cold?
6 Does Donald have a drink?
7 Do they have any money?
8 I only have a penny.
9 Isn't Donald happy?
10 Doesn't he have a car?

8 Adverbs

Adverbs are frequently formed by placing **gu** before adjectives:

math	good	**gu math**	well
dona	bad	**gu dona**	badly
snog	nice	**gu snog**	nicely

Other adverbs with **gu** are:
gu dòigheil   fine
gu luath   quickly
Watch out for more examples which follow.

8a 'How are you?'

Study the following phrases:

Ciamar a tha thu?	How are you?
tha gu math	well
tha gu dòigheil	fine
chan eil gu dona	not bad
chan eil gu math	not well
chan eil ach meadhanach	only middling, so-so
tha thu fhéin gu math?	are you well yourself?
	(*lit* 'you are well yourself?')

Vocabulary

cuideachd	/kudʲəxg/	also
brèagha	/brʲia-ə/	lovely
fios	/fis/	knowledge
Am bheil fios agad?	/ə vel fis agəd̪/	Do you know?
gu dearbh	/gə dʲ[ɛrɛ]v/	indeed
nis	/niʃ/	now
ach	/ax/	but
no	/nɔ/	or
rùm	/ʁu:m/	room
idir	/idʲərʲ/	at all
uile	/ulə/	all
an-diugh	/əɲ dʲu/	today
slàinte mhath	/sl̪a:ɲdʲə vã/	good health

COMHRADH (CONVERSATION)

Iain   Am bheil taigh aig Seumas an-seo?
Anna   Tha, tha taigh aig Seumas an-siud. Tha taigh aig Domhnall cuideachd agus tha e brèagha.
Iain   Am bheil cù agus cat aca, am bheil fios agad?
Anna   Chan eil, chan eil cù no cat aca.
Iain   Gu dearbh! Nis, am bheil càr agad?
Anna   Tha, tha càr agam ach chan eil e mór idir.

Iain	Agus am bheil taigh agad?
Anna	Chan eil, chan eil taigh agam. Chan eil airgead agam. Agus chan eil taigh aig Uilleam no aig Màiri. Tha caileag agus balach aca.
Iain	Am bheil Raghnall an-seo?
Anna	Tha, tha Raghnall an-seo. Tha rùm aige. Tha e toilichte an-seo. Tha leabhar aige agus tha e math.
Iain	Am bheil sibh uile toilichte an-seo?
Anna	Chan eil, chan eil sinn uile toilichte idir. Tha e fuar agus fliuch an-diugh agus tha sinn sgìth.
Iain	Am bheil deoch agad?
Anna	Tha, tha deoch agam an-seo – blàth agus làidir. Slàinte mhath!

TRANSLATION

John	Does James have a house here?
Ann	Yes, James has a house over there. Donald has a house also and it's lovely.
John	Do they have a dog and a cat, do you know?
Ann	No, they don't have a dog or a cat.
John	Indeed! Now, do you have a car?
Ann	I have a car but it's not big at all.
John	And do you have a house?
Ann	I have no house. I have no money. And neither William nor Mary have a house. They have a girl and a boy.
John	Is Ronald here?
Ann	Ronald is here. He has a room. He is happy here. He has a book and it's good.
John	Are you all happy here?
Ann	We aren't all happy here at all. It's cold and wet today and we are tired.
John	Do you have a drink?
Ann	I have a drink here – warm and strong. Good health!

Lesson 2

9 Emphatic pronouns

mise	I
t(h)usa	you
esan	he
ise	she
sinne	we
sibhse	you
iadsan	them

Gaelic normally uses emphatic suffixes (rather than tone or stress) for emphatic and contrastive purposes.

Tha Iain beag ach tha mise mór.	John is small but *I'm* big.
Tha Anna sgìth ach chan eil mise.	Ann is tired but *I'm* not.
Ciamar a tha thu?	How are you?
Ciamar a tha thusa?	How are *you*?

9a 'Who are you?'

To ask who someone is, we use **có** 'who?' with either the emphatic or unemphatic form of the pronouns as follows:

Có thusa?	OR Có thu?	Who are you?
Có ise?	Có i?	Who is she?
Có esan?	Có e?	Who is he?
Có sibhse?	Có sibh?	Who are you? (*formal, polite* and *plural*)
Có iadsan?	Có iad?	Who are they?

10 The verb '*is*' ('to be')

There are two verbs 'to be' in Gaelic, **tha** and **is**. We met **tha** in Lesson 1. In sentences like 'I am John', 'you are Ann', 'he is James', we use the verb **is**. As with **tha**, **is** comes first in the sentence. You will note from the following examples that the emphatic forms of the pronouns are usually used with **is**:

Is mise Iain.	I am John.
Is tusa Anna.	You are Ann.

19

Is esan Seumas.	He is James.
Is ise Peigi.	She is Peggy.
Is sinne an clas Gàidhlig.	We are the Gaelic class.
Is sibhse an tidsear.	You are the teacher.
Is iadsan Màiri agus Calum.	They are Mary and Calum.

Note: **tusa** rather than **thusa** is used with **is**.

10a A note on the difference between '*tha*' and '*is*'

In sentences like 'John is young' and 'she is Ann' we refer to 'young' and 'Ann' as being predicates (i.e. that which is being said about the subject of the sentence) of the verb 'to be'. A useful rule on the use of **tha** and **is** is as follows:

> when the predicate is a noun, use **is**
> when the predicate is anything else (e.g. adjective, adverb, etc), use **tha**

Note: this is one of the most important rules of Gaelic grammar and is important to remember.

Another minor difference between the verbs **tha** and **is** is that **is** is unstressed and is usually pronounced as **s**.

10b Negative and interrogative forms of '*is*'

To negate **is** replace **is** with **cha** or **chan** as follows:

Cha mhise Iain.	I am not John.
Cha tusa Anna.	You aren't Ann.
Chan esan Seumas.	He isn't James.
Chan ise Peigi.	She isn't Peggy.
Cha sinne an clas Gàidhlig.	We aren't the Gaelic class.
Cha sibhse an tidsear.	You aren't the teacher.
Chan iadsan Màiri agus Calum.	They aren't Mary and Calum.

You will note that **cha** becomes **chan** before a following vowel (i.e. before **esan, ise, iadsan**) and that **cha** lenites **mise**.

To form the interrogative (positive) replace **is** with **an** (**am** before **mise**):

Am mise Iain?	Am I John?
An tusa Anna?	Are you Ann?
An esan Seumas?	Is he James?
An ise Peigi?	Is she Peggy?

An sinne an clas Gàidhlig?	Are we the Gaelic class?
An sibhse an tidsear?	Are you the teacher?
An iadsan Màiri agus Calum?	Are they Mary and Calum?

To form the interrogative (negative) replace **is** with **nach**:

Nach mise Iain?	Am I not John?
Nach tusa Anna?	Aren't you Ann?
Nach esan Seumas?	Isn't he James?

To answer any of the above **is** questions, the answer must always include either the positive or the negative form of **is** and also the appropriate unemphatic pronoun:

POSITIVE	NEGATIVE
is mi	**cha mhi**
is tu	**cha tu**
se (<**is** + **e**)	**chan e**
si (<**is** + **i**)	**chan i**
is sinn	**cha sinn**
is sibh	**cha sibh**
siad (<**is** + **iad**)	**chan iad**

Some examples:

An tusa Iain? Is mi.	Are you John? Yes.
An ise Anna? Si.	Is she Ann? Yes.
An sibhse Màiri agus Peigi?	Are you Mary and Peggy?
Cha sinn.	No.
An iadsan an clas Gàidhlig?	Are they the Gaelic class?
Chan iad.	No.

Exercise 1

Translate

1 I am Ann.
2 He is Calum.
3 She is Peggy.
4 You aren't James.
5 They aren't the Gaelic class.
6 She isn't Mary.
7 Aren't you Donald? No.
8 Are you John? Yes.
9 They are Peggy and Mary.
10 You are the teacher.

11 Gender

Scottish Gaelic has two genders – feminine and masculine. Nouns
are either feminine or masculine. The gender of a noun must be
learnt by heart as there is no easy way of telling a word's gender. A
good example of this is the word **boireannach** 'woman' which is
grammatically a masculine noun. The main difference between
masculine and feminine nouns is that (a) feminine nouns are
generally lenited after the definite article (nominative) and (b)
adjectives following feminine nouns are generally lenited, e.g.:

MASCULINE   FEMININE

an gille beag   the little boy   **a' chaileag bheag**   the little girl

Here are some useful phrases which illustrate the difference
between masculine and feminine nouns:

madainn mhath	good morning
feasgar math	good evening
oidhche mhath	good night

12 The pronouns *'fear'* and *'té'*

The words **fear** (*m*) and **té** (*f*) which normally mean 'man' and
'woman', respectively, can act as pronouns meaning 'one'. **Fear**
meaning 'one' is used when referring to masculine nouns; **té** is
used when referring to feminine nouns:

leabhar (*m*)	book	**fear mór**	a big one
deoch (*f*)	drink	**té bheag**	a small one

13 Case in Gaelic

There are three cases in Gaelic: nominative, prepositional and
genitive. The nominative is the dictionary form of a word (article,
noun, adjective) and corresponds to the traditional cases of
nominative (subjects) and accusative (objects). The prepositional
corresponds partly to the traditional dative case and is used only
after prepositions. The prepositional and genitive will be discussed
in Lessons 6 and 7.

14 Definite article ('the')

The definite article always precedes the noun it qualifies and agrees
in gender, number and case with it. We can distinguish between

four main forms of the article in Gaelic: **an, an***, **na, nan**. As we will see, each capital form stands for a distinct set of forms (usually 2 or 3) of the article. We will deal only with the first two forms here.

NOMINATIVE FORMS

The article has two nominative forms: **an**, which is used before masculine nouns, and **an***, which is used before feminine nouns. The spelling of each form of the article changes slightly according to the initial sound of the following word. These changes are helpful as they reflect the pronunciation in each case.

(i) Masculine article *an*

The masculine article **an** is spelt:

am	before all labial sounds, i.e. **b f m p**
an t-	before all vowels
an	otherwise

am fear	the man	**an t-uisge**	the water	**an tidsear**	the teacher
am balach	the boy	**an t-airgead**	the money	**an sagart**	the priest
am ministear	the minister	**an t-ìm**	the butter	**an taigh**	the house
am peann	the pen	**an t-eilean**	the island	**an loch**	the lake

It will be seen that the change in spelling of **an** to **am** reflects the pronunciation of **an** before the labials **b f m p**. Compare your pronunciation of **n** in the English word **input**; you will more than likely pronounce this **n** as an **m**. A **t-** is prefixed before all masculine nouns beginning in a vowel after the masculine article **an**.

(ii) Feminine article *an***

The feminine article **an*** is spelt:

a' + lenition	before all lenitable consonants (except **d t s f**), i.e. **b c g m p**
an t-	before **s sl sr sn**, but NOT before **sg sp st**
an + lenition	before **f**
an	otherwise, i.e. before all vowels, **d n t l r** and **sg sp st**

Recall that the symbol * indicates that a word usually causes lenition (see Lesson 10).

a' chlach	the stone	an fhuil	the blood	an deoch	the drink
a' bhó	the cow	an fheòl	the meat	an teanga	the tongue
a' Bheurla	(the) English	an t-sùil	the eye	an obair	the work
a' Ghàidhlig	(the) Gaelic	an t-sràid	the street	an sgoil	the school

The feminine definite article generally lenites a following consonant, in which case the **n** of the article is not pronounced (except before **fh-**) and therefore dropped in spelling, hence **a'**. The **n** is pronounced and therefore retained before **fh-**. The dentals (i.e. sounds made at the teeth) **d t** are NOT lenited by the feminine article; the lenition is 'blocked' in such instances. This means that it is difficult to distinguish between masculine and feminine nouns beginning with **d t** when they are preceded by the article, e.g.:

an duine (*m*)	the man
an deoch (*f*)	the drink
an taigh (*m*)	the house
an tì (*f*)	the tea

The feminine article prefixes **t-** to feminine nouns beginning with **s** (**sl sr sn**), in which case the **s** is not pronounced. It follows that the groups **t-s, t-sl, t-sr, t-sn** are pronounced, respectively, as **t, tl, tr, tn**. The reason that **t** is not prefixed to feminine words beginning with **sg, sp, st** is that the initial groups **tg, tp, tt** are not possible in Gaelic.

14a Use of article

When a noun is used to designate an entire class, the singular article is often used, e.g.:

am bradan	salmon
an t-each	horses
am feur	grass

The article is always used before abstract nouns, e.g.:

an aois	age
an sgìos	tiredness
am blàs	warmth

Exercise 2

Put the proper form of the nominative article before the following nouns:

1 leabhar (*m*)	/ʎɔ-ər/	book
2 ceòl (*m*)	/kʲɔ:ʎ/	music

3 craobh (f)	/krɯːv/	tree
4 pìob (f)	/piːb/	pipe
5 bean (f)	/bɛn/	wife
6 feannag (f)	/fjaɲag/	crow
7 sràid (f)	/sd̪raːdʲ/	street
8 sporan (m)	/sbɔran/	purse
9 pàipear (m)	/pɛːhpɛrʲ/	paper
10 té (f)	/tʲeː/	woman

15 Possessive constructions

There are two possessive constructions in Scottish Gaelic, each involving the use of personal pronouns. The first construction involves the use of possessive pronouns which precede the noun they qualify. The second construction involves the use of the definite article and the prepositional pronouns formed from the preposition **aig**, 'at'.

(i) Possessive pronouns

Before consonants		Before vowels and f + vowel	
mo*		m'	my
do*		d' or t'	your
a*		a	his
a		a h-	her
ar		ar n-	our
ur		ur n-	your
an / am		an / am	their

mo mhàthair	my mother	m'athair	my father
do bhràthair	your brother	d'aodann	your face
a phiuthar	his sister	a athair	his father
a cas	her foot	a h-athair	her father
ar mac	our son	ar n-athair	our father
ur nighean	your daughter	ur n-athair	your father
an làmhan	their hands	an athair	their father

Note: **an** 'their' becomes **am** before labials, e.g.: **am bràthair** their brother.

Possessive pronouns are normally used with the so-called inalienables, i.e. parts of the body and blood relations, e.g.: **làmh** arm, **cas** leg, **sùil** eye, **màthair** mother, **athair** father, **mac** son, **nighean** daughter.

(ii) Alternative possessive construction involving prepositional pronouns

This construction involves the definite article, which precedes the noun, and the appropriate prepositional pronoun formed from the preposition **aig** 'at' which follows the noun. 'My cat' becomes **an cat agam** in Gaelic, *lit* 'the cat at-me'. Here are some further examples:

an cù agad	your dog
an leabhar aige	his book
an t-airgead aice	her money
a' bhó againn	our cow
an obair agaibh	your work
an deoch aca	their drink

This possessive construction is generally used with the so-called 'alienables', i.e. nouns which are not parts of the body or blood relations.

Exercise 3

Translate

1 my sister
2 your mother
3 her father
4 their son
5 his foot
6 our dog
7 their money
8 your cow
9 her work
10 her eye

16 Position and status of adjectives

Adjectives normally follow the noun they qualify. There is a small number of exceptions which precede the noun, and these will be discussed below. An adjective following a feminine noun is lenited (nominative form); an adjective following a masculine noun is not lenited (nominative form).

MASCULINE		FEMININE	
cù mór	a big dog	caileag bheag	a small girl
rùm dorcha	a dark room	slàinte mhath	good health
còta dearg	a red coat	léine gheal	a white shirt
taigh beag	a small house	uinneag shalach	a dirty window
òran math	a good song	oidhche mhath	a good night[1]

A noun can be followed by more than one adjective. There is a certain order in which these adjectives may occur. Adjectives denoting size (e.g.: mór 'big', beag 'small') tend always to appear first in a string of adjectives, e.g.:

cù mór dubh	a big black dog
léine bheag gheal	a small white shirt

You will note that a feminine noun lenites all (attributive) adjectives which follow it.

Note: it is only attributive and not predicative adjectives which are affected by lenition. Consider the following two examples which contain attributive adjectives:

bròg bheag	a small shoe
clach throm	a heavy stone

The following two examples, on the other hand, contain predicative adjectives:

Tha a' bhròg beag.	The shoe is small.
Tha a' chlach trom.	The stone is heavy.

The following example contains both attributive and predicative adjectives:

Tha [a' chlach bheag (attr)] trom (pred). The small stone is heavy.

(i) Adjectives which precede a noun

We have already mentioned that there are some adjectives which precede the noun they qualify, the most important of which are:

seann*	old
deagh*	good

[1]Oidhche mhath is also used to wish someone 'goodnight'.

droch*   bad

These adjectives lenite the initial consonant of a following noun (except **d t s** in the case of **seann**).

seann chroitear	an old crofter
seann duine	an old man
deagh sheinneadair	a good singer
droch bhiadh	bad food

The nominative article, when it appears, always precedes the adjectives **seann, deagh, droch**. It always appears as **an** before **deagh** and **droch**. **An** is used before **seann** when **seann** precedes a masculine noun; **an t-** is used when **seann** precedes a feminine noun. Study the following examples :

an deagh sheinneadair (*m*)	the good singer
an droch shìde (*f*)	the bad weather
an t-seann bhròg (*f*)	the old shoe
an seann chòta (*m*)	the old coat

(ii) 'The same'

The adjectives **aon*** and **dearbh*** also precede the noun they qualify and are usually preceded by the article **an** 'the', e.g.:

an aon bheachd	the same opinion
an aon chàr	the same car
an dearbh bhalach	the very boy
an dearbh rud	the very thing

(iii) 'Very' and 'too'

The words **glé*** 'very' and **ro*** 'too' lenite a following adjective. Study the following:

glé mhath	very well
glé bheag	very small
glé mhór	very big
ro mhath	too good
ro bheag	too small
ro mhór	too big

Vocabulary

bòrd (*m*)	/bɔːɾsd̪/	table
bó (*f*)	/boː/	cow
balach (*m*)	/baɫəx/	boy
bàta (*m*)	/baːht̪ə/	boat
sìde (*f*)	/ʃiːdʲə/	weather
gorm	/g[ɔrɔ]m/	blue

Exercise 4

Remove the brackets, make the necessary adjustments and translate:

1 bòrd (beag)
2 bó (mór)
3 balach (math)
4 oidhche (dorcha)
5 bròg (salach)
6 bàta (dearg)
7 seann (bàta)
8 deagh (caileag)
9 droch (sìde)
10 seann (càr) (gorm)

Vocabulary

madainn (*f*) **mhath**	/mad̪iɲ vaː/	good morning
ospadal (*m*)	/ɔsbəd̪əɫ/	hospital
nurs (*m*)	/nʏɾs/	nurse
goirt	/gɔɾsdʲ/	sore
ceàrr	/kʲaːɾ/	wrong
deas	/dʲes/	right
clì	/kliː/	left
beagan	/began/	a little
cuideachd	/kudʲəxg/	also
teann	/tʲauɲ/	tight
cruaidh	/kruəj/	hard
ùr	/uːr/	new
suidh (*vb*)	/suɪj/	sit down
an-sin	/əɲ ʃin/	there
basaidh (*m*)	/basi/	basin
an-seo	/əɲ ʃɔ/	here
blàth	/bɫaː/	warm
glan	/gɫan/	fine, nice
comhfhurtail	/kɔ-əɾsd̪al/	comfortable
tapadh leibh	/t̪ahpə lʏiv/	thank you

COMHRADH (CONVERSATION)

Iain aig an ospadal

Nurs	Madainn mhath. Is mise an nurs. Có thusa?
Iain	Is mise Iain.
Nurs	Ciamar a tha thu?
Iain	Chan eil mi gu math idir.
Nurs	Dé a tha ceàrr?
Iain	Tha mo chas goirt.
Nurs	A' chas dheas no a' chas chlì?
Iain	An té dheas ach tha an té chlì beagan goirt cuideachd.
Nurs	Am bheil a' bhròg agad ro theann?
Iain	Chan eil ach tha mo bhrògan ro chruaidh. Tha iad ùr, tha fios agaibh.
Nurs	Suidh an-sin, ma-tha. Tha basaidh agam an-seo.
Iain	O, tha sin glan. Tha an t-uisge blàth.
Nurs	Am bheil sin comhfhurtail?
Iain	Tha gu dearbh. Tapadh leibh.

TRANSLATION

John at the hospital

Nurse	Good morning. I'm the nurse. Who are you?
John	I'm John.
Nurse	How are you?
John	I am not well at all.
Nurse	What's the matter?
Nurse	My foot is sore.
Nurse	The right foot or the left foot?
John	The right foot but the left one is a little sore, too.
Nurse	Is your shoe too tight?
John	No, but my shoes are too hard. They are new, you know.
Nurse	Sit down here then. I've got a basin here.
John	Oh, that's nice. The water is warm.
Nurse	Is that comfortable?
John	It certainly is. Thank you.

Lesson 3

17 Verbal nouns

With every verb (except the verb **tha**), there is an associated verbal noun which corresponds to participles in other languages. In most cases the verbal noun is formed by adding a suffix to the verb, although this is not always the case. Here are some examples:

VERB		VERBAL NOUN	

(a) VERB + adh

leugh	→	leughadh	• reading
sgrìobh	→	sgrìobhadh	writing
geàrr	→	gearradh	cutting
mol	→	moladh	praising
pòs	→	pòsadh	marrying
buail	→	bualadh	striking

(b) VERB + (a)inn, sinn, tinn

faic	→	faicinn	seeing
faigh	→	faighinn	getting
feuch	→	feuchainn	trying
tuig	→	tuigsinn	understanding
cluinn	→	cluinntinn	hearing

(c) VERB + ail, tail

gabh	→	gabhail	taking
fàg	→	fàgail	leaving
cum	→	cumail	keeping
tog	→	togail	lifting, building
lean	→	leantail[1]	following

(d) VERB + achadh

smaoinich	→	smaoineachadh	thinking
lag	→	lagachadh	weakening

[1] Also **leantainn**.

31

(e) VERB + e

ith	→ ithe	eating
laigh	→ laighe	lying
suidh	→ suidhe	sitting
nigh	→ nighe	washing

(f) VERB = verbal noun

seinn	→ seinn	singing
òl	→ òl	drinking
falbh	→ falbh	going away
fàs	→ fàs	growing
ruith	→ ruith	running

(g) other forms

iarr	→ iarraidh	wanting
fuirich	→ fuireach	living
ceannaich	→ ceannach	buying
fairich	→ faireachdainn	feeling
eugh	→ eughachd	shouting
dèan	→ dèanamh	doing, making
seas	→ seasamh	standing
tuit	→ tuiteam	falling

Some irregular verbs form their verbal nouns from different roots:

rach	→ dol	going
thig	→ tighinn	coming
abair	→ ràdh	saying

18 The present tense

The present tense in Gaelic is formed by using the verbal noun
with the (auxiliary) verb **tha** as follows:

THA	SUBJECT	VERBAL NOUN PARTICLE	VERBAL NOUN
tha	**mi**	**ag**	**éisteachd**

I am listening, I listen

This literally means 'I am at listening'. In the present tense this
periphrastic ('long') construction covers both the continuous and
simple present. In other words, **tha mi ag éisteachd** can be
translated as 'I am listening' or 'I listen'.

The verbal noun is preceded by **ag** when used with **tha** to form the present tense. The final **g** of **ag** is not pronounced before a following consonant and is dropped in writing: **ag** → **a'**, e.g.:

tha mi a' sgrìobhadh	I am writing, I write
tha Anna a' leughadh	Ann is reading, Ann reads

Here are some further examples:

Tha Iain a' leughadh leabhar.
John is reading a book, John reads a book.

Am bheil Anna a' sgrìobhadh litir?
Is Ann writing a letter? Does Ann write a letter?

Chan eil mi a' faicinn sìon.
I don't see anything.

Tha mi a' cluinntinn ceòl brèagha.
I hear lovely music.

Chan eil iad a' dol a-mach.
They are not going out, they do not go out.

Am bheil Màiri a' fuireach ann an Glaschu?
Does Mary live in Glasgow?

Am bheil thu a' tuigsinn Gàidhlig?
Do you understand Gaelic?

Tha mi ag iarraidh ìm agus càise.
I want butter and cheese.

As the term implies, verbal nouns may function as either nouns or verbs. As nouns they may be preceded by the definite article, e.g.:

an leughadh (*m*)	the reading
an sgrìobhadh (*m*)	the writing
an t-òl (*m*)	the drinking
an fhaireachdainn (*f*)	the feeling

19 'What do you want?', etc.

To ask a question what . . . ?, put **dé a** ('what is it that') in front of the verb as follows:

Dé a tha thu ag iarraidh?	What do you want?
Dé a tha thu a' dèanamh?	What are you doing?
	What do you do?
Dé a tha thu ag òl?	What are you drinking?
	What do you drink?
Dé a tha thu a' faicinn?	What are you seeing?
	What do you see?

Vocabulary

Dùn Éideann	/d̪un e:dʲəŋ̊/	Edinburgh
Fraingeis (*m*)	/fraŋgʲəʃ/	French
bàrdachd (*f*)	/baːrsd̪əxg/	poetry
rannsachadh (*m*)	/r̪auŋsəxəɣ/	research
cupa cofaidh (*m*)	/kuhpə kɔfi/	a cup of coffee
obair (*f*)	/obərʲ/	work, working
ceart gu leòr	/kʲar̪sd̪ gə ʎɔːr/	all right, O.K.

Exercise 1

Translate

1 What are you thinking?
2 Ann lives in Edinburgh.
3 Do you understand French?
4 John is writing poetry.
5 Mary is doing research.
6 Are you coming out?
7 They want a cup of coffee.
8 James works in Glasgow.
9 Do you feel all right?
10 I don't understand.

20 Definite nouns: definition

We say that a noun is definite if it is (a) a proper noun, e.g.: **Iain** John, **Glaschu** Glasgow, (b) preceded by the article, e.g.: **an tidsear** 'the teacher', (c) preceded by a possessive pronoun, e.g.: **mo mhàthair** 'my mother'.

21 More on the verb '*is*' ('to be')

We have already dealt with **is** sentences of the following type:

IS	SUBJECT	PREDICATE	
Is	**mise**	**Iain.**	I am John.
Is	**tusa**	**an tidsear.**	You are the teacher.
Is	**esan**	**am ministear againn.**	He is our minister.
Is	**ise**	**mo mhàthair.**	She is my mother.

Our sentences so far have included those where the subject is a pronoun (**mise**, **tusa**, etc.) and the predicate is a definite noun.

If the subject, however, is a definite noun instead of a pronoun and the predicate remains a definite noun, we use **se** (<**is** + **e**) rather than **is** and the same order of elements as before, as follows:

IS	SUBJECT	PREDICATE	
Se	**Iain**	**an tidsear.**	John is the teacher.
Se	**m'athair**	**am ministear.**	My father is the minister.
Se	**Màiri**	**mo phiuthar.**	Mary is my sister.
Se	**Seumas**	**an sagart againn.**	James is our priest.

To negate **se** sentences, replace **se** with **chan e**:

Chan e do bhràthair an sagart.	Your brother is not the priest.
Chan e Iain an tidsear.	John is not the teacher.
Chan e Seumas mo bhràthair.	James is not my brother.

To form the interrogative (positive), replace **se** with **an e**:

An e Domhall an tidsear?	Is Donald the teacher?
An e Anna do mhàthair?	Is Ann your mother?
An e am post d'athair?	Is the postman your father?

To form the interrogative (negative), replace **se** with **nach e**:

Nach e Iain am ministear?	Isn't John the minister?
Nach e Uilleam do bhràthair?	Isn't William your brother?
Nach e an sagart an caraid agad?	Isn't the priest your friend?

To answer any of the above questions beginning **an e** or **nach e**, the answer forms are always as follows:

POSITIVE		NEGATIVE	
se	yes	**chan e**	no

In Lesson 2 we learnt several simple **is** sentences:

Is mise Iain.	I am John.
Is tusa Anna.	You are Ann.
Is esan Seumas.	He is James.
Is ise Peigi.	She is Peggy.
Is sinne an clas Gàidhlig.	We are the Gaelic class.
Is sibhse an tidsear.	You are the teacher.
Is iadsan Màiri agus Calum.	They are Mary and Calum.

We may note at this stage that **se** can replace **is** before the personal pronouns as follows:

Se mise Iain.	I am John.
Se thusa Anna.	You are Ann.

Se esan Seumas.	He is James.
Se ise Peigi.	She is Peggy.
Se sinne an clas Gàidhlig.	We are the Gaelic class.
Se sibhse an tidsear.	You are the teacher.
Se iadsan Màiri agus Calum.	They are Mary and Calum.

Note: **thusa** follows **se**, not **tusa**.

Similarly, **cha, an, nach** may be replaced by **chan e, an e, nach e** in which case **thu** (not **tu**) is used. Note also that **mise** is not lenited when it is preceded by **chan e**; **cha mhise** becomes **chan e mise**.

Here are some further examples:

Chan e mise Domhnall.	I am not Donald.
Chan e thusa Anna.	You are not Ann.
An e esan Iain?	Is he John?
An e ise Peigi?	Is she Peggy?
Nach e sibhse am ministear?	Aren't you the minister?
Nach e iadsan an clas Gàidhlig?	Aren't they the Gaelic class?

Exercise 2

Translate

1 I am John.
2 She is Ann.
3 Is he the teacher? Yes.
4 James is not my teacher.
5 Mary is the nurse.
6 Donald is her father.
7 Isn't William your son? No.
8 Catherine is the big sister.
9 You are small George.
10 Mary is their new minister.

22 Demonstratives

Gaelic, like Lowland Scots (a language related to English), distinguishes between 'this', 'that' and 'yon'; and also between 'here', 'there' and 'yonder'. The main difference between 'that' and 'yon' and between 'there' and 'yonder' in Gaelic is that the former are generally more specific in their reference, whereas the latter are usually more 'remote' in either spatial, temporal or emotional terms.

(a) Demonstrative adjectives

These adjectives, like most other adjectives, follow the noun they qualify. However, they are not affected by lenition. Nouns followed by demonstrative adjectives are usually preceded by the definite article. The forms are as follows:

an dealbh seo	this picture
an taigh sin	that house
a' bheinn ud	yon mountain

The plural form of the article is na:

na taighean seo	these houses
na dealbhannan sin	those pictures
na caileagan ud	yon girls

In a string of adjectives, the demonstrative adjectives usually appear in final position:

a' bheinn mhór àrd sin	that big high mountain
an dealbh bheag bhrèagha seo	this small fine picture

(b) Demonstrative pronouns

seo	this
sin	that
siud	that (yon)

There is a distinction between singular and plural forms. These are formed by placing the third person plural pronoun iad before the above demonstrative forms:

iad seo	these
iad sin	those
iad siud	those (yon)

It is also possible to distinguish between masculine and feminine singular forms although the basic demonstrative forms normally suffice. The forms are as follows:

e seo	this (*masculine*)
i seo	this (*feminine*)
e sin	that (*masculine*)
i sin	that (*feminine*)
e siud	that/yon (*masculine*)
i siud	that/yon (*feminine*)

The demonstrative pronouns act like other pronouns and nouns and therefore can be the subject (or object) of a verb, e.g.:

Tha seo math.	This is good.
Tha sin blasda.	That is tasty.
Tha siud dìreach àlainn.	That is just beautiful.

Note: the demonstrative pronouns **seo**, **sin** and **siud** may also be used as the subject of an **is** sentence, in which case the **se** construction introduced earlier in this lesson is used, e.g.:

Se seo Màiri.	This is Mary.
Se sin Iain.	That is John.
Se siud Anna.	That (yon) is Ann.

Se may be omitted before the demonstrative pronouns and so the following sentences often replace the above: (note that we can translate; 'this is' or 'here is', etc.)

Seo Màiri.	This is Mary; here is Mary.
Sin an tidsear.	That is the teacher; there is the teacher.
Siud Iain.	That (yon) is John; there (yonder) is John.

(c) **Demonstrative adverbs**

an-seo	here
an-sin	there
an-siud	yonder

'Where is . . .?'

Study the following phrases:

Càite am bheil a' bhùth?	Where is the shop?
Càite am bheil am banca?	Where is the bank?
Càite am bheil oifis a' phuist?	Where is the post office?
Càite am bheil an stèisean?	Where is the station?
Càite am bheil an taigh-beag?	Where is the toilet?

Note the difference between:

Tha an cat an-sin	The cat is there.
Sin an cat	That is the cat; there is the cat.

Vocabulary

a' chaileag (f)	/ə xalag/	the girl
am balach (m)	/əm baɫəx/	the boy
a' bhùth (f)	/ə vu:/	the shop

an duine (*m*)	/əŋ ɖuɲə/	the man
am boireannach (*m*)	/əm bɔrʲəŋəx/	the woman
an t-aran (*m*)	/əŋ t̪aran/	the bread
an sgian (*f*)	/əŋ sgʲiən/	the knife
am baile (*m*)	/əm balə/	the town
am baga (*m*)	/əm bagə/	the bag
a' bhasgaid (*f*)	/ə vasgɛdʲ/	the basket
an t-airgead (*m*)	/əŋ t[ɛrʲɛ]gʲəɖ/	the money
am manaidsear (*m*)	/əm manədʲʃɛrʲ/	the manager
a' bhròg (*f*)	/ə vrɔːg/	the shoe
an làmh (*f*)	/əŋ ɫãːv/	the hand
a' chas (*f*)	/ə xas/	the foot, leg
an t-sùil (*m*)	/əɴ t̪uːl/	the eye
a-rithist	/ə rʲi-əʃdʲ/	again

Exercise 3

Translate

1 this girl
2 that shop
3 yon town
4 that woman there
5 this is my sister
6 there is the knife
7 the bread is yonder
8 there is that mountain again
9 this is cold
10 that is very good

23 Numerals

The basic numerals from zero to ten are as follows:

0 **neoini**
1 **aon**
2 **dà**
3 **trì**
4 **ceithir**
5 **cóig**
6 **sia**
7 **seachd**
8 **ochd**
9 **naoi**
10 **deich**

40

If counting, and when there is no following noun, the numbers between one and ten prefix **a**, which lenites **dà** and prefixes **h-** to **aon** and **ochd**:

1 **a h-aon** or **aonan**
2 **a dhà**
3 **a trì**
4 **a ceithir**
5 **a cóig**
6 **a sia**
7 **a seachd**
8 **a h-ochd**
9 **a naoi**
10 **a deich**

The numbers from eleven to nineteen are formed by adding **deug** which corresponds to 'teen' in English as follows:

11 **a h-aon deug**   eleven
12 **a dhà dheug**   twelve
13 **a trì deug**   thirteen
14 **a ceithir deug** fourteen
15 **a cóig deug**   fifteen
16 **a sia deug**   sixteen
17 **a seachd deug**   seventeen
18 **a h-ochd deug**   eighteen
19 **a naoi deug**   nineteen

Exercise 4

Complete the following sums, writing the answers in words:

(a) $1 + 8 =$ (e) $14 \div 2 =$
(b) $2 + 3 =$ (f) $12 + 7 =$
(c) $8 - 2 =$ (g) $10 \div 10 =$
(d) $6 \times 3 =$ (h) $7 + 8 =$

24 Adverbs of direction

Adverbs which denote position in relation to the speaker generally distinguish between forms which imply <u>location</u> and forms which imply <u>motion</u>. In some cases, motion to and away from the speaker is also differentiated.

(a) 'Up' and 'down'

In words for 'up' and 'down', Gaelic makes a distinction between (i) position of being up or down and (ii) going 'up' and 'down', i.e. motion away from/towards the speaker.

(i)	**shuas**	up (location)
(ii)	**suas**	up, upwards (away from the speaker)
(iii)	**a-nuas**	up, upwards (towards the speaker)
(i)	**shìos**	down (location)
(ii)	**sìos**	down, downwards (away from the speaker)
(iii)	**a-nuas**	down, downwards (towards the speaker)

Note: **a-nuas** is used for both 'up' and 'down' which can be confusing at first. It is also useful to note that it is incorrect to say **a' dol a-nuas** or **a' tighinn sìos**, although younger speakers sometimes use them. Note also that some dialects do distinguish between 'up' and 'down' (towards the speaker); these dialects use **a-nìos** 'up', 'from below' (towards the speaker).

Examples:

Tha Iain shuas an staighre. John is upstairs.
Tha Anna a' dol suas an staighre. Ann is going up the stairs.
Tha Màiri a' tighinn a-nuas. Mary is coming up,
Mary is coming down.

(b) 'Over here' and 'over there'

Gaelic makes a distinction in words for 'over here' and 'over there' between location and motion:

a-bhos	over here (location at speaker)
a-nall	(coming) over here (motion towards speaker)
thall	over there (location not at speaker)
a-null	(going) over there (motion away from speaker)

Examples:

Tha Anna a-bhos ann an Dùn Éideann.
Ann is over here in Edinburgh.

Tha Màiri a' tighinn a-nall á Glaschu.
Mary is coming over here from Glasgow.

Tha Màiri thall ann an Glaschu.
Mary is over there in Glasgow.
Tha Anna a' dol a-null a Ghlaschu.
Ann is going over there to Glasgow.

These adverbs of motion are frequently used with the demonstrative adverbs **an-seo, an-sin** and **an-siud** which we met earlier in this lesson, e.g.:

Tha Màiri a-bhos an-seo.	Mary is over here.
Tha Iain thall an-sin.	John is over there.

There is a difference between **a-bhos** and **an-seo** on the one hand and between **thall** and **an-sin** (**an-siud**) on the other. The demonstrative adverbs are definite and specific in their reference; the directional adverbs **thall** and **a-bhos** are non-specific in their reference. **Thall** means 'not in the vicinity of the speaker'; **a-bhos** means 'in the vicinity of the speaker' without specifying the exact location.

'Here and there' is translated in Gaelic as **'thall is a-bhos'**.

(c) 'In' and 'out'

Gaelic makes a distinction in words for 'in' and 'out' between location and motion:

a-staigh	in, inside (location)
a-steach	in, inwards (motion)
a-muigh	out, outside (location)
a-mach	out, outwards (motion)

Not all varieties of Gaelic use **a-steach**. Indeed there is a tendency to use **a-staigh** to convey both location and motion.

Tha mi a-staigh an-dràsta.	I am in now.
Tha Anna a' tighinn a-steach.	Ann is coming in.
Tha Iain a-muigh a' cluich ball-coise.	John is out playing football.
Tha Màiri a' dol a-mach.	Mary is going out.

25 Days, months and seasons

Days

Di-Luain	Monday
Di-Màirt	Tuesday

Di-Ciadaoin	Wednesday
Diar-Daoin	Thursday
Di-hAoine	Friday
Di-Sathairne	Saturday
Di-Domhnaich/Latha na Sàbaid	Sunday

Note that all of the days of the week are stressed on the second syllable as the hyphen indicates.

The use of **Di-Domnaich** and **Latha na Sàbaid** depends to a certain extent on social factors although there are no absolutely clear lines of demarcation between the use of both. Generally speaking **Di-Domhnaich** tends to be used by Catholics and by Episcopalians, **Latha na Sàbaid** by Presbyterians.

Months

am Faoilteach	January
an Gearran	February
am Màrt	March
an Giblean	April
an Céitean	May
an t-Ògmhìos	June
an t-Iuchar	July
an Lùnastal	August
an t-Sultain	September
an Damhair	October
an t-Samhain	November
an Dubhlachd	December

Note that the names of the months all appear with the article.

Seasons

an t-Earrach	Spring
an Samhradh	Summer
am Foghar	Autumn
an Geamhradh	Winter

The seasons are all masculine. Study the following:

as t-Earrach	in Spring
as t-Samhradh	in Summer
as t-Fhoghar	in Autumn
BUT	
anns a' Gheamhradh	in Winter

26 Emphatic suffixes

We saw in Lesson 2 how Scottish Gaelic uses emphatic suffixes to give emphatic or contrastive power to the pronouns, e.g.:

Tha Iain beag ach tha <u>mise</u> mór.   John is small but *I* am big.

The emphatic pronouns consist of the pronoun followed by an emphatic suffix as follows:

PRONOUN		EMPHATIC SUFFIX		EMPHATIC PRONOUN	
mi	+	se	→	mise	*I*
thu	+	sa	→	thusa	*you*
e	+	san	→	esan	*he*
i	+	se	→	ise	*she*
sinn	+	ne	→	sinne	*we*
sibh	+	se	→	sibhse	*you*
iad	+	san	→	iadsan	*they*

Emphatic suffixes are also used with other parts of speech to give them emphatic or contrastive power. They are principally used with (a) prepositional pronouns and (b) following nouns preceded by possessive pronouns. In each case they emphasise the pronominal element. The emphatic suffixes are the same as those used with the pronouns listed above except that **-sa** rather than **-se** is used with the first person singular. Note that the hyphen does not indicate a change in stress. The italics in the English translations indicate emphatic or contrastive use:

an cù agamsa	**mo chù-sa**	*my* dog
an cat agadsa	**do chat-sa**	*your* cat
an taigh aigesan	**a thaigh-san**	*his* house
an càr aicese	**a càr-se**	*her* car
an t-aodach againne	**ar n-aodach-ne**	*our* clothes
an leabhar agaibhse	**ur leabhar-se**	*your* book
an sgoil acasan	**an sgoil-san**	*their* school

Note that a hyphen is not usually used with prepositional pronouns.

Vocabulary

thig (*vb*)	/higʲ/	come
an toiseach	/ əɲ t̪ɔʃəx/	first
siùcar (*m*)	/ʃuːhkərʲ/	sugar
mas e ur toil e	/maʃ e ər t̪ɔl ɛ/	please (polite, formal)

doras (*m*)	/d̪ɔrəs/	door
eile	/elə/	other, else
a-nis	/ə niʃ/	now
bainne (*m*)	/baɲə/	milk
ugh (*f*), **uighean** (*pl*)	/u/, /ɯjən/	egg, eggs
orainsear (*m*), **orainsearan** (*pl*)	/ɔrəɲʃɛrʲ/, /ɔrəɲʃɛrʲən/	oranges
có mheud?	/ko: v̄iā̯d̪/	how many (+ singular form of the noun)
brot (*m*)	/brɔht̪/	soup
duine (*m*), **daoine**	/d̪uɲə/, /d̪ɯ:ɲə/	man/person, men/people
a-nochd	/ə n̪ɔxg/	tonight
gu	/gɔ/	to
biadh (*m*)	/biəɣ/	food
dad (*m*)	/d̪ad̪/	anything
salann (*m*)	/sal̪ən̪/	salt
sceilp (*f*)	/sgʲɛlp/	shelf
banca (*m*)	/baŋgə/	bank
oifis a' phuist (*f*)	/ɔfiʃ ə fuʃdʲ/	post office
beannachd leibh	/bjan̪əxg lʲiv/	good-bye
mar sin leibh	/mər ʃin lʲiv/	good-bye to you

COMHRADH

Anna ann am bùth

Fear na bùtha	Thig a-staigh. Tha e fuar an-diugh.
Anna	Tha, tha e fuar agus fliuch.
Fear na bùtha	Dé a tha sibh ag iarraidh?
Anna	An toiseach, ma-tha, tha mi ag iarraidh siùcar. Càite am bheil e, mas e ur toil e?
Fear na bùtha	Tha thall an-sin aig an doras. Dé eile a tha sibh ag iarraidh?
Anna	Bainne agus uighean agus orainsearan.
Fear na bùtha	Có mheud ugh?
Anna	A sia, tha mi a' smaoineachadh.
Fear na bùtha	Glé mhath. Có mheud orainsear?
Anna	A seachd. Tha mi ag iarraidh uinneanan cuideachd. Tha mi a' dèanamh brot. Tha daoine a' tighinn a-nochd gu biadh.
Fear na bùtha	A-nis seo bainne, uighean, orainsearan agus uinneanan. Am bheil sibh ag iarraidh dad eile?

Anna	Tha. Tha mi ag iarraidh salann. Càite am bheil e?
Fear na bùtha	Tha e shuas air an sceilp sin. Am bheil sibh ag iarraidh dad eile?
Anna	Chan eil, tapadh leibh. Tha gu leòr agam. O, am bheil fios agaibh càite am bheil am banca agus oifis a' phuist?
Fear na bùtha	Tha, shìos an rathad. Beannachd leibh.
Anna	Mar sin leibh.

TRANSLATION

Ann in a shop

Shopkeeper	Come in. It's cold today.
Ann	Yes, it's cold and wet.
Shopkeeper	What do you want?
Ann	Well, first I want sugar. Where is it please?
Shopkeeper	It's over there at the door. What else do you want?
Ann	Milk and eggs and oranges.
Shopkeeper	How many eggs?
Ann	Six, I think.
Shopkeeper	Very good. How many oranges?
Ann	Seven. I want onions too. I'm making soup. People are coming to dinner tonight.
Shopkeeper	Now here are milk, eggs, oranges and onions. Do you want anything else?
Ann	Yes. I want salt. Where is it?
Shopkeeper	It's up there on that shelf. Do you want anything else?
Ann	No, thank you. I have enough. Oh, do you know where the bank and the post-office are?
Shopkeeper	Yes, down the road. Good-bye.
Ann	Good-bye.

Lesson 4

27 Past tense of 'tha'

We have already met the present tense of the verb **tha** 'to be'. The past tense forms are listed below with the present tense forms for comparison:

	Past	*Present*
Positive	**bha**	**tha**
Negative	cha **robh**	chan **eil**
Interrogative (positive)	an **robh**?	am **bheil**
Interrogative (negative)	nach **robh**?	nach **eil**

27a Independent and dependent verbal forms

It will be clear that there is a correspondence between **tha** and **bha** on the one hand, and between **(bh)eil** and **robh** on the other. **Tha** and **bha** appear 'independently' and usually appear at the beginning of an utterance. **Tha** and **bha** are therefore called independent verbal forms. **(Bh)eil** and **robh** on the other hand only appear after certain particles (e.g.: **cha, an, nach**) and their occurrence 'depends' on the occurrence of these particles. **(Bh)eil** and **robh** are therefore called dependent verbal forms. The distinction between independent and dependent forms is fundamentally important in the verbal system of Gaelic.

Here are some examples of the past tense of **tha**:

Bha Iain sgìth	John was tired
Cha robh e blàth	It was not warm
An robh Seumas an-seo?	Was James here?
Nach robh an t-airgead agad?	Did you not have the money?

27b Past tense of 'tha' with the verbal noun

In Lesson 3 we saw that the periphrastic construction (in the present tense) involving the verb **tha** and the verbal noun covered both the continuous tense and the simple present tense. When the past tense of **tha** is used in the periphrastic construction, however, the meaning is continuous past, not simple past. In other words,

bha mi ag òl means 'I was drinking' and not 'I drank'. Here are some further examples:

Bha Iain a' sgrìobhadh litir.	John was writing a letter.
Cha robh Anna a' dèanamh sìon.	Ann wasn't doing anything.
An robh sibh a' seinn an-raoir?	Were you singing last night?
Bha mi ag ithe mo bhracaist.	I was eating my breakfast.

The following verbal nouns when used in the periphrastic construction in the past correspond to the simple past tense in English: **iarraidh** 'wanting', **fuireach** 'living', **tuigsinn** 'understanding', **smaoineachadh** 'thinking'. Consider the following examples:

bha mi ag iarraidh aran	I wanted bread
bha Anna a' fuireach ann an Glaschu	Ann lived in Glasgow
bha mi a' tuigsinn	I understood
bha Iain a' smaoineachadh	John thought

28 Irregular verbs: simple past tense

The simple past tense is not formed by using a periphrastic construction; the simple past consists of one-word (short) verbal forms. There are 12 irregular verbs in Scottish Gaelic. We have already met the verbs 'to be' **is** and **tha**. One of the distinguishing features of irregular verbs, as we will see, is that their independent and dependent forms are frequently formed from different roots. It is possible to group the past tense formation of irregular verbs into the following four groups:

(i) Verbs whose independent and dependent forms differ substantially:

INDEPENDENT	DEPENDENT	
bha	**robh**	was
chunnaic	**faca**	saw
chaidh	**deach**	went

(ii) Verbs whose independent and dependent forms begin with **th-** and **d-** respectively:

INDEPENDENT	DEPENDENT	
thàinig	**dàinig**	came
thug	**dug**	gave, brought
thuirt	**duirt**	said

Note: some prefer to spell the dependent forms with an initial **t-** or even **d'th.**

(iii) Verbs whose dependent form is formed by prefixing **do** (or **d'**) to the independent form:

INDEPENDENT	DEPENDENT	
ràinig	do ràinig	reached
rug	do rug	caught
rinn	do rinn	did, made
fhuair	d'fhuair	got

(iv)

INDEPENDENT	DEPENDENT	
chuala	cuala	heard

Subjects including subject pronouns follow the above verbal forms as follows:

chuala mi	I heard
chuala t(h)u	you heard
chuala e, i	he, she heard
chuala sinn	we heard
chuala sibh	you heard
chuala iad	they heard

Bha Seumas an-seo.	James was here.
Cha robh Anna sgìth.	Ann was not tired.
Chunnaic sinn Màiri.	We saw Mary.
Am faca iad an cù.	Did they see the dog?
Chaidh Iain a-mach.	John went out.
Cha deach Uilleam a-mach.	William did not go out.
Ràinig i Dùn Éideann.	She reached Edinburgh.
An do ràinig sibh Glaschu?	Did you reach Glasgow?
Thàinig iad dhachaigh.	They came home.
Cha dàinig iad riamh.	They never came.
Thug Anna pòg do Raghnall.	Ann gave a kiss to Ronald.
An dug a mhàthair airgead dha?	Did his mother give him money?
Thuirt Iain sin.	John said that.
Cha duirt mise sin.	I did not say that.
Rug mi air Catrìona.	I caught Catherine.
An do rug thu air Uilleam?	Did you catch William?
Rinn mi an obair agam.	I did my work.

An do rinn thusa an obair agadsa.	Did *you* do *your* work?
Fhuair mi an t-airgead.	I got the money.
An d'fhuair e sìon?	Did he get anything?
Chuala mi an t-òran brèagha.	I heard the beautiful song.
An cuala sibh Màiri an-raoir?	Did you hear Mary last night?

Note: **nach** lenites f in **faca**, e.g.:

Nach fhaca Iain am bus?	Did John not see the bus?

Note: **cha*** becomes **chan*** before **faca**, e.g.:

Chan fhaca mi Seumas.	I didn't see James.

Note: **cha*** lenites only the dependent form **cuala**, e.g.:

Cha chuala mi thu.	I didn't hear you.

Note: both **tu/thu** may be used with the following verbal forms: **chunnaic, faca; thàinig, dàinig; ràinig, do ràinig; chuala, cuala.**

Note that the simple past tense can sometimes be translated as a perfect, e.g.:

an dàinig Iain fhathast?	has John come yet?
an cuala t(h)u an naidheachd?	have you heard the news?

The following text contains instances of all of the irregular verbs (in **bold**) in the past tense (positive). Study it carefully. Learning it by heart may be a useful way of learning the irregular verbs:

POSITIVE:

Am Meàirleach ('the Robber')

Bha mi aig an taigh Di-Luain. **Chuala** mi fuaim shuas an staighre. **Chaidh** mi suas. **Chunnaic** mi meàirleach. **Rinn** e bùrach. **Thuirt** mi: 'Có thusa?'. **Thàinig** am Poileas agus **rug** iad air a' mheàirleach. **Fhuair** am meàirleach buille. **Thug** e an t-airgead air ais. **Ràinig** iad an stèisean. **Bha** e duilich.

> I was at home on Monday. I heard a noise upstairs. I went up. I saw a robber. He made a mess. I said: 'Who are you?'. The police came and they caught the robber. The robber got a thump. He gave the money back. They reached the station. He was sorry.

NEGATIVE:

Cha robh mi aig an taigh Di-Luain. **Cha chuala** mi fuaim shuas an staighre. **Cha deach** mi suas. **Chan fhaca** mi meàirleach. **Cha do rinn** e bùrach. **Cha duirt** mi: 'Có thusa?'. **Cha dàinig** am Poileas agus **cha do rug** iad air a' mheàirleach. **Cha d'fhuair** am meàirleach buille. **Cha dug** e an t-airgead air ais. **Cha do ràinig** iad an stèisean. **Cha robh** e duilich.

I wasn't at home on Monday. I didn't hear a noise upstairs. I didn't go up. I didn't see a robber. He didn't make a mess. I didn't say: 'Who are you?'. The police didn't come and they didn't catch the robber. The robber didn't get a thump. He didn't give the money back. They didn't reach the station. He wasn't sorry.

Exercise 1

Rewrite the above passage in the interrogative (positive and negative).

Vocabulary

chuir mi seachad bliadhna	/xurʲ mi ʃɛxəd bliəŋə/	I spent a year
fhathast	/ha-əsd/	yet
an-raoir	/əŋ ɼɤirʲ/	last night

Exercise 2

Translate

1 I was happy.
2 I saw Ann yesterday.
3 John went out.
4 They came in.
5 We spent a year there.
6 You didn't do your work.
7 Did you get the money?
8 Did you not reach Edinburgh yet?
9 She didn't say anything.
10 I heard Mary last night.

29 Answering questions

In Lesson 1 we saw that when answering a question in Scottish Gaelic, we simply repeat the main verb of the question, usually without the subject. To answer 'yes', we simply repeat the independent form of the verb. To answer 'no', we repeat the dependent form of the verb preceded <u>always</u> by the negative particle **cha.** Consider the following examples:

An robh thu aig a' chéilidh?	Were you at the ceilidh?
Bha	Yes
Cha robh	No
Am faca t(h)u Seumas?	Did you see James?
Chunnaic	Yes
Chan fhaca	No
An do rinn thu an obair?	Did you do the work?
Rinn	Yes
Cha do rinn	No

30 Imperative

The imperative form of the verb is the form which is used for giving orders. It is also the most basic form of the verb. It is the imperative form which appears as the head word in dictionaries. We will see later that all tenses (other than periphrastic constructions) of regular verbs are derived from the imperative form. For this reason the imperative is sometimes referred to as the verbal root.

The two imperative forms which are most frequently used in Gaelic are the 2nd person singular and plural forms, corresponding to the use of the pronouns **thu** and **sibh.** The plural (also the polite or formal) form is formed by adding **-(a)ibh** to the singular form as follows:

SINGULAR		PLURAL
òl	drink	**òlaibh**
glan	clean	**glanaibh**
seas	stand	**seasaibh**
suidh	sit	**suidhibh**
ith	eat	**ithibh**
dùin	close	**dùinibh**

The singular imperative form is made emphatic by using the pronoun **thusa** as follows:

Òl thusa an tì agad.	<u>you</u> drink your tea.
Suidh thusa an-sin.	<u>you</u> sit there.

30a Negative imperative

To negate the imperative forms, simply place **na** before the above forms e.g.:

Na òl sin.	Don't drink that.
Na suidh an-sin.	Don't sit there.
Na dùin an doras fhathast.	Don't close the door yet.
Na gabh thusa dragh.	Don't <u>you</u> be worried.

The most commonly used imperative forms of the irregular verbs are as follows:

SINGULAR	PLURAL	
bi	**bithibh**	be
rach	**rachaibh**	go
dèan	**dèanaibh**	do, make
faigh	**faighibh**	get
thig	**thigibh**	come
thoir	**thoiribh**	give, bring (to)

The last two verbs, **thig** and **thoir** become **dig** and **doir** after the negative **na**:

Na dig an-seo.	Don't come here.
Na digibh an-seo.	Don't (*pl*) come here.
Na doir airgead dha.	Don't give him money.
Na doiribh airgead do Pheigi.	Don't (*pl*) give money to Peggy.

30b Other imperative forms

There are also first person plural and third person imperatives. The first person plural imperative is formed by adding **(e)amaid** to the verbal root (= imperative second singular form):

seasamaid	let us stand
suidheamaid	let us sit

The third person imperative is formed by adding **(e)adh** to the verbal root. This imperative form must always be followed either by one of the pronouns **e** (**esan**), **i** (**ise**), **iad** (**iadsan**) or by a noun, e.g.:

seinneadh e	let him sing
suidheadh ise	let *her* sit
seasadh iad	let them stand
thigeadh Anna	let Ann come

Example of the imperative

cuir	put
cuireadh e	let him put
cuireamaid	let us put
cuiribh	put
cuireadh iad	let them put

Vocabulary

tì (*f*)	/tiː/	tea
dìnnear (*m*)	/dʲiːɲɛrʲ/	dinner
suas	/suəs/	up
sìos	/ʃiəs/	down
sàmhach	/sãːvəx/	quiet
sìon; càil (*m*)	/ʃĩãn/, /ʃĩ̃n/; /kaːl/	anything
an-diugh	/ən dʲu/	today
an-dé	/ən dʲeː/	yesterday
a-màireach	/ə maːrʲəx/	tomorrow
mas e do thoil e	/mə ʃe də hɔl e/	please (*lit* 'if it is your wish') (*informal*)

Exercise 3

Translate

1 drink your tea
2 eat your dinner
3 stand up
4 sit down
5 be quiet
6 come in
7 give that to James
8 don't do anything
9 find it today
10 close the door please

31 Past tense of '*is*'

The Gaelic verb **is** is a defective verb since it only occurs in the present, past and conditional tenses. It has no future tense forms. The past and conditional forms are identical. The past tense of **is** is bu* (b' before vowels and f + vowel). **Bu** does not usually lenite a following **d**, **t**, **s**. Here are some examples:

Bu mhise an tidsear.	I was the teacher.
Bu tusa am ministear.	You were the minister.
B'esan an saor.	He was the joiner.
B'ise an dotair.	She was the doctor.
Bu sinne an clas Gàidhlig.	We were the Gaelic class.
Bu sibhse an clas Beurla.	You were the English class.
B'iadsan an clas Gearmailtis.	They were the German class.

31a Idioms with '*is*'

There are very many idioms in Gaelic involving the use of nouns, adjectives and prepositions with the verb **is**. Here is one example which we will study in more detail in the next lesson:

is	toil	le	Iain	cofaidh
is	pleasing	with	John	coffee

John likes coffee

This could be translated literally as 'it (i.e. coffee) is pleasing to John'

If we substitute **bu** for **is** in the above idiom, we get past or 'conditional' meaning:

bu toil le Iain cofaidh   John would like coffee

OR   John liked coffee

Watch out for other examples of **bu** below in our discussion of idioms involving the preposition **do** 'to'. We will translate **bu** as 'conditional' in what follows.

32 Prepositional pronouns: '*do**' ('to, for')

dhomh	to me	**dhuinn**	to us
dhut	to you	**dhuibh**	to you (*pl*)
dha	to him	**dhaibh**	to them
dhi	to her		

32a Idioms involving '*do*'

The preposition **do** lenites a following noun, e.g.: **do Sheumas** 'to James'.

(a) can

The basic pattern is:

IS	+	URRAINN	+	DO*	+	SUBJ
is		**urrainn**		**do**		**Chalum**
is		capability		to		Calum

'Calum can'

Study the following phrases:

Is urrainn do Sheumas.	James can.
Is urrainn dhomh.	I can.
B'urrainn do Mhàiri.	Mary could.
B'urrainn dha.	He could.

NEGATIVE FORMS:

Chan urrainn do Dhomhnall.	Donald cannot.
Cha b'urrainn dhi.	She couldn't.

INTERROGATIVE (POSITIVE) FORMS:

An urrainn dhut?	Can you?
Am b'urrainn do Shìle?	Could Sheila?

INTERROGATIVE (NEGATIVE) FORMS:

Nach urrainn do Dhomhnall?	Can't Donald?
Nach b'urrainn dhaibh?	Couldn't they?

ANSWERS:

an urrainn ...? / nach urrainn ...?	**is urrainn**	yes
	chan urrainn	no
am b'urrainn ...? / nach b'urrainn ...?	**b'urrainn**	yes
	cha b'urrainn	no

(b) to know (a person)

The basic pattern is:

IS	+	AITHNE	+	DO	+	SUBJ	+	OBJ
is		**aithne**		**do**		**Sheumas**		**Màiri**
is		knowledge		to		James		Mary

James knows Mary

Study the following phrases:

Is aithne do Mhàiri Seumas. Mary knows James.
Is aithne dhomh e. I know him.

NEGATIVE FORMS:

Chan aithne do Dhomhnall an duine sin.
Donald doesn't know that man.
Chan aithne dha Seumas.
He doesn't know James.

INTERROGATIVE (POSITIVE) FORMS:

An aithne dhut Peigi? Do you know Peggy?
An aithne dhuibh a chéile? Do you know one another?

INTERROGATIVE (NEGATIVE) FORMS:

Nach aithne dhut am ministear? Do you not know the minister?
Nach aithne dhi e? Does she not know him?

ANSWERS:

an/nach aithne do . . .?   **is aithne**   yes
                          chan aithne   no

(c) **should**

The basic pattern is:

BU	+	CHÒIR +	DO*	+	SUBJ	+
bu		**chòir**	**do**		**Mhàiri**	
is		proper	for		Mary	

Mary should

Study the following phrases:

Bu chòir dha. He should.
Bu chòir do Pheigi. Peggy should.

NEGATIVE FORMS:

Cha bu chòir do Dhomhnall. Donald shouldn't.
Cha bu chòir dhut. You shouldn't.

INTERROGATIVE (POSITIVE) FORMS:

Am bu chòir dhomh? Should I?
Am bu chòir do Mhàrtainn? Should Martin?

58

INTERROGATIVE (NEGATIVE) FORMS:

Nach bu chòir dhuinn? Shouldn't we?
Nach bu chòir dhomh? Shouldn't I?

ANSWERS:

am bu chòir ...? / nach bu chòir ...? **bu chòir** yes
  cha bu chòir no

33 Vocative (or address form)

When addressing a person or calling them by their name, Gaelic uses a special form of the noun, called the vocative (or address form). All vocative forms are preceded by the unstressed vocative particle **a*** which lenites.[1] **A***, like other unstressed particles is usually elided (i.e. not pronounced) in the vicinity of other vowels in speech and frequently in writing, but is retained here for reasons of clarity.

(a) Feminine personal nouns

Feminine personal nouns are simply lenited in the vocative.

VOCATIVE

a Mhórag	Morag
a Chatrìona	Catherine
a Mhàiri	Mary
a Sheonag	Joan
a Sheonaid	Janet
a Anna[2]	Ann

(b) Masculine proper nouns

Masculine proper nouns are lenited and the final consonant slenderised:

[1]Recall that an asterisk is used in this Course to show that a word lenites. See Pronunciation pages 9–11.
[2]Pronounced Anna.

VOCATIVE

a Sheumais	James
a Dhomhnaill	Donald
a Raghnaill	Ronald
a Chaluim	Calum
a Iain³	John
a Mhata	Mathew

Exercise 4

Put the following names into the vocative:

1 Donnchadh (*m*)	Duncan
2 Mairead (*f*)	Margaret
3 Mìcheal (*m*)	Michael
4 Murchadh (*m*)	Murdo
5 Sìne (*f*)	Sheena

34 The reflexive pronoun *'fhéin'* ('self')

The reflexive pronoun **fhéin** is used with personal, possessive and prepositional pronouns as follows. Note that **fhìn** (or **fhèin** in some dialects) is used with the first person singular and plural.

mi fhìn	myself
thu fhéin	yourself
e fhéin	himself
i fhéin	herself
sinn fhìn	ourselves
sibh fhéin	yourselves
iad fhéin	themselves

Note that **sibh** + **fhéin** is generally pronounced as **si** + **péin**.

The reflexive pronoun **fhéin** is used with both possessive constructions as follows:

an cù agam fhìn	OR	mo chù fhìn	my own dog
an cat agad fhéin		do chat fhéin	your own cat
an taigh aige fhéin		a thaigh fhéin	his own house
an càr aice fhéin		a càr fhéin	her own car
an t-aodach againn fhìn		ar n-aodach fhìn	our own clothes
an leabhar agaibh fhéin		ur leabhar fhéin	your own book
an sgoil aca fhéin		an sgoil fhéin	their own school

³Pronounced Iain.

Note that **agaibh** + **fhéin**, etc. is generally pronounced as **aga** + **péin**.

Fhéin is also used adverbially with emphatic meaning. Study the following:

gu dearbh	certainly
gu dearbh fhéin	certainly (more emphatic)
tha am biadh fhéin daor	the food itself is expensive/even the food is expensive
tha an deoch daor fhéin	the drink is terribly expensive

Vocabulary

oileanach (*m*), oileanaich (*pl*)	/ɣlanəx/, /ɣlaniç/	student, students
coinneachadh (*vn*)	/kɣɲəxəɣ/	meeting
taigh-òsta (*m*)	/tɣj ɔːsdə/	hotel, pub
guth (*m*)	/gu/	voice
a-staigh	/ə sd̪ɣj/	inside, in
fhathast	/ha-əsd̪/	yet
a dh'aithghearr	/ə ɣaçaɾ/	soon
naidheachd (*f*)	/n̪ɛ-əxg/	news
suas ri chéile	/suəs rʲi çeːlə/	going out together, courting
fìrinn (*f*)	/fiːrʲiɲ/	truth
ged-ta	/gə t̪aː/	though, however
inntinneach	/iːɲtʲiɲəx/	interesting
mar-tha	/mər haː/	already
uisge-beatha (*m*)	/ɯʃgʲə bɛhə/	whisky
gloine (*f*)	/gl̪aɲə/	glass
fìon (*m*)	/fian/, /fiən/	wine
dearg	/dʲ[ara]g/	red
geal	/gʲal̪/	white
siuga (*m*)	/ʃɣgə/	jug
falamh	/fal̪əv/	empty
deigh (*f*)	/dʲɣj/	ice
mas urrainn dhut	/mas uɾiɲ ɣuht̪/	if you can
leth-phinnt (*f*)	/ʎe fiːɲtʲ/	a half pint
draibheadh (*vn*)	/d̪raivəɣ/	driving

COMHRADH

Oileanaich a' coinneachadh ann an taigh-òsta

    Anna   An dàinig Beathag fhathast? Chuala mi an guth aice, bha mi a' smaoineachadh.

Màiri	Tha i a-muigh an-sin a' bruidhinn ach cha dàinig i a-staigh fhathast. Tha i a' tighinn a dh'aithghearr.
Anna	An cuala tu an naidheachd? Tha Beathag agus Iain suas ri chéile.
Màiri	O, chan eil mi a' creidsinn sin.
Anna	An fhìrinn, ged-ta.
Màiri	Nach eil sin inntinneach?
Anna	A-nis càite am bheil Domhnall?
Màiri	Thàinig esan mar-tha. Tha e thall an-sin a' ceannach uisge-beatha.
Anna	A Dhomhnaill, an d'fhuair thu gloine dhomhsa?
Domhnall	Fhuair. Fhuair mi fìon dearg dhut, a Anna. Agus seo fìon geal dhutsa a Mhàiri. Thoir dhomh siuga uisge, a Sheumais, agus faigh dhomh gloine fhalamh agus deigh mas urrainn dhut.
Anna	Dé a tha thu fhéin ag òl an-sin a Dhomhnaill?
Domhnall	Chan eil agam ach leth-phinnt agus gloine orains. Tha mi a' draibheadh a-nochd.

TRANSLATION

Students meeting in a pub

Ann	Has Rebecca come yet? I heard her voice, I thought.
Mary	She's out there talking but she hasn't come in yet. She's coming soon.
Ann	Have you heard the news? Rebecca and John are courting.
Mary	Oh, I don't believe that.
Ann	The truth, though.
Mary	Isn't that interesting.
Ann	Now where's Donald?
Mary	He has come already. He's over there buying whisky.
Ann	Donald, did you get a glass for me?
Donald	Yes. I got red wine for you Ann. And here's white wine for you, Mary. Give me a jug of water, James, and fetch me an empty glass and some ice if you can.
Ann	What are you drinking there yourself, Donald?
Donald	I've only got a half pint and a glass of orange. I'm driving tonight.

Lesson 5

35 Preposition 'ann an' ('in')

So far we have met the prepositional pronouns associated with the preposition **aig** 'at' and **do** 'to'. The prepositional pronouns associated with the preposition **ann an** 'in' are as follows:

annam	in me	**annainn**	in us
annad	in you	**annaibh**	in you (pl)
ann	in him/it	**annta**	in them
innte	in her/it		

Note: **ann** 'in it' can be used as an adverb meaning 'there' and in statements concerning 'existence', e.g.: **bha Iain ann an-raoir** 'John was there last night'. **Tha thu ann** 'you are there/in existence' is often used as an initial statement in a conversation or as a form of address.

The preposition **ann an**, unlike other prepositions, combines with the possessive pronouns **mo★**, **do★**, **a★**, **a**, **ar**, **ur**, **an/am**. The forms are as follows:

'nam★	in my	**'nar**	in our
'nad★	in your	**'nur**	in your (pl)
'na★	in his	**'nan/m**	in their
'na	in her		

35a Some idioms

These forms (i.e. **'nam**, **'nad**, etc.) are used in a small number of idioms involving the verb **tha** and verbal nouns. The idioms involved normally denote a state or a condition such as: sleep, being awake, lying, running, standing, stretching out, sitting:

Tha mi 'nam chadal.	I am asleep.
Tha thu 'nad dhùisg.	You are awake.
Tha e 'na laighe.	He is lying down.
Tha i 'na ruith.	She is running.
Tha sinn 'nar seasamh.	We are standing (up).
Tha sibh 'nur sìneadh.	You are stretched out.
Tha iad 'nan suidhe.	They are sitting (down).

Exercise 1

1 John is asleep.
2 Are you awake?
3 Mary is lying down.
4 He was standing there.
5 They are sitting down.

36 More on the use of '*is*'

We have already dealt with the following types of **is** sentence:

IS	SUBJECT	PREDICATE	
Is/se	**mise**	**Iain**	I am John
Se	**Seumas**	**an tidsear**	James is the teacher
Se	**Anna**	**mo phiuthar**	Ann is my sister

So far we have only dealt with cases where the predicate is a definite noun. We will now deal with sentences where the predicate is an indefinite noun, i.e. a noun which is (a) not a proper noun, (b) not preceded by the article and (c) not preceded by a possessive pronoun. We will therefore be dealing with sentences like 'John is a teacher' and 'she is a doctor'.

So far our **is** sentences have involved the order: **is + subject + predicate**. When the predicate is indefinite, however, the order is reversed and becomes: **is + predicate + subject**. In such sentences the verb **tha** and the preposition **ann an** are used as follows:

Se	Predicate	Relative	tha	ann an	Subject
se	tidsear	a	tha	ann an	Iain
it is	a teacher	that	is	in	John

'John is a teacher'

The **a** which appears before **tha** is a relative pronoun meaning 'that'. It is explained further in Lesson 9. More examples:

Se croitear a tha ann an Seumas.	James is a crofter.
Se nurs a tha ann an Anna.	Ann is a nurse. .
Se ministear a tha ann an Uilleam.	William is a minister.
Se oileanach a tha ann am Màiri.	Mary is a student.
Se seinneadair a tha ann an Ailean.	Alan is a singer.
Se actair a tha ann an Seonag.	Joan is an actor.

If the subject is a personal pronoun, we use the prepositional pronouns associated with the preposition **ann an**. 'I am a teacher' in Gaelic is literally 'it is a teacher that is in-me': **se tidsear a tha annam**. Here are some further examples:

Se oileanach a tha annam.	I am a student.
Se seinneadair a tha annad.	You are a singer.
Se actair a tha ann.	He is an actor.
Se dotair a tha innte.	She is a doctor.

Note: there is a certain amount of ambiguity in cases like **Se nurs a tha ann**, since **ann** can refer to 'him' or 'it'. **Se nurs a tha ann** could therefore be translated as 'he is a nurse' or 'it is a nurse'. It depends on what **ann** refers to.

Vocabulary

croitear (*m*)	/krɔhtʲɛrʲ/	crofter
dotair (*m*)	/d̪ɔht̪ɛrʲ/	doctor
borbair (*m*)	/b[ɔrɔ]bɛrʲ/	barber, hairdresser

Exercise 2

Translate

1 John is a minister.
2 Ann is a singer.
3 Joan is a teacher.
4 William is a crofter.
5 Donald is a student.
6 I am a student also.
7 She is a doctor.
8 You (*pl*) are a hairdresser.
9 Are you a teacher?
10 Is he a minister?

36a Negative and question forms of '*se*'

To negate **se**, replace **se** with **chan e**. To form the positive interrogative, replace **se** with **an e**. To form the negative interrogative, replace **se** with **nach e**.

Study the following forms:

An e tidsear a tha annad?	Are you a teacher?
Chan e saor a tha annam.	I am not a carpenter.
Nach e ministear a tha ann an Iain?	Isn't John a minister?

Answering questions an e ... / nach e ...

We have already noted that there is no single word for 'yes' or 'no' in Scottish Gaelic. To answer a question beginning **an e ...?** or **nach e ...?**, the answer for 'yes' and 'no' is **se** and **chan e**, respectively. Study the following examples:

An e tidsear a tha annad?	Are you a teacher?
Se.	Yes.
Chan e.	No.
An e saor a tha ann an Iain?	Is John a carpenter?
Se.	Yes.
Chan e.	No.
Nach e seinneadair a tha ann an Anna?	Isn't Ann a singer?
Se.	Yes.
Chan e.	No.

36b Alternative construction

There is an alternative way of dealing with the above type of 'is' sentence by using the verb **tha** instead of the verb **is**.

THA + SUBJECT + {ANN AN + POSS PRON (agreeing with subject)}
               + PREDICATE

Tha	**Iain**	**'na**	**mhinistear**

John is in his minister
John is a minister

Here are some further examples:

Tha Anna 'na seinneadair.	Ann is a singer.
Tha Seonag 'na tidsear.	Joan is a teacher.
Tha Uilleam 'na chroitear.	William is a crofter.
Tha Domhnall 'na oileanach.	Donald is a student.
Tha mi 'nam oileanach cuideachd.	I am a student also.
Tha i 'na seinneadair.	She is a singer.
Tha sibh 'nur tidsear.	You (*formal*) are a teacher.
Am bheil e 'na mhinistear?	Is he a minister?

36c 'It is . . .'

To translate any sentence 'it is . . .', we use the formula **se . . . a tha ann**, irrespective of the nature of the predicate . . . (i.e. whether it is definite or indefinite):

Se cù a tha ann.	It's a dog.
Se Seumas a tha ann.	It's James.
Se an tidsear ùr a tha ann.	It's the new teacher.

To negate or ask questions, we simply replace **se** with **chan e, an e, nach e** as usual:

Chan e ministear a tha ann.	It's not a minister.
An e càr a tha ann?	Is it a car?
Nach e call a tha ann?	Isn't it a loss/pity?

37 Past tense

The past tense of sentences like **se tidsear a tha ann an Iain** 'John is a teacher' or **se Iain a tha ann** 'it is John' is formed by putting **tha** in the past tense, e.g.:

Se tidsear a bha ann an Iain.	John was a teacher.
Se oileanach a bha annam.	I was a student.
Se Anna a bha ann.	It was Ann.
Chan e Màiri a bha ann.	It wasn't Mary.
An e Uilleam a bha ann?	Was it William?

38 'This is', 'that is'

We have already learnt (see Lesson 3) how to translate 'this is. . .' and 'that is . . .' sentences when the predicate is a definite noun, e.g.:

(Is) seo Iain	OR	**Se seo Iain**	this is John
(Is) sin an tidsear	OR	**Se sin an tidsear**	that is the teacher

When the predicate is an indefinite noun, we use the construction, introduced earlier on in this lesson, i.e. **se X a tha (ann an) seo/sin/siud**, the only difference being that the preposition **ann an** is omitted:

SE	+	PREDICATE	+	A THA	+	SEO/SIN/SIUD
se		**cù**		**a tha**		**seo**

this is a dog

Here are some further examples:

Se ionad-spòrs a tha sin.	That's a sports centre.
Se sionnach a bha siud.	That was a fox.

39 To ask the question: 'What is ...?':

Dé a tha ann?	What is it?
Dé a tha seo?	What is here/what is this?
Dé a tha sin?	What is there/what is that?
Dé a tha siud?	What is there (yonder)/what is that (yon)?

40 Fronting

Fronting occurs when a word is moved from its usual position nearer to the front of the sentence. The normal order of elements in a Gaelic sentence is as follows:

VERB	+	SUBJECT	+	OBJECT	+	IND OBJECT	+	ADVERB
chunnaic		**mi**		**Seumas**		**air a' bhus**		**an-dé**
saw		I		James		on the bus		yesterday

'I saw James on the bus yesterday'

It is, however, possible to place any of these elements at the beginning of the sentence for special emphasis. Such fronted sentences are very common indeed in Gaelic and are therefore important to learn at this stage. Fronted elements are preceded either by **se** or **sann** and are 'joined' to the remainder of the sentence by a relative pronoun **a** 'that'. The use of **se** and **sann** (<**is** + **ann**) is straightforward and is as follows:

(a) **se** is used to front pronouns and nouns
(b) **sann** is used to front everything else, e.g.: adjectives, adverbs, prepositional phrases, verbal phrases, etc.

Here is how we would front each of the elements in the sentence:

Chunnaic mi Seumas air a' bhus an-dé:

mi
Se mise a chunnaic Seumas air a' bhus an-dé. OR
Is mise a chunnaic Seumas air a' bhus an-dé.
It is I who saw James on the bus yesterday.

Note that the emphatic forms of the pronoun are used with **se** as before.

Seumas
Se Seumas a chunnaic mi air a' bhus an-dé.
It is James that I saw on the bus yesterday.

air a' bhus
Sann air a' bhus a chunnaic mi Seumas an-dé.
It is on the bus that I saw James yesterday.

an-dé
Sann an-dé a chunnaic mi Seumas air a' bhus.
It is yesterday that I saw James on the bus.

chunnaic
Sann a chunnaic mi Seumas air a' bhus an-dé.
I *saw* James on the bus yesterday.

Here are some further examples of fronted sentences:

Se Seumas a thàinig a-staigh.	It is James that came in.
Se cù a chunnaic mi.	It is a dog that I saw.
Se ise a chuala mi.	It is she that I heard.
Sann sgìth a tha Seumas.	It is tired that James is.
Sann an-dé a chunnaic mi Anna.	It is yesterday that I saw Ann.
Sann an Glaschu a tha Màiri.	It is in Glasgow that Mary is.
Sann agamsa a tha an leabhar.	It is at me that the book is/ *I* have the book.
Sann a thàinig Iain anmoch.	It is that John came late/ John (really) did come late.

Note that all 'it is' sentences involve the relative **a** 'that'.

Study the following negative and interrogative forms:

Chan ann sgìth a tha mi.	It is not tired that I am.
An ann an-dé a chunnaic thu Seumas?	Was it yesterday that you saw James?
Nach ann agadsa a bha an iuchair?	Did you not have the key? (*lit* 'Was it not at you that the key was?'

*** IMPORTANT ***

Compare:

Se Seumas a tha ann.	It is James.
Se Seumas a chunnaic mi.	It is James that I saw.

In 'it is . . .' sentences when the predicate is followed by a relative clause, **a tha ann** is not used.

Exercise 3

Front each of the elements **sinn, Anna a' seinn, aig a' chéilidh, an-raoir, chuala** *in the following sentence:*

Chuala sinn Anna a' seinn aig a' chéilidh an-raoir.
We heard Ann singing at the ceilidh last night.

41 Answering questions

To answer a question beginning with **an e?** ('Is it?'), **nach e?** ('Is it not?') or **an ann?** ('Is it?'), **nach ann?** ('Is it not?'), the answers are:

QUESTION	ANSWER	
	YES	NO
an e, nach e?	se	chan e ˋ
an ann, nach ann?	sann	chan ann

42 Ownership

We have already learnt how to translate 'have' sentences; we use the verb **tha** and the preposition **aig** 'at'. However, if we want to say that something 'belongs to' someone as opposed to someone 'having' something, we use **sann** and the preposition **le** 'with'. To say 'James owns the book' or 'the book belongs to James', in Scottish Gaelic we use a fronted sentence: 'it is with James that the book is':

Sann le Seumas a tha an leabhar.   The book belongs to James.

Study the following phrases:

Sann le Màiri a tha an càr.   The car belongs to Mary.
Sann le mo bhràthair a tha   The shop belongs to my
  a' bhùth.   brother.

42a 'Who owns?'

To ask the question 'who owns . . .?', we say:

Có leis a tha an leabhar?   Who owns the book? (*lit* 'With whom
                  is the book?')
Có leis a tha seo?   Who owns this?

42b Prepositional pronouns 'le' ('with')

leam	with me	**leinn**	with us
leat	with you	**leibh**	with you
leis	with him	**leotha**	with them
leatha	with her		

Study the following phrases:

Sann leamsa a tha an cat sin.	That cat is mine/belongs to me.
Sann leatsa a tha an cù sin.	That dog is yours/belongs to you.
Sann leinne a tha an t-airgead.	The money is ours/belongs to us.

Note that the prepositional pronouns are usually used with the emphatic suffixes in this construction.

42c Idioms involving 'le' ('with')

(i) Thank you

Study the following phrases:

tapadh leat	thank you (*informal*)
tapadh leibh	thank you (*pl* or *formal*)

(ii) I like, I would like

Study the following phrases:

Is toil le Ailean ceòl-mór.	Alan likes 'pibroch' (*lit* 'big music').
Is toil leinn dealbhchluich.	We like drama.
Bu toil le Catrìona deoch orains.	Catherine would like a drink of orange.
Bu toil leotha geama ball-coise.	They would like a game of football.

Some dialects use **is caomh** and **bu chaomh** instead of **is toil** and **bu toil** repectively in the above phrases.

NEGATIVE FORMS:

Cha toil (cha chaomh) leam uisge-beatha.	I don't like whisky
Cha bu toil leam rola.	I wouldn't like a bread roll.

INTERROGATIVE (POSITIVE) FORMS:

An toil (an caomh) leat an fhidheall? Do you like the fiddle?
Am bu toil leat pinnt? Would you like a pint?

INTERROGATIVE (NEGATIVE) FORMS:

Nach toil le Alasdair lionn? Doesn't Alasdair like beer?
Nach bu toil leat aran? Wouldn't you like (some) bread?

ANSWERS:

an toil ...?/nach toil ...?	is toil	yes
	cha toil	no
am bu toil .../am bu toil ...	bu toil	yes
	cha bu toil	no

(iii) I prefer, I would prefer

Study the following phrases:

Is fheàrr le Iain aran donn. John prefers brown bread.
Is fheàrr leatha tì na cofaidh. She prefers tea to coffee.

B'fheàrr le Anna feòil na iasg. Ann would prefer meat to fish.
B'fheàrr liom sgadan. I would prefer herring.

NEGATIVE FORMS:

Chan fheàrr le Sìle golf. Sheila doesn't prefer golf.
Cha b'fheàrr leis drama. He wouldn't prefer a dram (drink).

INTERROGATIVE (POSITIVE) FORMS:

An fheàrr leat am buntàta? Do you prefer potatoes?
Am b'fheàrr leat fìon? Would you prefer wine?

INTERROGATIVE (NEGATIVE) FORMS:

Nach fheàrr le Anna dannsa? Doesn't Ann prefer dancing?
Nach b'fheàrr le Uilleam buntàta? Wouldn't William prefer potatoes?

ANSWERS:

an fheàrr ...?/ nach fheàrr ...?	is fheàrr	yes
	chan fheàrr	no
am b'fheàrr ...?/ nach b'fheàrr ...?	b'fheàrr	yes
	cha b'fheàrr	no

(iv) I don't mind, it doesn't matter to me

Study the following phrases:

Is caingeis le Calum. Calum doesn't mind, it doesn't matter to Calum.

Is caingeis leam. I don't mind.

Tha mi caingeis is also used for the latter.

Vocabulary

lionn (*m*)	/ʎuːṇ/	beer
donn	/douṇ/	brown
dannsa (*m*)	/dauṇsə/	dancing
feòil (*f*)	/fjɔːl/	meat
ceòl-mór (*m*)	/kʲɔḷ moːr/	pibroch

Exercise 4

Translate the following:

1 Is toil leam a' Ghàidhlig.
2 Is fheàrr leatha Iain.
3 Am b'fheàrr leat lionn?
4 Am bu toil leat cupa tì?
5 Chan fheàrr leotha aran donn.
6 Nach toil le Anna dannsa?
7 Cha toil leamsa feòil.
8 B'fheàrr liom lionn na uisge-beatha.
9 An toil leat Run Rig?
10 Nach b'fheàrr leat ceòl-mór?

43 The weather

The weather **sìde** (*f*) or **aimsir** (*f*) is an important part of daily conversation in Gaelic. Most conversations begin with comments on the weather. Here are some useful examples:

Se latha brèagha a tha ann.	It is a lovely day.
Se latha fuar a tha ann.	It is a cold day.
Se latha fliuch a tha ann.	It is a wet day.
Se latha blàth a tha ann.	It is a warm day.

Alternatively, we can simply use the verb **tha** as follows:

Tha e brèagha an-diugh.	It is fine today.
Tha e fuar an-diugh.	It is cold today.
Tha e fliuch an-diugh.	It is wet today.
Tha e blàth an-diugh.	It is warm today.

The feminine pronoun **i** rather than **e** is used in some dialects to refer to the weather in the above phrases.

44 Prepositions

Prepositions may be classified into two groups according to whether they lenite a following noun or not:

DO NOT LENITE A FOLLOWING NOUN		LENITE A FOLLOWING NOUN	
aig	at	**bho**★	from
air	on	**fo**★	under
á	out of, from	**do**★	to, into, for
ann an	in	**de**★	of
le	with, by	**mu**★	about
ri	against†	**ro**★	before
gu	to (the point of)	**tro**★	through

†The meaning of **ri** changes according to idiom, e.g.: **bruidhinn ri** 'speak to', **tachair ri** 'meet with', etc.

Some examples

aig balla	at a wall	**bho Sheumas**	from James
air séithear	on a chair	**fo bhaga**	under a bag
á Glaschu	from Glasgow	**do Mhàiri**	to Mary
ann an cabhag	in a hurry	**ro chàr**	before a car
le Seumas	with James	**tro dhoras**	through a doorway

Note: **do** and **de** prefix **dh'** to a following vowel or **fh-** e.g.: **do dh'Anna** 'to Ann', **de dh'fhalt** 'of hair', **do dh'Iain** 'to John'.
Do★ is frequently reduced to **a**★ especially before place names, e.g.:

a Ghlaschu	to Glasgow
a Dhùn Éideann	to Edinburgh

The preposition **ann an** is frequently reduced to **an** (**am** before labials) before placenames, e.g.:

an Glaschu	in Glasgow
an Dùn Éideann	in Edinburgh

Vocabulary

taigh (*m*)	/t̪ɤj/	house
bòrd (*m*)	/bɔːɾsd̪/	table
duine (*m*)	/d̪uɲə/	man
baile (*m*)	/balə/	town
àm (*m*)	/aum/	time
Inbhir Nis	/iɲər ɲiʃ/	Inverness
geata (*m*)	/gʲeht̪ə/	gate
càr (*m*)	/kaːr/	car

Exercise 5

Translate

1 in a house
2 on a table
3 with a man
4 through a town
5 before James
6 from time to time
7 to Inverness
8 from Edinburgh
9 at a gate
10 under a car

45 More prepositional pronouns: '*air*'

orm	on me	**oirnn**	on us
ort	on you	**oirbh**	on you (*pl*)
air	on him/it	**orra**	on them
oirre	on her/it		

(i) The preposition **air** is frequently used in the following expressions expressing hunger, thirst, etc. or physical conditions which are generally to one's disadvantage.

Tha an t-acras orm.	I am hungry. (*lit* 'The hunger is on-me')
Tha am pathadh ort.	You are thirsty.
Tha an cnatan air.	He has a cold.
Tha an t-eagal oirre.	She is afraid.
Tha cabhag oirnn.	We are in a hurry.

(ii) **Air** is also used to express 'wearing clothes, etc.':

Tha còta snog oirre.	She is wearing a nice coat.
Tha peitein air Iain.	John is wearing a jumper.

Tha bròd gan àrda orra.	They are wearing boots.
Tha ad air.	He is wearing a hat.

(iii) **Air** is also used to ask someone's name:

Dé an t-ainm a tha ort?	What is your name?
	(*lit* 'What name is on you?')
Se Iain a tha orm.	John is my name.
OR	
Tha, Iain.	John.

(iv) **Dislikes, loathes**

IS	+	BEAG	+	AIR	+	SUBJ	+	OBJ
is		beag		air		Màiri		feòil

Mary dislikes meat

Here are some further examples:

is beag air Seumas còcaireachd	James dislikes/loathes cooking
is beag orm an leabhar sin	I dislike that book

(v) **Hurry up**

Greas ort!	Hurry up! (*informal*)
Greasaibh oirbh!	Hurry up! (*pl* or *formal*)

Vocabulary

port-adhair (*m*)	/pɔʁsd̪ a-ər^j/	airport
a-null thairis	/ə ṇu:ḻ har^jiʃ/	abroad (motion to)
Paras	/parəs/	Paris
seall dhomh	/ʃauɫ ɣɔ̃/	show (to) me
cairt-shiubhail (*f*)	/kaʁsd^j çu-əl/	passport
mas e do thoil e	/maʃ e d̪ə hɔl ɛ/	please (informal)
ceart gu leòr	/k^jaʁsd̪ gə ʎɔ:r/	fine, right enough
Glaschu	/gɫasəxɔ/	Glasgow
Dùn Éideann	/d̪un e:d^jəṇ/	Edinburgh
obair (*f*)	/obər^j/	work
tidsear (*m*)	/tid^jʃɛr^j/	teacher
fear-lagha (*m*)	/fɛr ḻɤɣə/	lawyer
baga (*m*), bagaichean (*pl*)	/bagə/, /bagiçən/	bag, the bags
suidheachan (*m*)	/suɪjəxan/	seat
faisg air	/faʃg^j ɛr^j/	near

uinneag (f)	/uɲag/	window
is caingeis leam	/əs kaiŋʲgʲəʃ lə:m/	I don't care, it's all the same
cadal (vn)	/kaḍəɫ/	sleep
is beag orm	/s beg [ɔrɔ]m/	I dislike, I don't care for
plèan (m), plèanaichean (pl)	/plɛ:n/, /plɛ:niçən/	plane, planes
co-dhiubh	/ko ju:/	anyway, however
na gabh dragh	/n̪a gav ḍrɤɣ/	don't worry
sam bith	/səm bi/	any, at all
aimsir (f)	/[ɛmɛ]ʃərʲ/	weather
turas (m)	/ṭurəs/	trip, journey
beannachd leat	/bjaṉəxg lahṭ/	good-bye, farewell
mar sin leat fhéin	/mər ʃin lahṭ he:n/	the same to you

COMHRADH

Port-adhair

Oifigeach Càite am bheil thu a' dol?

Iain Tha mi a' dol a-null thairis a Pharas.

Oifigeach Seall dhomh an tiocaid agad agus do chairt-shiubhail, mas e do thoil e.

Iain Seo agad i.

Oifigeach Ceart gu leòr. Sann á Glaschu a tha thu, an ann?

Iain Sann. Ach tha mi a' fuireach ann an Dùn Éideann.

Oifigeach Agus dé an obair a tha agad an-sin?

Iain Se tidsear a bha annam ach tha mi 'nam fhear-lagha a-nis.

Oifigeach An ann leatsa a tha na bagaichean sin uile?

Iain Sann ach am fear seo.

Oifigeach Am bu toil leat suidheachan faisg air uinneag?

Iain B'fheàrr leam suidheachan eile ach is caingeis leam. Tha an cadal orm agus is beag orm plèanaichean co-dhiubh.

Oifigeach Na gabh thusa dragh sam bith. Tha an aimsir math. Turas math dhut agus beannachd leat.

Iain Mar sin leat fhéin.

TRANSLATION

At the airport

Officer Where are you going?

John I'm going abroad to Paris.

Officer	Show me your ticket and your passport, please.
John	Here it is.
Officer	Fine. You're from Glasgow?
John	Yes. But I live in Edinburgh.
Officer	And what's your job there?
John	I was a teacher, but I'm now a lawyer.
Officer	Are all those bags yours?
John	Yes, except this one.
Officer	Would you like a seat near a window?
John	I'd prefer another seat but it's all the same. I'm sleepy and I don't like planes anyway.
Officer	Don't you worry at all. The weather's good. Good journey to you and good-bye.
John	The same to you.

Lesson 6

46 The prepositional case

Gaelic has a prepositional case, which is used after most prepositions. The only parts of speech which regularly change form after prepositions are feminine nouns and the article. Masculine nouns do not change form in the prepositional case. The use of the prepositional case of feminine nouns is disappearing in Gaelic and in many dialects is confined to a handful of singular feminine nouns and then usually only when the definite article precedes.

The prepositional form of the article may affect the initial consonant of a following noun. We have actually met the prepositional form of the article already; it is **an*** (irrespective of the gender of the following noun), which as you will recall is the form of the feminine nominative singular article. The forms are:

a' + lenition	before all lenitable consonants (except **d t s f**), i.e. **b c g m p**
an t-	before 's' (**s sl sr sn**, NOT **sg sp st**)
an + lenition	before 'f'
an	otherwise, i.e. before **d n t l r** and all vowels

Some examples

am bòrd	the table	**air a' bhòrd**	on the table
an céilidh	the ceilidh	**aig a' chéilidh**	at the ceilidh
an sagart	the priest	**air an t-sagart**	on the priest
an t-sràid	the street	**air an t-sràid**	on the street

Note that the above applies to all prepositions whether they themselves lenite an immediately following noun or not, e.g.:

air càr	on a car	**air a' chàr**	on the car
fo chàr	under a car	**fon a' chàr**	under a car

Most prepositions change form before the article with the exception of **air** and **aig**. These may be classified into two groups as follows:

(a) Prepositions which add -s before the definite article:

Preposition		Preposition before the article
á	→	**ás**
ann an	→	**anns**

78

le	→	leis
ri	→	ris
gu	→	gus

(b) Prepositions which add **-n** before the definite article:

Preposition		Preposition before the article
bho	→	bhon
fo	→	fon
mu	→	mun
ro	→	ron
tro	→	tron

Note that the prepositions **do** and **de** change form slightly:

| do | → | dhan |
| de | → | dhen |

Before we proceed to look at more examples, it will be well to explain what we mean by some feminine nouns changing form in the prepositional case, especially when preceded by the article. Feminine nouns which end in a consonant are slenderised following prepositions (see **Introduction**: sounds). Note that this slenderisation may alter the preceding vowel (see **Appendix 1**).

Some examples:

Nominative singular feminine		Prepositional form: singular	
cas	→	cois	foot
bas	→	bois	palm
làmh	→	làimh	hand
cluas	→	cluais	ear
bròg	→	bròig	shoe
caileag	→	caileig	girl
cailleach	→	caillich	old woman

LITERARY GAELIC

In practice this slenderisation of nouns following prepositions is confined to a handful of nouns, including the above examples. The slenderisation is far more common in literary Gaelic.

Watch out for more examples in the samples below (marked with **P**).

Some examples of prepositions + article:

ás a' bhaile   out of the town

anns a' Ghàidhlig	in the Gaelic[1]
leis a' mhinistear	with the minister
ris an t-sagart	against/with† the priest
fon a' bhòrd	under the table
dhan a' chaileig (P)	to the girl
ron an fhear	before the man
mun an taigh	about the house
tron an latha	through the day
anns an òran	in the song
aig an uinneig (P)	at the window

†Recall the translation of **ri** depends on the idiom with which it is used.

Note: **bhon an, fon an, dhan an** etc. are frequently reduced to **bhon, fon, dhan,** e.g.:

fon bhòrd	under the table
dhan chaileig (P)	to the girl

Vocabulary

seòmar (*m*)	/ʃɔːmər/	chamber, room
airgead (*m*)	/[ɛrʲɛ]gʲəd̪/	money
Beurla (*f*)	/bjɤːɫ̪ə/	English
craobh (*f*)	/krɯːv/	tree

Exercise 1

Translate

1 at the door
2 in the room
3 with the boy
4 to the girl
5 before the ceilidh
6 with the money
7 in the car
8 in (the) English
9 under a tree
10 through the town

[1]Gaelic uses both **ann an Gàidhlig** 'in Gaelic' and **anns a' Ghàidhlig** 'in the Gaelic' for English 'in Gaelic'.

47 Prepositions which are followed by the nominative: '*gun*' ('without'); '*mar*' ('like'); '*gu ruige*' ('to')

Most, but not all, prepositions are followed by the prepositional form. Some prepositions are followed by the genitive as we will see later (see **Section 62a**). Others are followed by the nominative, e.g.: **gun**(*) 'without', **mar*** 'like' and **gu ruige** 'to'. **Gun** may or may not lenite according to dialect. **Mar*** does lenite a following noun. (Some northern dialects use **man** for **mar**; it does not lenite.) Here are some examples:

gun f(h)acal	without a word
gun sgilling	without a penny
gun an t-airgead	without the money
mar dhuine	like a man
mar chat	like a cat
mar am fiadh	like the deer
gu ruige an t-Òban	to Oban
gu ruige a' Ghearmailt	to Germany

The difference between the use of the prepositional and the nominative form after certain prepositions is seen in the following examples:

leis a' chaillich (P)	with the old woman
mar a' chailleach	like the old woman
anns an Òban (P)	in (the) Oban
gu ruige an t-Òban	to Oban

Note the following idioms involving **gun**:

gun teagamh	without doubt, certainly
gun fhiosta do	unknown to
Thàinig Iain gun fhiosta dhomh.	John came unknown to me.

48 The past tense of regular verbs: independent forms

In Lesson 4 we met the continuous past (a periphrastic construction) and also the simple past tense of irregular verbs. The simple past tense of regular verbs is derived from the root of the verb, which in Gaelic is the imperative 2nd singular form. We will see later that the simple future and conditional/past habitual tenses are also derived from the verbal root.

To form the independent form of the past tense of a regular verb, lenite (see **Introduction**: sounds) the initial consonant of the root, e.g.:

Imperative	*Past*	
brist	**Bhrist Seumas an uinneag.**	James broke the window.
dùin	**Dhùin Anna an doras.**	Ann closed the door.
ceannaich	**Cheannaich Iain am pàipear.**	John bought the paper.
gabh	**Ghabh am balach òran.**	The boy sang a song.
coisich	**Choisich an nighean a-mach.**	The girl walked out.
bruidhinn	**Bhruidhinn Màiri.**	Mary spoke.

Note: some dialects have **bris** rather than **brist** for the verb 'break'.

If the verb begins with an unlenitable consonant, e.g.: **l, n, r,** the initial remains unchanged in writing, e.g.:

leugh	**Leugh Domhnall an leabhar.**	Donald read the book.
nigh	**Nigh Màiri a làmhan.**	Mary washed her hands.
ruith	**Ruith Calum a-mach.**	Calum ran out

If the verb begins with a **vowel** or **f** followed by a vowel, then the verb is preceded by **dh'** as follows:

innis	**Dh'innis Mórag dhomh.**	Morag told (to) me.
ith	**Dh'ith Seòras am biadh aige.**	George ate his food.
òl	**Dh'òl Uilleam pinnt.**	William drank a pint.
fón	**Dh'fhón Iain.**	John phoned.

Note: the past is a simple past tense. It implies a completed action in the past and does **not** have continuous or progressive meaning. **Bhrist Seumas** means 'James broke', **not** 'James was breaking'.

The pronouns are used just as with the verb **tha**. Note that the subject always follows the verb in Scottish Gaelic.

Dhùin mi an doras.	I closed the door.
Ghabh thu òran.	You sang a song.
Dh'ith e am biadh aige.	He ate his food.
Ruith i a-mach.	She ran out.
Cheannaich sinn aran.	We bought (some) bread.
Choisibh sibh air a' chabhsair	You walked on the pavement.
Dh'ionnsaich iad a' Ghàidhlig.	They learnt (the) Gaelic.

Exercise 2

Translate

1 James closed the window.
2 Ann walked home.
3 Mary bought the paper.
4 Catherine drank her tea.
5 John sang a song.
6 Calum read the paper.
7 He told me.
8 I learnt Gaelic.
9 She ate bread.
10 William ran and closed the door.

49 Some more prepositional pronouns

ri 'to'

rium	to me	**ruinn**	to us
riut	to you	**ruibh**	to you
ris	to him	**riutha**	to them
rithe	to her		

It is difficult to translate the preposition **ri** exactly as its sense varies according to idiom. See below for examples.

do 'to, for'

dhomh	to me	**dhuinn**	to us
dhut	to you	**dhuibh**	to you
dha	to him	**dhaibh**	to them
dhi	to her		

50 Verbs and prepositions

There are very many verbs in Gaelic which are complemented by prepositions. **Ri** is frequently used with the verbs **can** 'say' and **bruidhinn** 'speak', e.g.: **can rium** 'say to me', **bhruidhinn Seumas ris** 'James spoke to him'. **Do** is frequently used with the irregular verb **thoir** 'give, bring', e.g.: **thoir dhomh** 'give (to) me'. Note that when using the following verbs and prepositions that the subject follows the verb directly and not the preposition, e.g.: **bhruidhinn Seumas (subject) ri Anna** 'James spoke to Ann'. Here are some more examples consisting mostly of regular verbs which are

complemented by prepositions. In each case the verbal root, i.e.
the imperative 2nd singular form is given.

can ri	say to
bruidhinn ri	speak to
tachair ri	meet (with)
innis do	tell (to)
thoir do	give to
iarr air	ask
faighnich de	ask (information) of
còrd ri	enjoy (to accord with)

Such prepositions combine in the usual way with nouns and
pronouns. Here are some sample sentences in the past tense:

Thuirt Iain ri Domhnall.	John said to Donald.
Thug Anna pòg do Chalum.[2]	Ann gave a kiss to Calum.
Bhruidhinn mi ri Seumas an-raoir.	I spoke to James last night.
Thachair Anna ri Màiri an-dé.	Ann met (with) Mary yesterday.
Dh'innis mi an naidheachd do Sheumas.	I told the story to James.
Dh'iarr mi air an tidsear.	I asked the teacher.
Chòrd an céilidh rium.	I enjoyed the ceilidh.

51 More on the past tense: dependent

You will recall from Lesson 4 the distinction between independent
and dependent verbal forms. The forms given above for the past
tense are the independent forms which are used independently and
in other instances to be discussed shortly. The dependent past
forms are formed by prefixing **do** to the independent past form:

Cha do dh'òl mi an tì.	I did not drink the tea.
An do bhrist Anna an uinneag.	Did Ann break the window?
Nach do cheannaich thu am pàipear?	Did you not buy the paper?
Cha do bhruidhinn Iain rithe.	John did not speak to her.
An do thachair thu ris an tidsear fhathast?	Did you meet the teacher yet?
Nach do dh'innis mi dhut mar-thà.	Did I not tell you already?
Cha do chòrd an oidhche riutha.	They did not enjoy the night.

[2]Recall that **do** lenites a following noun. See Lesson 5 page 73.

51a 'Never', 'ever'

The Gaelic word for 'never', **riamh** is used with verbs in the past tense, e.g.:

Cha do dh'òl mi lionn riamh.	I never drank beer.
Cha do shreap mi Beinn Nibheis riamh.	I never climbed Ben Nevis.
An do dh'ith thu bradan riamh?	Did you ever eat salmon?
Nach do thachair thu ri Iain riamh?	Did you never meet John?

Riamh can mean 'ever, always', e.g.:

Bha sinn a' fuireach an Glaschu riamh	We have always lived in Glasgow

51b 'Only'

The word for 'only' in Gaelic is **ach** which means literally 'but'. **Ach** is usually placed immediately before the subject or the object of the sentence. Consider the following examples:

Cha dàinig ach Anna. (*subj*)	Only Ann came.
Cha do dh'òl mi ach gloine fìon. (*obj*)	I only drank a glass of wine.
Chan eil mi ag iarraidh ach pìos beag. (*obj*)	I only want a small piece.

52 Independent and dependent verbal particles

We have defined independent verbal forms as being forms which occur 'independently', i.e. at the beginning of sentences or phrases. Similarly we have defined dependent verbal forms as forms whose occurrence is 'dependent' upon the presence of particles like **cha** 'not', **an** 'is?', **nach** 'is . . . not?' We refer to these particles as **dependent particles**. We will learn some other dependent verbal particles shortly. Independent verbal forms can also occur after certain verbal particles e.g.: **ciamar a** 'how' and **cuine a** 'when'; such particles are referred to as **independent particles**. Consider the following examples:

INDEPENDENT VERBAL FORMS:

Bha Iain ann.	John was there.
Ciamar a **bha** an céilidh?	How was the ceilidh?

Cuine a bha an céilidh ann? When was the ceilidh?
Bhrist thu an iuchair. You broke the key.
Ciamar a bhrist thu an iuchair? How did you break the key?
Cuine a bhrist thu an iuchair? When did you break the key?

INDEPENDENT PARTICLES		DEPENDENT PARTICLES	
a	that, who, which (*rel pron*)	cha	not
dé a?	what?	an	*interr particle positive*
có a?	who?	nach	*interr particle*
ciamar a?	how?		*negative*, etc.
cuine a?	when?	càite an?	where?
ged a	although	far an	where (the place that)
nuair a	when (the time that)	gun	that (conjunction)
ma	if		
na	what, that which		

Examples:

INDEPENDENT:

An duine a chunnaic **mi an-raoir.** The man that I saw last night.
Có a bhrist **an uinneag?** Who broke the window?
Ciamar a chòrd **an céilidh riut?** How did you enjoy the ceilidh?
Cuine a thill **thu dhachaigh?** When did you return home?
Chan aithne dhomh e ged a I don't know him although
  thachair **mi ris.** I met him.
Dé a thuirt **Anna?** What did Ann say?
Ma cheannaich **thu am pàipear.** If you bought the paper.
Seo na tha **agam** Here's what I have.

DEPENDENT:

Càite an do dh'fhalbh **iad.** Where did they go?
Cha do choisich **sinn an** We did not walk that night.
  oidhche ud.
An do thachair **thu ri** Did you ever meet Norman?
  Tormod riamh.
Nach do leugh **thu an leabhar** Did you not read John's book?
  aig Iain?
Càite an do cheannaich **thu** Where did you buy the sweets?
  na suiteis?
Tha an còta agad far an do Your coat is where you left it.
  dh'fhàg **thu e.**

52a How to recognise an independent verbal particle

All independent particles (with the exception of **ma** 'if' and **na** 'that which') end in the particle **a**, which as we will see in a later lesson is in fact the relative pronoun **a** 'that'. However, the **a** is frequently dropped in writing following the vowels in **có** 'who' and **dé** 'what' in order to reflect pronunciation, but is retained here for reasons of clarity.

USEFUL RULE

Verbal particles which end in **a** are independent particles and are therefore followed by independent verbal forms. All other verbal particles (except **ma** and **na**) are dependent and are followed by dependent verbal forms.

---

53 Understanding the difference between:

có	who?	~	a	who
cuine a	when?	~	nuair a	when
càite an	where?	~	far an	where
dé a	what?	~	na	what

The question mark following the words in the first column indicates that these forms are question (also called interrogative) forms. Note that they all begin with **c-** (compare English **wh-**). The forms without question marks are not question forms. **A** 'who' is a relative pronoun for which sometimes 'that' is used. **Nuair a** means 'when' in the sense 'the time that'. **Far an** means 'where' in the sense 'the place that'. **Na** means 'what' in the sense 'that which' or 'all that'.

The question forms of 'who, when, where, what' are usually used with the idiom **tha fios aig** 'know', e.g.:

Chan eil fios agam có a chuir an litir.
I don't know who sent the letter.
Am bheil fios agaibh cuine a thàinig an trèan?
Do you know when the train came?
Am bheil fios agad càite am bheil an stèisean?
Do you know where the station is?
Chan eil fios aig Anna dé a thachair.
Ann doesn't know what happened.

Note: some dialects use **far an** 'where' and **na** 'what' in indirect questions like the above.

The difference between **ma** 'if' and **an** 'if, whether' is discussed in Lesson 10 **Section 88.**

Vocabulary

dùin	/d̪u:ɲ/	close
doras (*m*)	/d̪ɔrəs/	door
iuchair (*f*)	/juxərʲ/	key
ceilidh (*m*)	/kʲe:li/	ceilidh
leabhar (*m*)	/ʎɔ-ər/	book
òg	/ɔ:g/	young
seinn (*vb*)	/ʃeiɲ/	sing
sgìth	/sgʲi:/	tired

Exercise 3

Translate

1 Who closed the door?
2 When did they go out?
3 Where did you put the key?
4 I didn't tell him
5 Did you enjoy the ceilidh?
6 I read that book when I was young
7 Leave it where you found it
8 There's the man that sang at the ceilidh
9 I didn't see James if he was there
10 He came although he was tired

54 Time

Dé an uair a tha e? What time is it?
Tha e ... It is ...

In telling the time, the word which corresponds to 'o'clock' in English is **uair**, which means 'hour' or 'time'. The singular form **uair** is used with **dà** 'two', but the plural **uairean** is used with the numerals from three to ten. Note that **aon** is not used to translate 'one (o'clock)' but is used in the translation of 'eleven (o'clock)'. The time in simple hours is therefore as follows:

uair one o'clock
dà uair two o'clock

trì uairean	three o'clock
ceithir uairean	four o'clock
còig uairean	five o'clock
sia uairean	six o'clock
seachd uairean	seven o'clock
ochd uairean	eight o'clock
naoi uairean	nine o'clock
deich uairean	ten o'clock
aon uair deug	eleven o'clock
dà uair dheug	twelve o'clock

Note the lenition of **deug** in **dà uair dheug**; it is often pronounced as if it were **dà reug**. **Meadhan latha** is used for 'midday' and **meadhan oidhche** is used for 'midnight'. If we want to indicate time a.m., we usually add **anns a' mhadainn**, literally 'in the morning'. If we want to indicate p.m., we usually add **feasgar** which literally means 'evening'. However, there is some overlap between **feasgar** and **as t-oidhche** which literally means 'at night'. **Feasgar** is generally used up to about 6 o'clock and in some cases possibly up until 9 o'clock. **As t-oidhche** is generally used from about 9 o'clock onwards although when using **feasgar** there is some overlap, with 9 o'clock as a rough boundary.

54a Other times of the year

Study the following:

a' Bhliadhna Ùr	(the) New Year
Oidhche Challainn	Hogmanay, New Year's Eve
an Nollaig	Christmas
a' Chàisg	Easter
Latha Bealltainn	May Day
Oidhche Shamhna	Halloween
am bliadhna	this year
an-uiridh	last year
a-bhòn-uiridh	the year before last
an-dé	yesterday
an-raoir	last night
a-bhòin-dé	the day before yesterday
a-màireach	tomorrow

54b 'Last', 'next'

Study the following phrases:

a' bhliadhna seo a chaidh	last year
an t-seachdain seo a chaidh	last week
a' mhìos seo a chaidh	last month

A' bhliadhna seo a chaidh literally means 'this year that has passed'. The **a** before **chaidh** is usually elided in speech.

an ath bhliadhna	next year
an ath sheachdain	next week
an ath mhìos	next month
an ath-oidhch	tomorrow night

Ath* 'next' is a leniting word and is usually preceded by the article.

Here are some other useful phrases involving **ath***:

an ath dhuine	the next person
an ath fhear (m)/t(h)é (f)	the next one (m, f)
an ath dhoras	(the) next door
an ath latha	(the) next day

'Next' can also be translated as follows:

a' bhliadhna seo a' tighinn	next year
an t-seachdain seo a' tighinn	next week
a' mhìos seo a' tighinn	next month

A' bhliadhna seo a' tighinn literally means 'this year coming'. The **a'** before **tighinn** is usually elided in speech.

55 'Some'

The word for 'some' in Gaelic is **eigin** which is affixed to a small number of nouns, e.g.:

cuid-eigin	some person, someone
rud-eigin	something
uair-eigin	sometime
àit-eigin	somewhere
té-eigin	someone (f)
fear-eigin	someone (m)

The phrase **air choireigin** 'some . . . or other' can also be used with this group and is regularly used with other nouns, e.g.:

taigh air choireigin	some house or other
leabhar air choireigin	some book or other
rud air choireigin	some thing or other

55a 'Feadhain'

The indefinite pronoun **feadhain** can mean 'some people' or 'some things', e.g.:

Dh'fhalbh feadhain a Ghlaschu agus thill feadhain eile á Peairt.
Some people went away to Glasgow and others returned from Perth.

Tha dealbhannan aig Màiri agus tha feadhain aig Anna cuideachd.
Mary has photographs and Ann also has some.

56 'Every'

The word for 'every' in Gaelic is **a h-uile** which prefixes **h-** to vowels, e.g.:

a h-uile rud	every thing
a h-uile duine	every man, everyone
a h-uile h-àite	every place
a h-uile h-uair	every time

Vocabulary

leugh (*vb*)	/ʎe:(v)/	read
pàipear-naidheachd (*m*)	/pɛ:hpɛrʲ n̪ɛ-əxg/	newspaper
an-diugh	/ən dʲu/	today
cothrom (*m*)	/kɔɾəm/	chance
dad as ùr?	/d̪ad̪ as u:r/	anything new?
Telebhisean na Gàidhlig	/tɛləviʃən nə ga:ligʲ/	Gaelic Television
muilleanan	/muʎɛnən/	millions
gu sealladh sealbh ort	/gə ʃaɫ̪ə ʃ[aɫ̪a]v ɔɾst̪/	asseveration of surprise or disbelief: good lord!
teich (*vb*)	/tʲeç/	escape, flee
prìosanach (*m*), **prìosanaich** (*pl*)	/prʲi:sanəx/, /prʲi:saniç/	prisoners
gu ruige	/gə ɾugʲə/	to
cùirt (*f*)	/ku:ɾsdʲ/	court
taghadh-pàrlamaid (*m*)	/tɤ-əɣ pa:ɾɫ̪əmɛdʲ/	parliamentary election
an Fhraing (*f*)	/ən ɾaiŋʲgʲ/	France
tagh (*vb*)	/tɤɣ/	elect, select
ceann-suidhe (*m*)	/kʲaun̪ sujə/	president

a h-uile duine	/ə hulə d̪uɲə/	everyone
dùthaich (f)	/d̪u:-iç/	country, district
bho chionn ghoirid	/ɔ çu:ꬻ ɣɤrʲəd̪ʲ/	recently
móran	/mo:ran/	much
meàirleach (m),	/mja:r̯ɫəx/,	thief, robber
meàirlich (pl)	/mja:r̯ɫiç/	
an t-Òban (m)	/əꬻ t̪ɔ:ban/	Oban
goid (vb)	/gɤd̪ʲ/	steal, rob
mìltean	/mi:ltʲən/	thousands
cuid-eigin	/kud̪ʲigʲin/	somebody
a' bhòin-dé	/ə vɔ:ɲ d̪ʲe:/	the day before yesterday
poileas (m)	/pɔləs/	police
bruidhinn (vb)	/brɯ-iɲ/	speak
manaidsear (m)	/manad̪ʲʃɛrʲ/	manager
aithnich (vb)	/aɲiç/	recognise, know
sgeul (m)	/sgʲiaɫ/	sign, news

COMHRADH

Am bheil dad as ùr?

Anna An do leugh thu am pàipear-naidheachd an-diugh?

Sìm Cha do leugh. Cha d'fhuair mi cothrom fhathast. Am bheil dad as ùr ann?

Anna Tha. Fhuair Telebhisean na Gàidhlig airgead mór: muilleanan.

Sìm Gu sealladh sealbh ort!

Anna Agus theich prìosanaich a bha a' dol gu ruige cùirt. Thachair sin an t-seachdain seo a chaidh.

Sìm Agus nach robh taghadh-pàrlamaid anns an Fhraing?

Anna Bha agus thagh iad ceann-suidhe ùr air a' phàrlamaid aca. Ach cha do chòrd sin ris a h-uile duine.

Sìm Dé a thachair anns an dùthaich seo bho chionn ghoirid?

Anna Cha do thachair móran. Bhrist meàirlich a-staigh dhan a' bhanca anns an Òban. Agus ghoid iad mìltean.

Sìm Dh'innis cuid-eigin sin dhomh a' bhòin-dé ceart gu leòr. Cha do rug am poileas orra fhathast, chuala mi.

Anna Cha do rug. Bhruidhinn am poileas ris a' mhanaidsear ach ged a dh'aithnich esan na meàirlich, chan eil sgeul aca orra.

TRANSLATION

Anything new?

    Ann   Have[3] you read the newspaper today?

  Simon No. I haven't had a chance yet. Is there anything new in it?

    Ann   There is. Gaelic Television got a lot of money: millions.

  Simon Good lord!

    Ann   And prisoners who were going to court escaped. That happened last week.

  Simon And wasn't there a parliamentary election in France?

    Ann   Yes, and they elected a new president for their parliament. But that didn't please everyone.

  Simon What happened in this country recently?

    Ann   Not much happened. Robbers broke into a bank in Oban. And they stole thousands.

  Simon Somebody told me that the day before yesterday right enough. The police didn't catch them yet, I heard.

    Ann   No. The police spoke to the manager but although he recognised the thieves, they don't have a sign of them.

---

[3]Note that Scottish Gaelic uses the simple past tense here where English uses the perfect.

Lesson 7

57 The genitive case

Gaelic, besides having a nominative and a prepositional case also has a genitive case, denoted here by (G). The genitive has various functions. It can be used (a) to express possession and (b) to give adjectival force to a noun.

(a) **taigh Dhomhnaill (G)**   Donald's house
(b) **sgian-arain (G)**   bread-knife

(a) Possession

There are two ways of expressing that something belongs to someone, only one of which involves the genitive case:

(i) POSSESSEE   +   POSSESSOR (GEN)
    taigh   **Dhomhnaill**
    Donald's house

Here are some other examples:

leabhar Sheumais (G)	James' book
cat Mòraig (G)	Morag's cat
mac ministeir (G)	a son of a minister
ad caileige (G)	a girl's hat

It will be clear from the above that the genitive of masculine proper names is formed by leniting the initial consonant of the noun and by slenderising the final consonant. The genitive of feminine proper names is formed by slenderising the final consonant of the noun. This applies only when there are initial consonants to lenite and/or when there are non-slender final consonants to slenderise. Consider the following examples whose genitive and nominative forms are identical:

leabhar Iain	John's book
cat Alasdair	Alasdair's cat
cù Anna	Ann's dog
càr Catrìona	Catherine's car

The alternative possessive construction is formed as follows:

(ii) ART   +   POSSESSEE   +   AIG   +   POSSESSOR
an   **taigh**   **aig**   **Domhnall**
Donald's house

This construction should be familiar to you. It is essentially the 'alternative possessive construction' which we learnt in Lesson 2. Here are some further examples:

an leabhar aig Seumas	James' book
an cat aig Mórag	Morag's cat
an leabhar aig Iain	John's book
an cat aig Aonghas	Angus' cat
an cù aig Anna	Ann's dog
an càr aig Catrìona	Catherine's car

(b) Adjectival force

The genitive is also used to give adjectival force to a noun. In other words, if a noun is used adjectivally, it appears in the genitive case. Let us compare the following two noun phrases:

sgian bheag	a small knife
sgian-arain (G)	a bread-knife

It is clear that both **beag** and **arain** are adjectives: they both tell us more about **sgian** 'knife' and as adjectives they naturally both follow the noun they qualify. However, **beag** is an adjective proper and **ara(i)n** is a noun. When **aran** 'bread' is used adjectivally it appears in the genitive case. The genitive of **aran** is **arain**. Hyphens are sometimes used in such compounds. Here are some further examples with the genitive noun underlined:

leabhar-sgoile	a school book
solas-sràide	a street light
seòmar-leughaidh	a reading-room

Even when the genitive indicates possession, the genitive noun also acts as an adjective. Consider the following examples, the genitive noun being underlined in each case:

mac ministeir	a minister's son
còta balaich	a boy's coat
ad caileige	a girl's hat

57a Forming the genitive case

Leaving aside irregular nouns, there are five types of genitive formation, the most important of which are numbers 1 and 2 below.

Type	Formation	
1	+ **slenderisation**	applies to masculine nouns only
2	+ **slenderisation** + **e**	applies to feminine nouns only
3	+ **a**	applies to masculine and feminine nouns
4	+ **ach**	applies to feminine nouns (usually ending in **-ir**)
5	**no change**	applies to masculine and feminine nouns

+ slenderisation means that the genitive is formed by slenderising the nominative singular form, etc. The process of slenderisation may affect the preceding vowel (as was pointed out in the introduction; see also Appendix 1) e.g.: **cas** > **coise**; **bòrd** > **bùird**; **mac** > **mic**; **caileag** > **caileige**; **cailleach** > **cailliche**; **ceòl** > **ciùil** etc. Watch out for examples below.

Here are some examples:

TYPE 1: + SLENDERISATION

Masculine nouns only

Nominative	Genitive	Example	
cat cat	**cait**	**biadh cait**	cat or cat's food
ministear minister	**ministeir**	**taigh ministeir**	a minister's house
balach boy	**balaich**	**ad balaich**	a boy's hat
bòrd table	**bùird**	**cas bùird**	leg of a table
ceòl music	**ciùil**	**fear ciùil**	a music man, musician

TYPE 2: + SLENDERISATION + E

Feminine nouns only

Nominative	Genitive	Example	
cluas ear	**cluaise**	**fàinne cluaise**	an earring
caileag girl	**caileige**	**còta caileige**	a girl's coat
cas foot, leg	**coise**	**ball-coise**	football
sgoil school	**sgoile**	**maighistear sgoile**	school teacher

TYPE 3: + A

Masculine and feminine nouns

Nominative	Genitive	Example	
pìob (f) pipe	**pìoba**	**ceòl pìoba**	pipe music
loch (m) lake	**locha**	**uisge locha**	lake water

fiodh (*m*) wood	fiodha	each fiodha	a wooden horse
fuil (*f*) blood	fala	dòrtadh fala	bloodshed
muir (*f*) sea	mara	iasg mara	sea-fish

TYPE 4: (+ SYNCOPE) + (E)ACH

Feminine nouns only

Note that the final syllable is lost (called syncope) when (**e**)**ach** is added.

Nominative	*Genitive*	*Examples*	
obair work	obrach	latha obrach	a work day
litir letter	litreach	bogsa-litreach	a letter-box

TYPE 5: NO CHANGE

Masculine and feminine nouns

Nominative	*Genitive*	*Examples*	
baile (*m*) town	baile	meadhan baile	middle of a town
duine (*m*) man	duine	ad duine	a man's hat
bus (*m*) bus	bus	draibhear bus	a bus driver
bainne (*m*) milk	bainne	gloine bainne	a glass of milk
tì (*f*) tea	tì	cupa tì	a cup of tea
colaiste (*f*) college	colaiste	cùrsa colaiste	a college course

Types 1 and 2 are by far the most commonly used. Type 5 is used for all nouns with final vowels or final -**chd** and also for the majority of recent loan-words from English. The final -**e** in type 2 is sometimes dropped with disyllabic words, thus bringing the genitive formation of such nouns into line with type 1, e.g.:

| ad caileige | OR | ad caileig | a girl's hat |
| còta cailliche | OR | còta caillich | an old woman's coat |

Note: all subsequent nouns in this lesson will have a number attached to indicate which genitive formation they have.

57b The article in the genitive case

The article changes form in the genitive. We must distinguish between masculine and feminine forms. The masculine forms are **an**⋆ which we have met before (see nominative feminine singular and prepositional singular forms of the article, Lessons 2 and 6). The feminine forms are **na** which are discussed below.

MASCULINE: *an**
a' + lenition	before all lenitable consonants (except **d t s f**), i.e. **b c g m p**
an t-	before 's' **sl sr sn**, NOT **sg sp st**
an + lenition	before 'f'
an	otherwise, i.e. before **d n t l r** and all vowels

FEMININE: *na*
na h-	before all vowels
na	otherwise

58 Double definite article

We have seen that when two nouns come together where the second noun is adjectival with respect to the first (e.g.: **leabhar Sheumais** 'James' book', **sgian-arain** 'a bread-knife'), the second noun appears in the genitive case. When the second noun is a definite noun (i.e. a proper noun or a noun preceded by the article or a possessive pronoun, see **Section 20**) the first noun i.e. the possessee may NOT be preceded by the definite article.

Am mac 'the son' and **am ministear** 'the minister' combine to give **mac a' mhinisteir** (with only one article) which means 'the son of the minister' or 'the minister's son'. The definiteness of such noun phrases is marked by the definiteness of the second noun only. Here are some more examples:

MASCULINE
fear an taighe	the man of the house, compère
fear a' bhainne	the man of the milk, the milkman
ceann a' chait	the head of the cat, the cat's head
meadhan a' bhaile	the centre of the town
leabhar a' ghille	the book of the boy, the boy's book

FEMININE
gloine na h-uinneige	the glass of the window
mac na caileige	the son of the girl, the girl's son
solas na gréine	the light of the sun, the sunlight
duilleagan na craoibhe	the leaves of the tree

DDA RULE

The DDA rule (the Double Definite Article rule) states that if the possessor is a definite noun the preceding noun (the possessee) will not be preceded by the article.

In a string of nouns connected in a genitival relation only the last noun (the possessor) appears in the genitive, e.g.:

bràthair a' bhalaich (*gen*) — the boy's brother
taigh bràthair a' bhalaich (*gen*) — the boy's brother's house
doras taigh bràthair a' bhalaich (*gen*) — the door of the boy's brother's house

Irregular nouns

Nominative		*Genitive*	*Examples*	
athair (*m*)	father	**athar**	**càr an athar**	the father's car
màthair (*f*)	mother	**màthar**	**athair mo mhàthar**	my mother's father
bràthair (*m*)	brother	**bràthar**	**taigh do bhràthar**	your brother's house
piuthar (*f*)	sister	**peathar**	**caraid mo pheathar**	my sister's friend
mac (*m*)	son	**mic**	**bean do mhic**	your son's wife
taigh (*m*)	house	**taighe**	**doras an taighe**	the door of the house
bean (*f*)	wife	**mnà**	**còta na mnà**	the wife's coat
cù (*m*)	dog	**coin**	**biadh a' choin**	the dog's food
bó (*f*)	cow	**bà**	**bainne na bà**	the cow's milk
leabaidh (*f*)	bed	**leapa**	**aodach leapa**	bed clothes
ceòl (*m*)	music	**ciùil**	**fear ciùil**	a man of music
biadh (*m*)	food	**bidhe**	**taigh bidhe**	a restaurant

Vocabulary

mac (*m, irreg*)	/maxg/	son
sagart (*m*, 1)	/sagəʁsd̪/	priest
dath (*m*, 3)	/d̪a/	colour
sneachd (*m*, 5)	/ʃɲɛxg/	snow
cnoc (*m*, 1)	/krɔ̃xg/	hill
doras (*m*, 1)	/d̪ɔrəs/	door
sgoil (*f*, 2)	/sgɔl/	school
biadh (*m, irreg*)	/biəɣ/	food
leabhar (*m*, 1)	/ʎɔ-ər/	book

Exercise 1

Translate

1 the son of the priest
2 the colour of the snow
3 the top of the hill
4 the door of the school
5 my brother's sister
6 the key of the house
7 my sister's car
8 the cat's food
9 James' father
10 Catherine's book

59 Surnames

In surnames the element following **Mac** is usually a noun in the genitive, e.g.:

MacDhomhnaill	MacDonald	(*lit* 'the son of Donald')
MacAonghais	MacInnes	(*lit* 'the son of Angus')
Mac a' Ghobhainn	Smith	(*lit* 'the son of the smith')
Mac an t-Saoir	Macintyre	(*lit* 'the son of the carpenter')

Nic rather than **Mac** is used for females, e.g.:

NicDhomhnaill	MacDonald
NicAonghais	MacInnes
Nic a' Ghobhainn	Smith
Nic an t-Saoir	Macintyre

60 Adverbs of quantity

On occasions you will need to talk about quantities; you may have too much, too little, a lot or not enough of something, etc.

Study the following:

móran	much, many
beagan	little, small amount
tòrr	a lot
cus	too much, too many (very many)
gu leòr/pailteas	enough, plenty

These words can be used on their own as nouns, e.g.:

Chan eil móran an-seo.	There is not much here.
Tha beagan agam.	I have a little.
Tha tòrr an-sin.	There is a lot there.
Dh'òl Domhnall cus an-raoir.	Donald drank too much last night.
Am bheil gu leor agad?	Do you have enough?

These words can also be used with a following noun in which case the following noun appears in the genitive:

móran airgid (G)	much money
beagan salainn (G)	a little salt
tòrr siùcair (G)	a lot of sugar
cus feòla (G)	too much meat
gu leòr/pailteas càise (G)	enough/plenty of cheese

However, **móran** and **beagan** may also be used with the preposition **de** 'of' :

móran de dh'airgead	much money
beagan de shalann	a little salt

61 The verbal noun and the genitive case

In Lesson 3, we discussed the periphrastic construction involving the verb **tha** and verbal nouns. The direct object of this periphrastic construction normally appears in the genitive when the object is a definite noun (see **Section 20**), e.g.:

Tha mi a' leughadh an leabhair (G).	I am reading the book.
Tha e a' seinn an òrain (G).	He is singing the song.
Tha i ag ithe na feòla (G).	She is eating the meat.

The use of the genitive is easily understood when we consider a literal translation of the above examples:

I am at the reading of the book.
He is at the singing of the song.
She is at the eating of the meat.

If, however, the verbal noun in question is complemented by a preposition, the (indirect) object of such verbs does not appear in the genitive since it follows a preposition. Here are some examples:

Bha mi a' bruidhinn ri Seumas.	I was talking to James.
Thug Calum pòg dhan a' chaileig (P).	Calum gave a kiss to the girl.
Dh'innis mi an naidheachd dhan a' chaillich (P).	I told the story to the old woman.
Chòrd an céilidh ri Domhnall.	Donald enjoyed the ceilidh.

Vocabulary

tì (*f*, 5)	/ti:/	tea
fosgladh (*vn*)	/fɔsgɫəγ/	opening
dùnadh (*vn*)	/d̪u:nəγ/	closing
doras (*m*, 1)	/d̪ɔrəs/	door
uinneag (*f*, 2)	/uɲag/	window

Exercise 2

Translate

1 We are leaving today.
2 Are they coming?
3 Who is singing?
4 They are not listening.
5 We were eating and drinking.
6 Were you working today?
7 She is drinking the tea.
8 They are buying the book.
9 I am opening the door.
10 She is closing the window.

62 Composite prepositions

The prepositions which we have met so far have been simple prepositions consisting of monosyllabic words. These prepositions are followed by the prepositional form (of the article and of feminine nouns) in Scottish Gaelic. There are, however, other prepositions which we may call **composite prepositions** which consist of two words, one of which is a simple preposition. There are two types, the distinction between them depending upon the position of the simple preposition; the simple preposition may be (A) the second element or (B) the first element.

Type A: word + preposition = new composite preposition

coltach ri	like
comhla ri	along with
timcheall air	around
tarsainn air	across, over
seachad air	past
faisg air	near, close to

The prepositional form of the article and of feminine nouns are used following these composite prepositions since their final element is a simple preposition:

coltach ri seann chù	like an old dog
comhla ri mo phiuthair (P)[1]	(along) with my sister
timcheall air a' chladach	around the shore
tarsainn air a' bhalla	over the wall
seachad air a' chaillich (P)	past the old woman
faisg air a' chathair	near the city

Type B: preposition + noun = new composite preposition

air cùl	behind
air beulaibh	in front
(air) feadh	throughout
an aghaidh	against
an deidh	after
mu dheidhinn	about, concerning
os cionn	over, above
ri taobh	beside
a dh'ionnsaigh	to, towards
as aonais	without, in the absence of
airson (< air + son)	for (the sake of)

A noun following these composite prepositions appears in the genitive. This is illustrated by the following example:

ri taobh a' chait (G)[2] beside the cat

Ri taobh means literally 'by side'. When a noun, e.g. **an cat** 'the cat' follows, this becomes 'by the side <u>of</u> the cat', hence the need for the genitive. Most of the above composite (type B) prepositions can be translated by using two words in English which would use 'of' before a following noun, e.g.: **air cùl** 'on back (of)', **air beulaibh** 'in front (of)', **an aghaidh** 'in face (of)', etc. Traditionally **air + son** is written as one word, **airson**.

Some examples:

airson do mhàthar (G)	for your mother
air cùl an taighe (G)	behind the house
air feadh na h-Alba (G)	throughout Scotland
an aghaidh na gaoithe (G)	against the wind

---

[1] P denotes prepositional form of the noun.
[2] G denotes the genitive form of the noun.

an deidh a' gheama (G)	after the game
mu dheidhinn a' ghaoil (G)	about love
os cionn an dorais (G)	above the door
ri taobh a' bhalaich (G)	beside the boy
a dh'ionnsaigh a' bhaile (G)	towards the town
as aonais mo pheathar (G)	without my sister

62a Prepositions which are followed by the genitive

There is a small number of **simple prepositions** which are followed by the genitive:

chun	to
far	off
ré	during
tarsainn	across
chun a' bhaile (G)	to the town
far a' bhùird (G)	off the table
ré na h-oidhche (G)	during the night
tarsainn na pàirce (G)	across the park

Do not confuse **far** 'off' which is a preposition and therefore only used before nouns, with **far an** 'where' which is a verbal particle and is therefore only used before verbs.

Composite prepositions with pronouns

Type A

Pronoun objects of type A composite pronouns combine in the usual way with the final preposition:

coltach rium	like me
comhla riut	along with you
timcheall oirnn	around us
tarsainn orra	across them
seachad oirbh	past you

Type B

Pronoun objects of type B composite prepositions do not follow the preposition as expected. Instead the pronoun appears as a possessive pronoun and precedes the noun part of the composite preposition. 'Behind me' is not **air cùl mi** but **air mo chùlaibh**, literally 'on my back'. Here are other examples:

AIR CÙL		AIR BEULAIBH	
air mo chùlaibh	behind me	air mo bheulaibh	in front of me
air do chùlaibh	behind you	air do bheulaibh	in front of you
air a chùlaibh	behind him	air a bheulaibh	in front of him
air a cùlaibh	behind her	air a beulaibh	in front of her
air ar cùlaibh	behind us	air ar beulaibh	in front of us
air ur cùlaibh	behind you	air ur beulaibh	in front of you
air an cùlaibh	behind them	air am beulaibh	in front of them

AN AGHAIDH		AN DEIDH	
nam aghaidh	against me	nam dheidh	after me
nad aghaidh	against you	nad dheidh	after you
na aghaidh	against him	na dheidh	after him
na h-aghaidh	against her	na deidh	after her
nar n-aghaidh	against us	nar deidh	after us
nur n-aghaidh	against you	nur deidh	after you
nan aghaidh	against them	nan deidh	after them

MU DHEIDHINN		RI TAOBH	
mu mo dheidhinn	about me	ri mo thaobh	beside me
mu do dheidhinn	about you	ri do thaobh	beside you
mu a dheidhinn	about him	ri a thaobh	beside him
mu a deidhinn	about her	ri a taobh	beside her
mu ar deidhinn	about us	ri ar taobh	beside us
mu ur deidhinn	about you	ri ur taobh	beside you
mu an deidhinn	about them	ri an taobh	beside them

AIRSON		OS CIONN	
air mo shon	for me	os mo chionn	over me
air do shon	for you	os do chionn	over you
air a shon	for him	os a chionn	over him
air a son	for her	os a cionn	over her
air ar son	for us	os ar cionn	over us
air ur son	for you	os ur cionn	over you
air an son	for them	os an cionn	over them

A DH'IONNSAIGH		AS AONAIS	
gam ionnsaigh	towards me	as m'aonais	without me
gad ionnsaigh	towards you	as d'aonais	without you
ga ionnsaigh	towards him	as a aonais	without him
ga h-ionnsaigh	towards her	as a h-aonais	without her
gar n-ionnsaigh	towards us	as ar n-aonais	without us
gur n-ionnsaigh	towards you	as ur n-aonais	without you
gan ionnsaigh	towards them	as an aonais	without them

Vocabulary

doras (*m*)   /d̪ɔrəs/   door

Exercise 3

Translate

1 behind me
2 in front of you
3 above him
4 beside her
5 without us
6 like them
7 along with me
8 around us
9 past it (*m*)
10 to the door

63 More on time

We have already learnt how to tell the time in simple hours. We will now learn how to tell other times. The word for 'after/past' is **an deidh** and the word for 'to' is **gu**. The counting form of the numerals follows both **gu** and **an deidh** i.e. **a** precedes the numerals from two to ten e.g.: **a dhà, a trì, . . ., a h-ochd** etc. However, the **a** is generally elided in speech and usually in writing following **gu**; it will be retained here for reasons of clarity. The word for 'quarter' is **cairteal** (**ceathramh** in some dialects) and the word for 'half' is **lethuair**.

cairteal an deidh a deich	quarter past ten
cairteal gu a sia	quarter to six
lethuair an deidh a h-ochd	half past eight
cairteal gu a h-ochd	quarter to eight
cairteal gu aon uair deug	quarter to eleven
lethuair an deidh dà uair dheug	half past twelve

You will note that **uair, uairean** are usually omitted in the above examples, except in the case of **aon uair deug**, 'eleven o'clock', and **dà uair dheug**, 'twelve o'clock'.

When using minutes the appropriate form of the word **mionaid** 'minute' is used, i.e. singular after **dà** and plural, **mionaidean**, after numerals from three to ten. The singular form of **mionaid** is always used with **fichead** 'twenty'.

mionaid an deidh uair	a minute past one
dà mhionaid an deidh a h-ochd	two minutes past eight
trì mionaidean gu a deich	three minutes to ten
cóig mionaidean gu meadhan latha	five (minutes) to midday
deich mionaidean an deidh a trì	ten (minutes) past three
fichead mionaid gu a ceithir	twenty (minutes) to four
cóig mionaidean fichead gu a seachd	twenty-five to seven

Note that **mionaidean** is generally <u>not</u> omitted in Scottish Gaelic as 'minute(s)' is in English.

Vocabulary

lathaichean saora (*m*)	/ḷa-içən sɯːrə/	holidays
taobh (*f*)	/ṭɯːv/	side, part
riamh	/rʲiəv/	ever
roimhe	/rɔ̃jə/, /rējə/	before
an-uiridh	/ə n̪ʲurʲi/, /ə n̪ʲuri/	last year
Beinn na h-Iolaire	/beiɲ nə çuḷərʲə/	the Mountain of the Eagle
sreap (*vb*)	/sṭrɛhp/	climb
shreap	/hrɛhp/	climbed
Cnoc a' Chapaill	/krɔ̃xk ə xahpəʎ/	the Hill of the Horse
còrd ri (*vb*)	/kɔːr̪ṣḍ rʲi/	enjoy, be pleasing to
gu sonraichte	/gə sɔ̃ːriçdʲə/	especially
coltas (*m*)	/kɔḷṭəs/, /kɔḷəs/	appearance
uabhasach	/ūāvasəx/	terribly (intensifier), very much
àite (*m*)	/aːhtʲə/	place
iasgach (*vn*)	/iəsgəx/	fishing
gu tric	/gə ṭriçgʲ/	often
Loch na Creige	/ḷɔx nə krʲegʲə/	the Loch of the Crag
Linne na Ciste	/ʎiɲə ūə kʲiʃtʲə/	the Pool of the Chest
abhainn (*f*)	/ā-iɲ/, /āviɲ/, /ān-iɲ/	river
Càrn Sheumais	/kaːr̪ṇ heːmiʃ/	the Cairn of James
le chéile	/lɛ çeːlə/	both, together
an Sìdhein (*m*)	/əɲ ʃiː-ɛn/	the Fairy Mound
muir (*f*), mara (G)	/murʲ/, /marə/	sea
rathad (*m*)	/r̪a-əḍ/	road
tachair ri (*vb*)	/ṭaxərʲ rʲi/	meet with
geamair (*m*)	/gʲɛmɛrʲ/	gamekeeper
dùthaich (*f*), dùthcha (G)	/ḍuː-iç/, /ḍuːxə/	country, district
eachdraidh (*f*)	/ɛxḍri/	history

COMHRADH

Lathaichean saora faisg air Beinn na h-Iolaire[3]

Domhnall	Tha mac mo pheathar agus bràthair m'athar a' tighinn gar n-ionnsaigh air an lathaichean saora.
Iain	An robh iad an taobh seo riamh roimhe?
Domhnall	O bha gu dearbh. Bha iad an-seo an-uiridh comhla ruinn.
Iain	Agus dé a rinn sibh?
Domhnall	Sheall sinn Beinn na h-Iolaire dhaibh agus shreap sinn Cnoc a' Chapaill.
Iain	An do chòrd sin riutha?
Domhnall	Chòrd, agus gu sonraichte chòrd coltas an àite riutha uabhasach math.
Iain	An robh sibh ag iasgach comhla riutha?
Domhnall	Bha gu tric air Loch na Creige agus aig Linne na Ciste.
Iain	An deach sibh tarsainn air an abhainn no seachad air Càrn Sheumais?
Domhnall	Chaidh, le chéile, agus timcheall air an t-Sìdhein agus ri taobh na mara ar an rathad dhachaigh.
Iain	An do thachair geamair na dùthcha ruibh?
Domhnall	Thachair agus dh'innis e eachdraidh an àite dhaibh. Bha e uabhasach coibhneil.

CONVERSATION

Holidays near Beinn na h-Iolaire

Donald	My nephew (sister's son) and my uncle (father's brother) are coming (to visit us) on their holidays.
John	Were they ever in these parts before?
Donald	Oh yes indeed. They were here last year with us.
John	And what did you do?
Donald	We showed them Beinn na h-Iolaire and we climbed Cnoc a' Chapaill.
John	Did they enjoy that?
Donald	They did, and especially they enjoyed the appearance of the place very much.
John	Were you fishing along with them?
Donald	Yes, often on Loch na Creige and at Linne na Ciste.
John	Did you go across the river or past Càrn Sheumais?

[3]A not uncommon place name throughout the Highlands and Islands.

Donald Yes we did,. both of them, and round the Sìdhein and beside the sea on the way home.

John Did the gamekeeper of the district meet you?

Donald Yes, he did and he told them the history of the place. He was terribly kind.

Lesson 8

64 'Tha': future

You will recall that Gaelic differentiates between independent and dependent verbal forms. Independent forms are used (i) independently and (ii) following independent verbal particles. Dependent forms are used following dependent verbal particles. In the future tense (of regular verbs) there are two independent verbal forms, the first of which is used independently and the second, following independent verbal particles. Here are the future forms of **tha**:

INDEPENDENT (i)	INDEPENDENT (ii) = Relative	DEPENDENT	
bidh	**bhios**	**bi**	
bidh mi	**bhios mi**	**bi mi**	I will be
bidh tu	**bhios tu**	**bi thu**	you will be
bidh e, i	**bhios e, i**	**bi e, i**	he, she will be
bidh sinn	**bhios sinn**	**bi sinn**	we will be
bidh sibh	**bhios sibh**	**bi sibh**	you will be
bidh iad	**bhios iad**	**bi iad**	they will be

Note also that **tu** is used with the independent forms and **thu** is used with the dependent form.

The future forms of **tha** may also be used to denote habitual actions, particularly when adverbs implying habit are present, e.g.:

Bidh mi ann an Glaschu a h-uile latha. I am in Glasgow every day.
Bidh mi a' snàmh a h-uile madainn. I swim every morning.

64a Regular verbs: future

The periphrastic construction involving **tha** and the verbal noun, when used in the future usually refers only to the continuous future, e.g.: **bidh mi ag òl** 'I will be drinking'. The simple future consists of short verbal forms derived from the verbal root. We must distinguish once again between independent and dependent forms in the future tense. Moreover, we must distinguish between

two independent forms in this case. You will recall that independent forms occur:

(i) in utterance initial position and
(ii) following independent particles.

The future uses separate verbal forms for each. We will refer to the first independent form as the independent form of the future and to the second independent form as the relative form of the future.

The independent form is made by adding -**(a)idh** to the verbal root e.g.: **cuiridh** 'will put'. The relative form is made by adding -**(e)as** to the verbal root and leniting the verbal root, e.g.: **chuireas**; if the verbal root begins with a vowel or f + vowel, **dh'** is prefixed to the verbal root, e.g. **dh'òlas, dh'fhalbhas.**

The endings -**aidh** and -**as** are used following verbal roots with final broad endings in accordance with the fundamental spelling rule of Gaelic: **Leathann ri Leathann is Caol ri Caol** 'Broad with broad and slender with slender'. Similarly, -**idh** and -**eas** are used following verbal roots with final slender endings.

The dependent form of the future is the verbal root itself. Here are some examples:

Imperative/ Verbal Root	*Independent* (i)	*Independent* (ii) = *Relative*	*Dependent*
cuir put	**cuiridh**	**chuireas**	**cuir**
gabh eat, etc.	**gabhaidh**	**ghabhas**	**gabh**
brist break	**bristidh**	**bhristeas**	**brist**
ceannaich buy	**ceannaichidh**	**cheannaicheas**	**ceannaich**
leugh read	**leughaidh**	**leughas**	**leugh**
òl drink	**òlaidh**	**dh'òlas**	**òl**
falbh go away	**falbhaidh**	**dh'fhalbhas**	**falbh**

Examples:

<u>**Cuiridh**</u> mi a-mach an cat. (Independent)
I will put the cat out.

Có <u>chuireas</u> a-mach an cat? (Relative)
Who will put the cat out?

Cha <u>chuir</u> Seumas a-amach e. (Dependent)
James won't put him out.

<u>**Gabhaidh**</u> mi buntàta is ìm. (Independent)
I will eat potatoes and butter.

Dé <u>ghabhas</u> Anna? (Relative)
What will Ann eat?

Nach gabh i an aon rud?	(Dependent) Will she not have the same (thing)?
Òlaidh mi uisge beatha.	(Independent) I will drink whisky.
Nuair a dh'òlas mi lionn.	(Relative) When I drink ale.
An òl thu balgam beag?	(Dependent) Will you drink a little drop?

64b Pronouns

The personal pronouns **mi, t(h)u, e, i, sinn, sibh, iad** are used with all future forms. However, **tu** is used with the independent forms **-(a)idh** and **-(e)as** and **thu** is used with the dependent forms, e.g.:

Bristidh tu a' ghloine.	You will break the glass.
Dé sheinneas tu?	What will you sing?
An ceannaich thu am pàipear?	Will you buy the paper?

Note that **cha** normally lenites a following consonant (except **d, t** and **s**) and becomes **chan** before vowels and **f** + vowels, e.g.:

Cha chuir mi a-mach an cù.	I will not put the dog out.
Cha ghabh e sìon.	He will not eat anything.
Chan òl mi uisge beatha.	I will not drink whisky.
Chan fhalbh iad gu bràch.	They will never leave.

*** IMPORTANT ***

Verbs with two syllables usually ending in **-r, -l, -n, -ng** lose their second syllable when the future endings are added. Here is a list of the most important examples, illustrated with the endings **idh, as**:

tachair	tachraidh, thachras	will happen
fosgail	fosglaidh, dh'fhosglas	will open
bruidhinn	bruidhnidh, bhruidhneas	will speak
tarraing	tàirrnidh, thàirrneas	will pull

Note also:

| innis | innsidh, dh'innseas | will tell |

Note: final **-nn** and **-ng** are reduced to **-n** when an ending is added

---

In English in sentences where the main clause is in the future tense, subordinate clauses introduced by 'when' and 'if' usually appear in the present tense. In Gaelic the future tense is retained throughout in both clauses, e.g.:

Leughaidh mi an leabhar nuair a bhios an ùine agam.
I will read the book when I have the time.

Òlaidh mise té ma ghabhas tu fhéin té.
I will drink one (a drink) if you take one.

64c Present habitual use of future tense

The future tense forms may, as in English, be used to denote present habitual actions, particularly when adverbs implying habit are present, e.g.

Ceannaichidh Iain am pàipear a h-uile latha.	John buys the paper every day.
Falbhaidh iad gach seachdain.	They go away every week.
Bidh mi an Glaschu gu math tric.	I am in Glasgow fairly frequently.

65 Ability

The future tense can imply 'ability', e.g.:

seinnidh Anna	Ann can sing
cluichidh Iain camanachd	John can play shinty

Vocabulary

ionnsaich (*vb*)	/jūːn̠siç/	learn
seinn (*vb*)	/ʃeiɲ/	sing
òran (*m*, 1)	/ɔːran/	song
aran (*m*, 1)	/aran/	bread
geal	/gʲaɫ/	white
gu moch	/gə mɔx/	early
uair sam bith	/uərʲ səm bi/	any time
anns a' mhadainn	/as ə vãḏiɲ/	in the morning
till (*vb*)	/tʲiːʎ/	return
fàg (*vb*)	/faːg/	leave
falbh (*vb*)	/f[aɫa]v]	go away, leave
airgead (*m*, 1)	/[ɛrʲɛ]gʲəḏ/	money
cuidich (*vb*)	/kudʲiç/	help

pàipear (*m*, 1)	/pɛ:hpɛrʲ/	paper
dùisg (*vb*)	/d̪u:ʃgʲ/	to wake up
dùin (*vb*)	/d̪u:ɲ/	to close
doras (*m*, 1)	/d̪ɔrəs/	door

Exercise 1

Translate

1 Ann will drink her tea.
2 I will learn Gaelic.
3 When will you sing the song?
4 She will not buy white bread any time.
5 Will they go away early in the morning?
6 I will speak to him if he returns.
7 Where will we leave the money?
8 Who will help me?
9 I will read the paper when I wake up.
10 How will you close the door?

66 Answering questions

As usual, we repeat the main verb of the question:

An òl thu am bainne?	Will you drink the milk?
Òlaidh.	Yes.
Chan òl.	No.
An dùin thu an doras?	Will you close the door?
Dùinidh.	Yes.
Cha dùin.	No.

67 Conjunctions

Conjunctions are words that join two sentences together. There are two types of conjunctions:

(a) co-ordinating conjunctions
(b) subordinate conjunctions

(a) Co-ordinating conjunctions

Co-ordinating conjunctions join two sentences or clauses together which are of <u>equal</u> importance. **Agus** 'and', **no** 'or' and **ach** 'but' are examples of co-ordinating conjunctions. Co-ordinating conjunctions are not strictly speaking either independent or dependent particles. This is clearly seen when they are used in future sentences where the independent (i) form of a following verb is used, not the independent (ii) = relative form. Here are some examples:

Bidh Iain ann agus bidh Anna ann cuideachd.
John will be there and Ann will be there also.

Chan eil am pathadh orm ach òlaidh mi fìon.
I am not thirsty but I will drink some wine.

Seinnidh e òran no innsidh e sgeulachd.
He will sing a song or he will tell a story.

(b) Subordinate conjunctions

Subordinate conjunctions introduce subclauses. A subclause is a clause which is dependent on a main clause. Subordinate clauses are marked in Gaelic either by the presence of the relative particle **a** 'that' or a dependent verbal form. The subordinate nature of independent verbal particles is shown by the presence of the relative pronoun **a** 'that'. See Lesson 6, **Section 52** where it was pointed out that all independent particles are followed by the relative particle **a** 'that'. Here are some examples:

Tha iad a' ràdh gun dàinig Iain.
They say that John came.

An aithne dhut an t-àite far am bheil Anna a' fuireach?
Do you know the place where Ann lives?

Cha deach Màiri air lathaichean saora ged a bha an t-airgead aice.
Mary didn't go on holiday even though she had the money.

67a 'Because', 'since'

There are many words in Gaelic which may be roughly translated as 'because', which can be classified into two types:

TYPE 1		TYPE 2	
a chionn	because, since	**a chionn is gun**	because
a thoradh	because, since	**a thoradh is gun**	because
airson	because, since		
oir	because, since		

Type 2 conjunctions are dependent verbal particles and are
followed by dependent verbal forms. However, type 1 conjunctions
are neither followed by the relative pronoun nor by dependent
verbal forms. They act, in effect, like co-ordinating conjunctions
and are followed by independent (non-relative) verbal forms. Here
are some examples of both:

Chaidh mi a Pheairt a chionn bha mo charaid a' fuireach ann.
I went to Perth since my friend was living there.

**Chaidh mi a Pheairt a chionn is gun robh mo charaid a'
fuireach ann.**
I went to Perth because my friend was living there.

67b 'Never', 'ever'

The Gaelic word **gu bràch** is used with the future and conditional.

Chan fhàg mi an t-Eilean Sgitheanach gu bràch.
I will never leave the Isle of Skye.

Chan òl mi lionn gu bràch a-rithist.
I will never drink beer again.

An ceannaich thu taigh ùr gu bràch?
Will you ever buy a new house?

Mairidh sin gu bràch.
That will last forever.

Gu bràch can be emphasised by adding **tuilleadh**, e.g.:

Cha cheannaich mi aran geal gu bràch tuilleadh.
I will never again buy white bread.

68 The plural

The majority of nouns have one plural form only which is used for
all forms, the nominative, prepositional and genitive. The
nominative and prepositional plural forms are identical for **all**
nouns. Some nouns, however, have a different genitive plural form
as we will see below. It is important to note that the plural form of
any noun may vary according to dialect, e.g.: **àiteachan** and
àitichean are both used as the plural form of **àite** (*m*) 'place'. There
are two main ways of forming the plural in Scottish Gaelic:

(A) by adding a suffix ending in **-(e)an**
(B) by slenderising the final consonant

There is no easy way of predicting what the plural form for any given noun will be. Plural forms must be learnt as vocabulary items.

**TYPE A
SUFFIXES ENDING IN -(E)AN**

1 (e)an
2 t(e)an
3 (e)achan
4 (a)ichean
5 (e)annan
6 slenderisation + ean

Examples

TYPE A1

	Singular	Plural	
(e)an	caileag	caileagan	girls
	uinneag	uinneagan	windows
	gille	gillean	boys
	craobh	craobhan	trees

TYPE A2

t(e)an	sgoil	sgoiltean	schools
	baile	bailtean	towns
	teine	teintean	fires
	coille	coilltean	woods

TYPE A3

(e)achan	gloine	gloineachan	glasses
	balla	ballachan	walls
	àite	àiteachan	places

Balla and **àite** also have plural forms **ballaichean** and **àitichean** respectively.

TYPE A4

(a)ichean	bliadhna	bliadhnaichean	years
	càr	càraichean	cars
	clas	clasaichean	classes
	latha	lathaichean	days
	nurs	nursaichean	nurses

TYPE A5

(e)annan	àm	amannan	times
	oidhche	oidhcheannan	nights
	dealbh	dealbhannan	pictures
	ainm	ainmeannan	names

TYPE A6

Slenderisation + ean	cladach	cladaichean	sea shores
	anart	anairtean	linens

TYPE B
SLENDERISATION

This applies to masculine nouns only. The process of slenderisation can affect the preceding vowel, as before. See Appendix 1.

Examples

SINGULAR	NOMINATIVE PLURAL	
bodach	bodaich	old men
òran	òrain	songs
cat	cait	cats
boireannach	boireannaich	women
Gàidheal	Gàidheil	Gaels
bòrd	bùird	tables
fiadh	féidh	deer
cnoc	cnuic	hills
Gall	Goill	Lowlanders
ceann	cinn	heads

68a Genitive plural

For type A suffix plurals (i.e. all plurals ending in **-an**), the genitive plural is the same as the nominative plural. For type B plurals, the genitive plural in Gaelic is different from the nominative plural and is in fact the same as the nominative singular.

Note that nouns with suffix plurals (i.e. type A) can also have genitive plural forms which are identical to the nominative singular. Such forms are particularly common in higher registers of the language but are not uncommon in local dialects.

Here are some examples which illustrate the two types of genitive plural formation:

NOM. SING.		NOM. PL.		GEN. PL.	
TYPE A					
caileag	girl	**caileagan**	girls	**caileagan**	girls'
sgoil	school	**sgoiltean**	schools	**sgoiltean**	schools'
càr	car	**càraichean**	cars	**càraichean**	cars'
dealbh	picture	**dealbhannan**	pictures	**dealbhannan**	pictures'
craobh	tree	**craobhan**	trees	**craobhan**	trees'
TYPE B					
bodach	old man	**bodaich**	old men	**bodach**	old men's
òran	song	**òrain**	songs	**òran**	songs'
boireannach	woman	**boireannaich**	women	**boireannach**	women's
Gàidheal	Gael	**Gàidheil**	Gaels	**Gàidheal**	Gaels'
cat	cat	**cait**	cats	**cat**	cats'

68b The plural article

As with nouns, the nominative and prepositional plural form of the article is identical; it is **na**. (This, you will recall, is also the form of the feminine singular genitive article; see Lesson 7, **Section 57b**.)

> **Nominative (= prepositional) article** (*pl*): **na**
> **na h-**   before vowels
> **na**   otherwise

The genitive plural form of the article is **nan**:

> **Genitive article: nan**
> **nam**   before the labials **b p f m**
> **nan**   otherwise

NOM. SING.		NOM. PL.	GEN. PL.
uinneag	window	na h-uinneagan	nan uinneagan
caileag	girl	na caileagan	nan caileagan
pìob	pipe	na pìoban	nam pìoban
cat	cat	na cait	nan cat
bodach	old man	na bodaich	nam bodach

68c Note on the genitive plural

When the article does not precede a genitive plural noun, the noun is automatically lenited. In other words indefinite genitive plurals are lenited, e.g.:

móran ghillean (G, *pl*)	a large number of boys, many boys
beagan bhòrd (G, *pl*)	a small number of tables

69 Prepositions before the article

We have already noted that the prepositional plural is always the same as the nominative plural. You will recall that most prepositions change form when they precede the singular article by adding -n or -s. Those prepositions which add -s before the singular article also add -s before the plural article. All other prepositions do **not** change form before the plural article except **do** and **de** which become **dha** and **dhe** respectively. Here are some examples:

anns na craobhan	in the trees
leis na gillean	with the boys
bruidhinn ris na nursaichean	speak to the nurses
ás na càraichean	out of the cars
bho na lathaichean sin	since those days
tro na dorsan	through the doorways
do na bodaich	to the old men
tro na h-uinneagan	through the windows

Vocabulary

cànan (*m*)	/ka:nan/	language
airgead (*m*, 1)	/[ɛrʲɛ]gʲəd̪/	money
an deidh (+ *genitive*)	/əɲ dʲe:/, /əɲ dʲɣ-i/	after

Exercise 2

Translate

1 the girls and boys
2 in the towns
3 under the tables
4 from the Gaels
5 on the hills
6 the teachers of the schools
7 the boys' books
8 the language of the Gaels
9 the women's money
10 after the nights

70 Irregular nouns: plural

There is a small handful of nouns whose plural formations are irregular and as such should be learnt separately:

NOMINATIVE SING.		NOMINATIVE PL.	GENITIVE PL.
bean (*f*)	wife	**mnathan**	**ban**
cù (*m*)	dog	**coin**	**con**
bó (*f*)	cow	**bà**	**bó**
beinn (*f*)	mountain	**beanntan**	**beann(tan)**
caora (*f*)	sheep	**caoraich**	**caorach**
sgian (*f*)	knife	**sgeinean**	**sgeinean**
leabaidh (*f*)	bed	**leapannan**	**leapannan**
duine (*m*)	man	**daoine**	**daoine**
piuthar (*f*)	sister	**peathraichean**	**peathraichean**
bràthair (*m*)	brother	**bràithrean**	**bràithrean**
athair (*m*)	father	**athraichean**	**athraichean**
màthair (*f*)	mother	**màthraichean**	**màthraichean**
mac (*m*)	son	**mic**	**mac**

71 Numerals with nouns

Note that **a** only precedes numerals when they are not used with nouns. When these numerals are used with nouns, **a** is usually dropped. The numerals from three to ten are normally followed by the plural form of the noun. **Aon** and **dà** are followed by the singular form of the noun which is lenited. The noun always precedes **deug**.

1	**aon chat**	one cat	11	**aon chat deug**	eleven cats
2	**dà chat**	two cats	12	**dà chat dheug**	twelve cats
3	**trì cait**	three cats	13	**trì cait deug**	thirteen cats
4	**ceithir cait**	four cats	14	**ceithir cait deug**	fourteen cats
5	**cóig cait**	five cats	15	**cóig cait deug**	fifteen cats
6	**sia cait**	six cats	16	**sia cait deug**	sixteen cats
7	**seachd cait**	seven cats	17	**seachd cait deug**	seventeen cats
8	**ochd cait**	eight cats	18	**ochd cait deug**	eighteen cats
9	**naoi cait**	nine cats	19	**naoi cait deug**	nineteen cats
10	**deich cait**	ten cats			

Deug is sometimes lenited when it follows a plural noun with final slenderised consonant but is always lenited following **d(h)à +** noun, e.g.:

trì cait d(h)eug	thirteen cats
naoi cnuic dheug	nineteen cats
dà chat d(h)eug	twelve cats

71a Dual number

There are remnants of a dual form in Scottish Gaelic. Only feminine nouns have a dual form. The dual form of feminine nouns is formed by slenderising the final consonant. This is in effect the same form as the prepositional form as we will see later.

dà bhròig	two shoes
dà chluais	two ears
dà uinneig	two windows

Recall that slenderisation can, in some instances, affect the preceding vowel (see **Appendix 1**), e.g.:

dà chois	two feet	(from **dà + cas**)
dà chloich	two stones	(from **dà + clach**)
dà chirc	two hens	(from **dà + cearc**)

The singular rather than the plural form of the noun **bliadhna** 'year' is used with all numerals, e.g.:

dà bhliadhna	two years
trì bliadhna	three years
deich bliadhna	ten years

Vocabulary

pìob (*f*), **pìoban** (*pl*)   /pi:b/, /pi:bən/   pipe, pipes

Exercise 3

Translate, writing the numerals in words:

(a)   3 windows
(b)   10 schools
(c)   7 girls
(d)   2 classes
(e)   8 trees

(f)   12 cars
(g)   15 pipes
(h)   18 songs
(i)   2 feet
(j)   12 windows

72 Verbal nouns with pronoun objects

Verbs which are complemented by prepositions are
straightforward; the object simply combines with the preposition in
the usual way. Here are some examples:

Bha mi a' bruidhinn ris an-dé.   I was speaking to him yesterday.
Thachair iad rithe an-uiridh.   They met her last year.
An do chòrd an oidhche riut?   Did you enjoy the night?
An dug Iain an t-airgead sin dhut? Did John give you that money?

When the verb is not followed by a preposition, things are not so
straightforward. If we want to say 'he is making bread', we say: **tha
e a' dèanamh aran**. If we want to say 'he is making it', we might
expect to be able to say: **tha e a' dèanamh e**, where the pronoun
object simply follows the verbal noun. While this has been a
possibility in some dialects since the last century at least, the
majority would say, **tha e ga dhèanamh**, literally 'he is at its
making', where **ga** = **aig** 'at' + **a** 'its'. The pronoun object
becomes the corresponding possessive pronoun.

Here is the full paradigm:

gam★ (me)   + lenition
gad★ (you)   + lenition
ga★ (him, it)   + lenition
ga (her, it)   prefixes **h-** to vowels
gar (our)   prefixes **n-** to vowels
gur (your)   prefixes **n-** to vowels
gan/gam (them)

124

Examples

Tha Iain gam bhualadh.	John is hitting me.
Tha sinn gad fhaicinn.	We see you.
Am bheil thu ga chluintinn?	Do you hear him/it?
Tha iad ga cluinntinn.	They hear her/it.
Tha Màiri gar coinneachadh.	Mary is meeting us.
Tha na balaich gur faighneachd.	The boys are asking for you.
Bha Anna gan iarraidh.	Ann wanted them.
Bha Seumas ga h-iarraidh.	James wanted her/it.
An robh sibh gar n-iarraidh?	Did you want us?

Vocabulary

freagairt (*vn*)	/frʲegəɾsdʲ/	answering
fàgail (*vn*)	/faːgal/	leaving
ceannach (*vn*)	/kʲaɲəx/	buying
seinn (*vn*)	/ʃeiɲ/	singing

Exercise 4

Translate

1 Do you hear me?
2 Do you (*pl*) see it?
3 John is meeting them.
4 Were the boys hitting you (*pl*)?
5 Who wants us?
6 Ann was asking for you.
7 I am answering him now.
8 Are you leaving us here?
9 Are you buying it (*fem*)?
10 They were singing it (*masc*).

73 'Duine'

Duine (*plural* **daoine**) can mean 'man', 'husband' or simply
'person'. Consider the following examples:

Tha duine ag obair anns a' gharaids.	A man is working in the garage.
Se Seumas an duine agam.	James is my husband.
Bha daoine gu leòr ann.	There were a lot of people there.

Duine can also be used impersonally. Consider the following examples:

Am bheil duine a-staigh?   Is there anyone in?
Chan eil fhios aig duine.   Nobody knows.

Vocabulary

co-latha breith sona dhut	/kɔ ḻa-ə brʲe sɔnə ɣuhṯ/	happy birthday (to you)
meal do naidheachd	/mjaḻ d̪ə nɛ-əxg/	congratulations (informal)
sìon (*m*)	/ʃīān/, /ʃīən/	a particle, a small bit
sìon a dh'fhios	/sian ə jis/	a bit of knowledge, not a clue, no idea
seinneadair (*m*)	/ʃeɲəd̪ɛrʲ/	singer
pìobaire (*m*)	/pi:bərʲə/	piper
fìdhlear (*m*)	/fi:lɛrʲ/	fiddler
an comhnaidh	/əŋ ko:ni/	always
math fhéin	/ma he:n/	great, splendid
dìnnear (*f*)	/d̪ʲi:ɲɛrʲ/	dinner
taigh-òsta (*m*)	/tɤj ɔ:sd̪ə/	hotel, pub
mus	/mas/	before
timcheall air	/tʲ[imi]çəḻ ɛrʲ/	around, about
freagarrach	/fregərəx/	suitable
gu mì-fhortanach	/gə mi: ɔɾsd̪anəx/	unfortunately
tràth	/t̪ra:/	early
idir	/id̪ʲərʲ/	at all
taghta	/tɤ:ht̪ə/	fine, great
ma-tha	/mə ha:/	then
an-dràsta	/ən̪ d̪ra:sd̪ə/	now, this minute
cairteal (*m*)	/kaɾsd̪ʲaḻ/	quarter
fiughar (*m*)	/fju-ər/	hope, expectation, looking forward to
laochan (*m*)	/ḻɤ:xan/	good lad, friend (used only of males)
a laochain	/ə lɤ:xaɲ/	good lad, friend (address form)

COMHRADH

Co-latha breith Anna

Iain Hallo, am bheil Anna a-staigh?

Anna Se Anna a tha a' bruidhinn. Có a tha agam an-seo?

Iain Se Iain a tha ann.

Anna Hallo a Iain.

Iain Co-latha breith sona dhut a Anna agus meal do naidheachd.

Anna Tapadh leat a Iain. Càite am bi sinn a' dol a-nochd?

Iain	Bidh chun a' chéilidh.
Anna	Có a bhios a' seinn aig a' chéilidh?
Iain	Chan eil sìon a dh'fhios agamsa ach tha seinneadairean is pìobairean is fìdhleirean ás an àite seo fhéin a' dol ann. Seinnidh Pàdraig agus Catrìona co-dhiubh. Tha òrain gu leòr acasan. Bidh iad gan seinn an comhnaidh.
Anna	Am bheil thu ag iarraidh dìnnear anns an taigh-òsta mus fhalbh sinn?
Iain	Bidh sin math fhéin. Cuin a ghabhas sinn ar dìnnear, ma-tha?
Anna	Timcheall air ochd uairean. Am bi sin freagarrach leatsa?
Iain	Cha bhi gu mì-fhortanach. Am bi seachd uairean ro thràth dhuibh?
Anna	Cha bhi idir. Tha sin taghta.
Iain	Glé mhath ma tha. Bidh mise gad fhàgail an-dràsta ach bidh mi gad fhaicinn ann an taigh-òsta Dhomhnaill timcheall air cairteal gu a seachd.
Anna	Bidh fiughar agam ri sin ma-tha, a laochain.

TRANSLATION

Ann's birthday

John	Hello, is Ann in?
Ann	It's Ann who is speaking. Who is this?
John	It's John.
Ann	Hello John.
John	Happy birthday Ann and congratulations.
Ann	Thank you John. Where will we be going tonight?
John	To the ceilidh.
Ann	Who will be singing at the ceilidh?
John	I've no idea, but there are plenty of singers and pipers and fiddlers from this place itself going there. Patrick and Catriona will sing anyway. They have songs galore. They're always singing them.
Ann	Do you want dinner in the hotel before we go?
John	That will be great. When will we have dinner then?
Ann	About eight o'clock. Will that be suitable for you?
John	No, unfortunately. Will seven o'clock be too early for you?
Ann	Not at all. That will be splendid.
John	Very good then. I'll be leaving you just now but I'll be seeing you in Donald's Hotel about quarter to seven.
Ann	I look forward to that then, my good friend.

Lesson 9

74 Irregular verbs: future

We learnt the past tense forms of the irregular verbs in lesson 4. We will now look at the (simple) future forms. As with the past tense, most irregular verbs distinguish between an independent and dependent form. We will see that the future forms are very different from the past forms. It is possible to group the future tense formation of irregular verbs into the following three groups:

(i) Verbs whose independent and dependent forms differ substantially:

Independent	Dependent	
their	**abair**	will say
nì	**dèan**	will do, make
chì	**faic**	will see
gheibh	**faigh**	will get
bheir	**doir**	will bring, give

(ii) Verbs whose independent and dependent forms begin with **th-** and **d-** respectively:

Independent	Dependent	
théid	**déid**	will go
thig	**dig**	will come

Note: some prefer to spell the dependent forms with an initial **t-** or even **d'th-**.

(iii) Verbs whose future formation is regular

Independent	Dependent	
beiridh	**beir**	will catch
bheireas (*rel*)		
cluinnidh	**cluinn**	will hear
chluinneas (*rel*)		
ruigidh	**ruig**	will reach
ruigeas (*rel*)		

Note: The personal pronouns are used as usual with these verbal forms except that **tu** rather than **thu** is used after **-idh** and **-as** with group (iii) verbs as with regular verbs.

127

Note also that the future forms can express capability. This is particularly true of the verbs **faic** 'see' and **cluinn** 'hear'. Here are some examples:

Cluinnidh mi an t-eun.   I can hear the bird.
Chì thu a' bheinn.   You can see the mountain.

Note that the regular verb **can** is used for **abair** in the future tense, the imperative and, as we will see, in the conditional also.

Examples

Their e riut a-màireach, nach abair.[1]
He will tell you tomorrow, won't he?

Cha bheir sinn air a' mheàirleach a-nis.
We will not get hold of the robber now.

Cluinnidh tu na h-eòin.
You will hear the birds.

Nì mi mo dhìcheall.
I will do my best.

Dé chì thu? Chan fhaic sìon.
What do you see? Nothing.

Cuine a gheibh iad am plèan?
When will they get the plane?

Théid sinn a Ghlaschu.
We will go to Glasgow.

An ruig sibh an taigh a-nochd?
Will you reach home tonight?

An dig thu a chéilidh orm a-nochd? Thig.
Will you come to visit me tonight? Yes.

Nach doir thu an t-airgead aige air ais?
Will you not give back his money?

In English in sentences where the main clause is in the future tense, subordinate clauses introduced by 'when' and 'if' usually appear in the present tense. In Gaelic the future tense is retained throughout in both clauses, e.g.:

Chì sinn thu nuair a thig thu.
We will see you when you come.

Dé ní sinn ma théid sinn air chall?
What will we do if we get lost?

[1]Commonly = **canaidh e riut a-màireach, nach can?**

Vocabulary

sìon (*m*)	/ʃīān/	anything
bean an taighe (*f*)	/bɛn əɳ t̪ɛhə/	the woman of the house
eun (*m*), eòin (*pl*)	/ian/, /jɔːɲ/	bird, birds
seinn (*vn*)	/ʃeiɲ/	singing
obair (*f*, 4)	/obərʲ/	work
lathaichean saora (*m*, *pl*)	/l̪a-içən suːrə/	holidays
dìreach	/dʲiːrʲəx/	directly
trèan (*f*, 5)	/trɛːn/	train
dìcheall (*m*)	/dʲiːçəl̪/	utmost, best

Exercise 1

Translate

1 I will not say anything to him.
2 What will you give to the woman of the house?
3 Do you hear the birds singing?
4 Will you do the work for me?
5 Will they get their holidays tomorrow?
6 We will see them when they reach Glasgow.
7 Will your brother go to the ceilidh?
8 They will not come home directly after school.
9 He will get the train when it comes.
10 Will you do your best this time John?

75 Answering questions

As usual, we repeat the main verb of the question:

An dèan thu e?	Will you do it?
Nì.	Yes.
Cha dèan.	No.
An cluinn thu an ceòl?	Do you hear the music?
Cluinnidh.	Yes.
Cha chluinn.	No.
An dig iad?	Will they come?
Thig.	Yes.
Cha dig.	No.

76 Present habitual use of future tense

As with the regular verbs, the future tense forms may, as in English, be used to denote habitual actions, particularly when adverbs implying habit are present, e.g.:

Chì mi Iain a h-uile latha.
I see John every day.

Théid Anna a Ghlaschu a h-uile Di-Màirt.
Ann goes to Glasgow every Tuesday.

77 The relative

We have already met the relative (= independent form (ii)) of the future tense of regular verbs (**Sections 64 and 64a**). In a typical relative construction we have the following elements in the following order:

ANTECEDENT+	RELATIVE PRONOUN +	RELATIVE CLAUSE
na balaich	**a**	**chluich**
the boys	who	played

The antecedent may be the object or the subject of a preceding verb, e.g.:

VERB	+	SUBJECT	+	OBJECT = ANTECEDENT	+	RELATIVE
chunnaic		**Iain**		**na balaich**		**a chluich**
saw		John		the boys		who played

'John saw the boys who played'

VERB	+	SUBJECT = ANTECEDENT	+	RELATIVE
dh'fhalbh		**na balaich**		**a chluich**
left		the boys		who played

'the boys who played left'

We will only be concerned with the relative construction itself and so our discussion below will be restricted to the relative clause and the order of its elements.

The relative pronoun is an independent particle and as such is followed by independent verbal forms (independent (ii) = relative in the case of the future). Here are some examples:

An duine a dh'fhalbh.	The man who left.
Na caileagan a sheinneas.	The girls who will sing.
An sgioba a bhuannaicheas.	The team that will win.

The relative clause has the following elements in the following order:

VERB + SUBJECT OR OBJECT OF RELATIVE VERB + ADVERB

To sum up, a relative construction consists of the following elements in the following order:

ANTECEDENT + REL PRONOUN + VERB + SUBJ OR OBJ OF RELATIVE VERB + ADVERB

ANTECEDENT	REL PRON	VERB	SUBJ OR OBJ OF REL VERB	ADVERB
a' chaileag	a	chaidh		a-mach
the girl	who	went		out
'the girl who went out'				
an t-òran	a	sheinn	Iain (*subj*)	
the song	that	sang	John	
'the song that John sang'				
am boireannach	a	dh'fhàg	an taigh (*obj*)	an-raoir
the woman	who	left	the house	last night
'the woman who left the house last night'				
am ministear	a	sheinneas	na sailm (*obj*)	
the minister	who	will sing	the psalms	
'the minister who will sing the psalms'				

It will be clear from the above examples that Gaelic unlike English does not distinguish between relative clauses which contain the subject or the object of the relative verb. In other words, phrases like 'the boy who hit the teacher (*obj*)' and 'the boy that the teacher (*subj*) hit' are identical in Gaelic: **an gille a bhuail an tidsear**. This does not lead to ambiguities as it is usually clear from the context which noun is the subject and which is the object of the relative verb.

77a Relative 'whose'

There is no one word in Gaelic to translate relative 'whose'. Instead Gaelic uses both the relative pronoun **a** and the third person possessive pronoun which agrees in gender and number with the antecedent. A typical sentence like 'the teacher whose son went to Perth, would in Gaelic become literally 'the teacher that his son went to Perth':

| An tidsear a chaidh a mhac a Pheairt. | The teacher whose son went to Perth. |

Here are some further examples:

| A' chaileag a tha a màthair tinn. | The girl whose mother is ill. |
| Na tidsearan a tha an clasaichean math. | The teachers whose classes are good. |

77b Relative 'in which', 'with whom', etc.

Gaelic has two relative pronouns which both precede the following 'relative' verb:

(i) **a**   direct relative pronoun
(ii) **an/am**   indirect relative pronoun

We have just met the direct relative pronoun **a** in the relative clauses discussed above. When the relative clause, however, contains a preposition, the indirect relative pronoun **an/am** is used. **Am** is used before verbs beginning with a labial **b, p, f, m**. **An/am** is a dependent particle and as such is followed by dependent verbal forms. The order of elements in indirect relative constructions is as follows:

ANTECEDENT	+ PREPOSITION	+ AN/AM	+ VERB (DEP)	+SUBJECT
an séithear	**air**	**an**	**do shuidh**	**Ailean**
the chair	on	which	sat	Alan
'the chair on which Alan sat'				
an duine	**aig**	**an**	**robh**	**an t-airgead**
the person	at	whom	was	the money
'the person who had the money'				

All prepositions (other than **air, aig**) change form slightly before the indirect relative pronoun **an/am**. We have learnt these forms already; they are exactly the same as the forms of the prepositions which occur before the singular article. See **Section 46**, Lesson 6.

Prepositions which add **-s**:

Preposition	Form of preposition before indirect relative pronoun
á	→	**ás**
ann an	→	**anns**
le	→	**leis**
ri	→	**ris**

Prepositions which add **-n**:

Preposition		Preposition before indirect relative pronoun:
bho	→	**bhon**
fo	→	**fon**
do	→	**dhan**
de	→	**dhen**
mu	→	**mun**
ro	→	**ron**
tro	→	**tron**

Here are some further examples:

na daoine ris an do bhruidhinn mi
the men to whom I spoke

am baile anns an robh sinn
the town in which we were

an rùm ás an do theich iad
the room out of which they fled

an toll dhan an do thuit an t-uaireadair
the hole into which the watch fell

a' chraobh fon am bheil an taigh aca
the tree under which their house is

am baile tron an deach sinn
the town through which we went

77c Relative 'in which', 'with whom': alternative construction

Like English, Gaelic has an alternative relative construction for relative clauses containing prepositions. The alternative to our first example above 'the chair on which Alan sat' would in English be 'the chair that Alan sat in'. The alternative construction in Gaelic is similar to the English alternative construction except that a prepositional pronoun, agreeing in person and number with the antecedent, appears instead of a simple preposition. The above example would in Gaelic literally be 'the chair that Alan sat in-it':

ANTECEDENT	+ REL PRON + (DIRECT)	VERB	+ SUBJECT	+ PREPOSITIONAL PRONOUN
an séithear	**a**	**shuidh**	**Ailean**	**ann**
the chair	that	sat	Alan	in-it (*m*)

'the chair that Alan sat in'

Here are some further examples:

na daoine a bhruidhinn mi riutha	the people that I spoke to (them)
am baile a bha sinn ann	the town that we were in (it)
an rùm a theich iad ás	the room that they walked out of (it)
a' chraobh a tha an taigh aca foidhpe	the tree that their house is under (it)
am baile a chaidh sinn troimhe	the town that we went through (it)

78 Negative relative clauses

To negate any of the above relative clauses, we replace **a** or **an/am**
with **nach** which is a dependent particle and as such is always
followed by a dependent verbal form.

Here are some examples:

am boireannach nach do dh'fhàg an taigh	the woman who did not leave the house
a' chaileag nach deach a-mach	the girl who did not go out
am balach nach robh a' bruidhinn	the boy that was not speaking
am ministear nach seinn na sailm	the minister who will not sing the psalms
an uinneag nach fhosgail Màiri	the window that Mary does not open
sin leabhar nach do leugh mi anns an sgoil	that's a book that I didn't read at school
am boireannach nach eil a màthair tinn	the woman whose mother is not ill
na daoine ris nach do bhruidhinn mi	the men to whom I did not speak
am baile anns nach robh sinn	the town in which we were not
an rùm ás nach do theich iad	the room out of which they did not flee
na daoine nach do bhruidhinn mi riutha	the men that I did not speak to
am baile nach robh sinn ann	the town that we were not in
an rùm nach do theich iad ás	the room that they did not flee from

Note that the relative pronoun is sometimes left out in English but
never in Gaelic, e.g. 'the man (that) I saw' **an duine a chunnaic mi**.

Vocabulary

clach (f, 2)	/kₜax/	stone
tilg (vb)	/tʲ[ili]gʲ/	throw
iuchair (f, 4)	/juxərʲ/	key
innis do (vb)	/ĩːʃ d̪a/	tell to
naidheachd (f, 5)	/nɛ̃-əxg/, /najəxg/	news, story
sgioba (m, 5)	/skʲibə/	team
cluich (vb)	/kₜuiç/	play
ceòl (m)	/kʲɔːₜ/	music
éisteachd (f, 5) ri	/e:ʃdʲaxg/	listening to
rathad (m, 1)	/ʁa-əd̪/	road
bruidhinn mu dheidhinn (vb)	/brɯ-iɲ ma je-iɲ/	speak about
tachair ri (vb)	/t̪axirʲ rʲi/	meet (with)
ceum (m, 5)	/kʲe:m/	degree
an-uiridh	/əɲ urʲi/	last year

Exercise 2

Translate

1 Do you know the boy who threw the stone?
2 There is the woman who sang that beautiful song last night.
3 Where is the book that you did not read?
4 This is the the room that I left the key in.
5 Is that the woman to whom you told the story?
6 I like the team with which I played.
7 Do you like the music that Donald was listening to?
8 The road that we were speaking about.
9 Is that the man you met?
10 Do you know the lawyer whose son got his degree last year?

79 Interrogatives involving prepositions

We will now learn how to ask questions involving verbs which are complemented by prepositions, i.e. how to say in Gaelic 'to whom did you speak?'. In Lesson 5 we learnt how to say in Gaelic 'who owns the book?', which as you will recall was:

có leis a tha an leabhar?

This can be literally translated as 'who with-him is the book' or more accurately 'to whom is the book'. This gives us the model for other interrogatives involving prepositions:

CÓ + PREP PRON,	+ REL PRON	+ VERB +	SUBJECT + DIR OBJ
3RD SING			
có **ris**	**a**	**bhruidhinn**	**Iain**
who to-him	that	spoke	John

'to whom did John speak'

| **có** **dha** | **a** | **dh'innis** | **Anna** **an naidheachd** |
| who to-him | that | told | Ann the news |

'to whom did Ann tell the news?'

| **có** **aige** | **a** | **tha** | **an iuchair** |
| who at-him | that | is | the key |

'at whom is the key?', 'who has the key?'

The last example gives us an example of an idiom which involves a
preposition in Gaelic but not in English. Watch out for others.
Here is one further example:

| **có** **dheth** | **a** | **dh'fhaighnich** | **thu** |
| who of-him | that | asked | you |

'of whom did you ask?', 'who did you ask?'

80 Relative form of '*is*'

Is usually combines with the relative pronoun **a** to give **as**. **Is** and
as are pronounced identically.

an rud as toil leam	the thing that I like
sin an fheadhain as fheàrr	these are the ones which I
leamsa	prefer
dé as fheàrr leat?	what do you prefer?
ged as e droch oidhche a tha ann	although it is a bad night
nuair as ann a' dol dhachaigh	when it is going home that
a bhios tu	you will be

The relative pronoun **a** does not combine with the past/conditional
forms of **is**:

| **an rud a bu toil leam** | the thing that I would like |
| **an rathad a b'aithne dhomh** | the road that I knew |

80a Negative relative forms of '*is*'

The negative relative form of **is** is **nach** in the present tense (which
lenites **f**); in the past/conditional it is **nach bu**. Here are some
examples:

an fheadhain nach toil leam	the ones that I don't like
sin am fear nach fheàrr	that's the one that Ann does
le Anna	not prefer
ged nach e Seumas a tha ann	although it's not James
sin rud nach bu toil leam	that's a thing that I wouldn't like
balach nach b'aithne dhomh	a boy whom I didn't know

81 Adjectives: singular

(a) Nominative

We have already learnt that adjectives are lenited when they follow feminine nouns in the nominative singular but are not lenited when they follow masculine nouns:

MASCULINE		FEMININE	
cat mór	a big cat	bròg bheag	a small shoe
càr dearg	a red car	cas mhór	a big foot
leabhar geal	a white book	deise dhubh	a black suit

(b) Prepositional

Adjectives are lenited when they follow (singular) nouns which are preceded by a preposition and the article. Adjectives are in addition also slenderised when they follow (singular) feminine nouns:

MASCULINE	FEMININE
air a' chat mhór	anns a' bhròig bhig
on the big cat	in the small shoe
fon a' chàr dhearg	air a' chois mhóir
under the red car	on the big foot
anns an leabhar gheal	leis an deise dhuibh
in the white book	with the black suit

Note: Adjectives following masculine nouns which are not preceded by the article are not lenited, e.g.: **fo chàr dearg** 'under a red car', **air bòrd mór** 'on a big table'.

(c) Genitive

Adjectives are lenited and slenderised when they follow a masculine noun in the genitive:

MASCULINE

a' chait mhóir	of the big cat
a' chàir dheirg	of the red car
an leabhair ghil	of the white book

Adjectives are slenderised and add **-e** when they follow a feminine noun in the genitive:

FEMININE

na bròige bige	of the small shoe
na coise móire	of the big foot
na deise duibhe	of the black suit

There is a tendency to use the lenited and slenderised form of the adjective following feminine nouns in the genitive, especially when disyllabic feminine nouns drop the final **-e** of the genitive. Compare:

na caileige móire OR	na caileig mhóir	of the big girl
na cailliche bige	na caillich bhig	of the small old woman

Vocabulary

solas (*m*)	/sɔ̧l̩əs/	light
geal	/gʲa̧l̩/	bright, white
dath (*m*)	/d̪a/	colour
deise (*f*)	/dʲeʃə/	suit
facal (*m*), faclan (*pl*)	/fahkəl̩/, /fahkᵗən/	word, words
òran (*m*)	/ɔ:ran/	song
ceòl (*m*)	/kʲɔ:l̩/	music
pìob-mhór (*f*)	/pi:b voːr/	bagpipe
cosgais (*f*)	/kɔsgəʃ/	cost
camara (*m*)	/kamərə/	camera
daor	/d̪ɯːr/	dear, expensive
laghach	/l̩ɣ-əx/	kind
càraid (*f*)	/ka:rɛdʲ/	couple
ceàrr	/kʲaːʀ/	wrong
rathad (*m*)	/ʀa-əd̪/	road

Exercise 3

Translate

1 with the small cat
2 on the white table
3 to the big girl
4 in the bright light

5 the colour of the new suit
6 the words of the beautiful song
7 the music of the bagpipe
8 the cost of the expensive camera
9 with the kind couple
10 on the wrong road

82 More on numerals

For numerals over 20, there are two ways of counting in Gaelic. The traditional system of counting operates with 20 as its base (hence it is called the vigesimal system). The Gaelic for 30 is **deich ar fhichead** which means literally 'ten on twenty'. A more modern, decimal system has been introduced into schools in very recent times. Both systems are given below:

	VIGESIMAL	DECIMAL
20	**fichead**	**fichead**
30	**deich ar fhichead**	**trithead**
40	**dà fhichead**	**ceathrad**
50	**dà fhichead is a deich**	**caogad**
60	**trì fichead**	**seasgad**
70	**trì fichead is a deich**	**seachdad**
80	**ceithir fichead**	**ochdad**
90	**ceithir fichead is a deich**	**naochad**
100	**ceud**	**ceud**

Lethcheud is also used for 50. **Is** is short for **agus** 'and' in the above and following lists of numbers.

The other numbers are formed as follows:

	VIGESIMAL	DECIMAL
21	**a h-aon ar fhichead**	**fichead is a h-aon**
22	**a dhà ar fhichead**	**fichead is a dhà**
29	**a naoi ar fhichead**	**fichead is a naoi**
31	**a h-aon deug ar fhichead**	**trithead is a h-aon**
38	**a h-ochd deug ar fhichead**	**trithead is a h-ochd**
41	**dà fhichead is a h-aon**	**ceathrad is a h-aon**
49	**dà fhichead is a naoi**	**ceathrad is a naoi**
51	**dà fhichead is a h-aon deug**	**caogad is a h-aon**
52	**dà fhichead is a dhà dheug**	**caogad is a dhà**
66	**trì fichead is a sia**	**seasgad is a sia**
77	**trì fichead is a seachd deug**	**seachdad is a seachd**

88	ceithir fichead is a h-ochd	ochdad is a h-ochd
99	ceithir fichead is a naoi deug	naochad is a naoi

You will see that multiples of **fichead** usually precede other numerals in such phrases; but between 21 and 39, in the vigesimal system – **fichead** comes last in the phrase. The forms given above are those which are used when counting i.e. without a following noun.

82a Numerals with nouns

VIGESIMAL
When these numbers are used with a noun, the noun follows multiples of **fichead** but precedes **fichead** in the numbers from 21 to 39. Note that singular forms of the noun are used with **fichead** and multiples of **fichead**, and also with **dà**. Otherwise, the plural form is used as before. Note that **a** is not used when a noun follows the numeral:

21 cats	aon chat ar fhichead
22 cats	dà chat ar fhichead
29 cats	naoi cait ar fhichead
31 cats	aon chat deug ar fhichead
38 cats	ochd cait deug ar fhichead
41 cats	dà fhichead cat is a h-aon
49 cats	dà fhichead cat is a naoi
51 cats	dà fhichead cat is a h-aon deug
52 cats	dà fhichead cat is a dhà dheug
66 cats	trì fichead cat is a sia
77 cats	trì fichead cat is a seachd deug
88 cats	ceithir fichead cat is a h-ochd
99 cats	ceithir fichead cat is a naoi deug

DECIMAL
The singular form of the noun is used with the decimal forms. The noun may either come right at the end or it may follow the numeral which is a multiple of ten as follows:

21 cats	fichead is a h-aon cat	fichead cat is a h-aon
22 cats	fichead is a dhà cat	fichead cat is a dhà
29 cats	fichead is a naoi cat	fichead cat is a naoi
31 cats	trithead is a h-aon cat	trithead cat is a h-aon
38 cats	trithead is a h-ochd cat	trithead cat is a h-ochd
41 cats	ceathrad is a h-aon cat	ceathrad cat is a h-aon

49 cats	ceathrad is a naoi cat	ceathrad cat is a naoi
51 cats	caogad is a h-aon cat	caogad cat is a h-aon
52 cats	caogad is a dhà cat	caogad cat is a dhà
66 cats	seasgad is a sia cat	seasgad cat is a sia
77 cats	seachdad is a seachd cat	seachdad cat is a seachd
88 cats	ochdad is a h-ochd cat	ochdad cat is a h-ochd
99 cats	naochad is a naoi cat	naochad cat is a naoi

The singular form of nouns is used with **ceud** '100' and multiples of **ceud**. This also applies for **mìle** '1,000' and **muillean** '1,000,000'. Here are some examples involving the higher numbers:

1,040	**mìle is dà fhichead**
3,789	**trì mìle, seachd ceud, ceithir fichead is a naoi**
80,453	**ceithir fichead mìle, ceithir ceud, dà fhichead is a trì deug**

The vigesimal system is used for years and dates. Note how years are normally broken up into two numbers as in English:

1990	**naoi deug, ceithir fichead is a deich**
1996	**naoi deug, ceithir fichead is a sia deug**

82b Age; 'how old are you?'

Study the following phrases. Note that **a dh'aois** 'of age' is optional in the following phrases:

Dé an aois a tha thu?	How old are you?
Tha mi deich bliadhna a dh'aois	I am ten years of age
Tha mi cóig bliadhna deug a dh'aois	I am fifteen years of age
Tha mi fichead bliadhna a dh'aois	I am twenty years of age
Tha mi aon bhliadhna ar fhichead	I am twenty one years of age
Tha mi dà fhichead bliadhna is a ceithir	I am forty four years of age

Exercise 4

Translate

(a) 45 books
(b) 76 horses
(c) 87 chairs
(d) 39 years of age
(e) 62 years of age
(f) 70 years of age

83 Use of *'de'* ('of')

In Lesson 7 we saw that the genitive corresponds in many cases to the use of the preposition 'of' in English or 'de' in French. Generally speaking, the corresponding Gaelic preposition **de** 'of' is not used in possessive contexts. However, **de** 'of' is used, particularly in partitive contexts. Here are some examples:

té de na boireannaich	one of the women
fear de na balaich	one of the boys
aon de na tidsearan	one of the teachers
cuid de na daoine	some of the people
punnd de shiùcar	a pound of sugar

84 Countries

In Gaelic, most countries are feminine in gender and are preceded by the article:

a' Bheilg	Belgium
a' Bhreatainn Bheag	Brittany
a' Chuimrigh	Wales
an Danmhairg	Denmark
an Eadailt	Italy
an Eilbheis	Switzerland
an Fhraing	France
an Fhionnlainn	Finland
a' Ghearmailt	Germany
a' Ghréig	Greece
an Òlaind	Holland
a' Phólainn	Poland
a' Phortaigeil	Portugal
an Ruis	Russia
an Roinn-Eòrpa	Europe
an t-Seapan	Japan
an Spàinn(t)	Spain
an t-Suain	Sweden

Ruisia without the article is also used for 'Russia'.

The following countries are not normally preceded by the article:

Alba or **Albainn**	Scotland
Breata(i)nn	Britain
Canada (*m*)	Canada
Éirinn	Ireland
Lucsamburg	Luxemburg
Lochla(i)nn/Nirribhidh	Norway
Sasa(i)nn	England
Sìna	China
an Rìoghachd Aonaichte	the United Kingdom
na Stàitean Aonaichte	the United States

Some dialects use **na Staidean** for the 'United States'.

In the genitive **Alba** and **Éirinn** may be preceded by the article, e.g.:

muinntir na h-Alba	the people of Scotland
ceòl na h-Éirinn	the music of Ireland

In literary Gaelic, **Alba** also has the following case forms:

Albainn (prepositional)
Albann (genitive)

Vocabulary

gabhaibh mo lethsgeul	/ga-əv mə leʃgʲaɫ/	excuse me (polite, formal form)
tiocaid (*f*)	/tʀgʲɛdʲ/	ticket
stèisean (*m*)	/sdɛːʃən/	station
eilean (*m*)	/elan/	island
an-iar	/ə ɲiər/	western
rathad (*m*), **rathaid** (G)	/ʀa-əd̪/, /ʀa-idʲ/	road
duilich	/d̪uliç/	sorry
aiseag (*m*)	/aʃəg/	ferry
trèan (*m*)	/trɛːn/	train
bàta (*m*)	/baːht̪ə/	boat
deagh*	/dʲoː/	good
àm (*m*), **amannan** (*pl*)	/aum/, /aməҩən/	time, times
bòrd-sanais (*m*)	/bɔːʀsd̪ saniʃ/	notice board
caismeachd (*f*)	/kaʃmaxg/	signal, announcement
an comain	/əŋ komɛɲ/	indebted, obliged
'nur comain	/nar komɛɲ/	in your debt, indebted to you

COMHRADH

Torcal   Gabhaibh mo lethsgeul. Càit an déid mi airson nan tiocaidean?

Anna   Théid chun an dorais anns am bheil fear an stèisein 'na sheasamh.

Torcal   Móran taing dhut.

Torcal a' bruidhinn ri fear an stèisein

Torcal   Am faigh mi tiocaid a bheir á seo gu ruige na h-Eileanan An-iar mi?

Fear an Stèisein   Gheibh agus bidh sin cóig notaichean ar fhichead, a' dol taobh an Òbain.

Torcal   An doir an tiocaid fad an rathaid mi?

Fear an Stèisein   Tha mi duilich. Cha doir. Gheibh thu tiocaid eile airson an aiseig nuair a ruigeas tu an t-Òban.

Torcal   Am beir an ath thrèan air a' bhàta?

Fear an Stèisein   Beiridh agus ann an deagh àm. Chì thu amannan nan trèanaichean air a' bhòrd-shanais ach cluinnidh tu caismeachd mus dig an trèan a-staigh dhan an stèisean.

Torcal   Tapadh leibhse. Tha mi fada 'nur comain.

TRANSLATION

Torquil   Excuse me. Where can I go for the tickets?

Ann   To the door where the station-master is standing.

Torquil   Many thanks to you.

Torquil speaking to the station-master

Torquil   Can I get a ticket that will take me from here to the Western Isles?

Station-master   Yes, and that will be £25, going via Oban.

Torquil   Will the ticket take me the whole way?

Station-master   I'm sorry. No. You will get another ticket for the ferry when you get to Oban.

Torquil   Will the next train catch the boat?

Station-master   Yes, and in good time. You will see the train times on the notice-board but you will hear an announcement before the train comes into the station.

Torquil   Thank you. I'm much obliged to you.

Lesson 10

85 Regular verbs: conditional/past habitual: independent forms

The forms of the conditional and the past habitual are identical in Scottish Gaelic. The conditional/past habitual is formed with short forms derived from the verbal root as with the simple past and future. The difference between independent and dependent conditional/past habitual forms is slight. They both share the same endings and differ only in that independent forms are lenited, dependent forms are not. The independent forms of the conditional/past habitual are formed as follows:

CONDITIONAL/PAST HABITUAL: REGULAR VERBS: INDEPENDENT

1 Lenite the initial consonant of verbal root
2 Prefix **dh'** to vowels and **f** + vowel
3 Add the following suffixes:

Singular	*Plural*
1 (a)inn	1 (e)amaid
2 (e)adh tu	2 (e)adh sibh
3 (e)adh e, i	3 (e)adh iad

Here are examples based on the verbs **cuir** put and **òl** drink:

chuirinn	I would put; I used to put
chuireadh tu	you would put; you used to put
chuireadh e, i	he, she would put; he, she used to put
chuireamaid	we would put; we used to put
chuireadh sibh	you would put; you used to put
chuireadh iad	they would put; they used to put
dh'òlainn	I would drink; I used to drink
dh'òladh tu	you would drink; you used to drink
dh'òladh e, i	he, she would drink; he, she used to drink
dh'òlamaid	we would drink; we used to drink
dh'òladh sibh	you would drink; you used to drink
dh'òladh iad	they would drink; they used to drink

To form the conditional/past habitual, we lenite the initial consonant of the verb or prefix **dh'** to vowels and **f** + vowel and add the following endings to the verbal root: **(a)inn** and **(e)amaid** for the first person singular and plural respectively; **(e)adh** + the appropriate pronoun for the other persons. Note **tu**, not **thu** is used with the conditional/past habitual. The ending **(e)adh** is also the form used with all noun subjects.

The pronouns **mi** and **sinn** are 'inbuilt' in the endings **(a)inn** and **(e)amaid** respectively. We refer to these as <u>synthetic</u> verbal forms. Verbal forms where the pronouns appear separated from or affixed to the verb are called <u>analytic</u> forms. Some dialects use analytic forms instead of **(e)amaid** for the first person plural e.g. **chuireadh sinn** instead of **chuireamaid**.

*** IMPORTANT ***

Verbs with two syllables usually ending in **-r, -l, -n, -ng** lose their second syllable when the conditional endings are added. Here is a list of the most important examples, illustrated with the ending **(e)adh**:

tachair	thachradh	would happen
fosgail	dh'fhosgladh	would open
bruidhinn	bhruidhneadh	would speak
tarraing	thàirrneadh	would pull

Note also:

innis	dh'innseadh	would tell

Note: final **-nn** and **-ng** are reduced to **-n** when an ending is added

---

85a Regular verbs: conditional/past habitual: dependent forms

The independent and dependent forms of the conditional/past habitual are the same except that dependent forms are not lenited and that **dh'** is not prefixed to vowels or **f** + vowel. Note, however, the exceptions of **cha***, and **nach** which lenites **f**. Here are some examples:

Nach canadh tu sin a Sheumais? Would you not say that, James?

Càite an cuireadh iad na beathaichean?	Where would they put the animals?
Cha ghlasainn an doras a h-uile h-oidhche.	I used not to lock the door every night.
Nach fhalbhadh Anna aig dà uair?	Wouldn't Ann leave at two o'clock?

85b '*Tha*': conditional/past habitual

The independent conditional/past habitual forms of the verb **tha** are:

bhinn	I would be; I used to be
bhiodh tu	you would be; you used to be
bhiodh e, i	he, she would be; he, she used to be
bhiomaid	we would be; we used to be
bhiodh sibh	you would be; you used to be
bhiodh iad	they would be; they used to be

The dependent forms are exactly the same except that they are unlenited:

binn
biodh tu
biodh e, i
biomaid
biodh sibh
biodh iad

When the conditional/past habitual forms of **tha** are used in the periphrastic (long) construction involving verbal nouns, the sense is usually continuous conditional/past habitual and not simple conditional/past habitual, e.g.:

bhinn ag òl	I would be drinking; I used to be drinking
bhiodh Anna a' seinn	Ann would be singing; Ann used to be singing

85c Answering questions

As usual, we repeat the main verb of the question:

Am biodh tu toilichte?	Would you be happy?
Bhiodh	Yes
Cha bhiodh	No

An òladh sibh seo?	Would you drink this?
Dh'òladh	Yes
Chan òladh	No
An glasadh Iain an doras?	Would John lock the door?
Ghlasadh	Yes
Cha ghlasadh	No

86 'If'

Gaelic has two words for 'if', namely **ma** and **nan**. **Nan** is only used with the conditional/past habitual. **Ma** is used with all other tenses, i.e. past, present and future. **Nan** in a dependent particle; **ma** is an independent particle.

86a 'Ma'

Ma dh'fhàg thu an-sin e, càite am bheil e?   (Past)
If you left it there, where is it?
Tha mise a' dol ann ma tha Anna a' tighinn.   (Present)
I am going (there) if Ann is coming.
Chì mi thu ma bhios tu ann.   (Future)
I will see you if you are (will be) there.

The clause containing 'if' is referred to as the <u>subordinate clause</u>; the remainder of the sentence is referred to as the <u>main clause</u>. When the main clause is in the past, present or future, the subordinate 'if' clause will have the same tense as the main clause and 'if' is translated with **ma**.

86b 'Nan'

In Gaelic, if the main clause of an 'if' sentence is in the conditional, then the 'if' clause will also be in the conditional and 'if' is translated by **nan**. Note that in English the 'if' clause appears in the past tense in such instances. Consider the following examples:

Sheinneadh Iain nan seinneadh tusa.
John would sing if you sang.
Cha ghlasadh iad an doras nam biodh fios aca.
They wouldn't lock the door if they knew.
Thogainn an iuchair nam fàgadh tu ann i.

I would pick up the key if you left it there.

Nan becomes **nam** before labials **b**, **p**, **f**, **m**.

87 *'Mura'*, 'if not'

English uses two words to express 'if not'. Gaelic uses one word: **mura**. We have seen that Gaelic has two words for 'if'. However, **mura** is used corresponding to both **ma** and **nan**. In other words, both **ma** and **nan** are negated by **mura**. **Mura** is a dependent particle:

Innis dhomh mura bheil thu a' tighinn.
Tell me if you aren't coming.

Chan fhaic mi thu mura bi thu ann.
I will not see you if you aren't there.

Cha seinneadh Iain mura seinneadh tusa.
John wouldn't sing if you didn't.

Leughainn am pàipear mura binn sgìth.
I would read the paper if I wasn't tired.

Mura becomes **mur** before **do** in the past tense of regular verbs and those irregular verbs which have **do** in their dependent forms:

Dèan an obair agad a Sheumais mur do rinn thu fhathast i
Do your work James if you haven't done it yet

Tha Domhnall ann an taigh Anna mur do dh'fhalbh e.
Donald is in Ann's house if he hasn't left (unless he has left).

87a 'If it were not for'

'If it were not for' is translated in Gaelic as **mura b'e**. Consider the following examples:

Dh'fhalbhamaid a-mach an-diugh mura b'e an droch shìde.
We would go out today if it weren't for the bad weather.

Bhiodh Anna toilichte mura b'e Seumas.
Ann would be happy if it weren't for James.

88 'If' meaning 'whether'

When 'if' is used in a non-conditional sense in English, i.e. when it means 'whether', neither **ma** nor **nan** is used; instead we simply use the interrogative particle **an**. Consider the following examples:

Chan eil fios agam an dàinig Seumas.
I don't know if/whether James has come.

Chì sinn an dig e a-nochd.
We will see if/whether he comes tonight.

Saoil an e Anna a tha ann.
I wonder if/whether it's Ann.

Faighnich do Shìle am bheil i a' tighinn.
Ask Sheila if/whether she is coming.

Vocabulary

cuir suas ri (*vb*)	/kurʲ suəs rʲi/	put up with
dùisg (*vb*)	/duːʃgʲ/	wake
madainn (*f*, 5)	/mãḍiɲ/	morning
nigh (*vb*)	/ɲi/	wash
abhainn (*f*)	/ãviɲ/, /ã-iɲ/, /ãũ-iɲ/	river
lorg (*vb*)	/ɫ[ɔrɔ]g/	find
àite (*m*)	/aːhtʲə/	place
gabh anail (*vb*)	/gav anaɫ/	rest, take a breather
ith (*vb*)	/i/, /iç/	eat
greim (*m*)	/grʲeim/	a bite
ach	/ax/	only
druthag (*f*, 5)	/ḍru-ag/	drop
dìreach	/dʲiːrʲəx/	just
post (*vb*)	/pɔsḍ/	post
litir (*f*, 4)	/ʎihtʲərʲ/	letter
dhomh	/ɣõ/	for me
cuid (*f*) **mhath**	/kudʲ vã/	a fair amount
gu dearbh	/gə dʲ[ɛrɛ]v/	certainly
tha fios agam	/ha fis agəm/, /ha fisəm/	I know

Exercise 1

Translate

1 I wouldn't put up with that.
2 When did you used to wake up in the morning?
3 Why would John believe that?
4 They used to wash themselves in the river.

5 We found a place where we could draw breath.
6 They wouldn't eat a bite.
7 I would only take a small drop.
8 Would you post this letter for me?
9 They would understand a fair amount of it, certainly.
10 I would open the door for you if I knew you were there.

89 Adjectives: comparative and superlative

(a) Equative

The pattern is as follows:

CHO	+	ADJECTIVE	+	RI	+	NOUN
cho		**sgìth**		**ri**		**seann chù**
as		tired		as		an old dog

Here are some other examples:

Tha Anna cho làidir ri Iain. Ann is as strong as John.
Tha Màiri cho seòlta ri sionnach. Mary is as cunning as a fox.

The equative forms can be used adverbially:

Tha an latha cho brèagha. The day is so beautiful.
Tha e cho fuar. It is so cold.
Tha a' chlann cho modhail. The children are so well-behaved.

(b) Comparative and superlative of adjectives

The comparative and superlative are identical in Gaelic and are differentiated only by the particle which precedes them, **nas** in the case of the comparative and **as** in the case of the superlative. For regular adjectives, the comparative/superlative is formed by slenderising the final consonant of the adjective and adding **e**. Slenderisation may affect the preceding vowel in the usual manner. (See Appendix 1.) **Nas** and **as** both lenite f. Here are some examples:

òg	òige	young
àrd	àirde	high
dearg	deirge	red
sean	sine	old
trom	truime	heavy
brònach	brònaiche	sad
tiugh	tighe	thick
fliuch	fliche	wet
geur	géire	sharp

Some adjectives drop their second syllable when the final -e is added:

ìseal	**ìsle**	low
uasal	**uaisle**	high, noble
dìleas	**dìlse**	loyal
milis	**mìlse**	sweet

Adjectives ending in a vowel show no change in the comparative/superlative:

brèagha	**brèagha**	beautiful, lovely
buidhe	**buidhe**	yellow
toilichte	**toilichte**	happy

90 Irregular adjectives

Here are some of the most important adjectives whose comparative/superlative forms are irregular:

mór	**motha**	big
beag	**lugha**	small
math	**feàrr**	good
dona	**miosa**	bad
fada	**faide**	long
gearr, goirid	**giorra**	short
furasda	**fasa**	easy
làidir	**treasa** (or **làidire**)	strong
duilich	**duilghe**	hard
teth	**teotha**	hot

(b1) Comparative

NAS + ADJECTIVE + SLENDERISATION + E + NA 'than'
nas **òige** **na**
younger than

Examples:

Tha mi nas fheàrr a-nis, tapadh leat. I am better now, thank you.
Tha na balaich sin a' fàs nas miosa. Those boys are getting worse.
Tha Anna nas sine na Catrìona. Ann is older than Catherine.
Am bheil Iain nas òige na Peigi? Is John younger than Peggy?
Tha stàilinn nas treasa na fiodh. Steel is stronger than wood.

(b2) Superlative

AS + ADJECTIVE + SLENDERISATION + E
as   **òige**
youngest

Examples:

an gille as òige	the youngest boy
an taigh as motha	the biggest house
sin a' chèic as mìlse a bhlais	that is the sweetest cake
mi riamh air	I ever tasted
Se Iain as miosa	John is the worst

Nas and **as** are used when the main verb of the clause in which they occur is in the present or future tense. When the main verb of the clause is in the past or conditional/past habitual, the forms **na bu★** and **a bu★** (**na b'** and **a b'** before vowels and **f** + vowel) are used respectively. However, there is a tendency among younger speakers to use **nas** and **as** in all contexts. Here are some examples:

Bha na balaich na bu mhiosa.	The boys were worse.
Bhiodh Anna na bu mhotha	Ann would be bigger at that
an uair sin.	time.
Bha Màiri na bu shine na Iain.	Mary was older than John.
Bhinn na bu t(h)oilichte ri sin.	I would be happier with that.
Thàinig an nighean a bu bhrèagha.	The most beautiful girl came.
Sin an ceòl a b'fheàrr a chuala	That is the best music that
mi riamh.	I ever heard.
Chunnaic mi an taigh a bu mhotha.	I saw the biggest house.
B'e Iain a bu mhiosa.	John was the worst.

Vocabulary

can (*vb*)	/kan/	say
sìde (*m/f*, 5)	/ʃiːdʲə/	weather
suidh (*vb*)	/suɪj/	sit
buinig (*vb*)	/buɲigʲ/	win
duais (*f*, 2)	/d̪uəʃ/	prize
an t-Òban (*m*)	/ən̪ t̪ɔːban/	Oban
teaghlach (*m*, 1)	/tʲɤːɫəx/	family
sgian (*f*, 2)	/sgʲiən/	knife
Ailean	/alan/, /ɛlan/	Alan
craobh (*f*, 2)	/krɯːv/	tree
riamh	/rʲiəv/	ever
doirbh, duilich	/d̪[ɤrʲɤ]v/	difficult

a' Ghàidhlig (*f*, 5)	/ə ɣaːligʲ/	Gaelic
a' Bheurla (*f*, 5)	/ə vjɤːɬʲə/	English
beairteach	/bɛɾsdʲəx/, /bjaɾsdʲəx/	rich
fear (*m*, 1) **lagha**	/fɛr ɬɤɣə/	lawyer

Exercise 2

Translate

1 I would say that John is older than Mary.
2 If the weather were better we would sit outside.
3 I told you that you would win the biggest prize.
4 William lived in Oban when he was younger.
5 James is the eldest in his family.
6 It is easier when the knife is sharper.
7 Peggy is stronger than Alan although she is smaller than him.
8 That is the highest tree that I ever saw.
9 Gaelic is as difficult as English. (say: *the* Gaelic and *the* English)
10 The teacher is not as rich as the lawyer.

91 'That': linking clauses and reported speech

It is important to distinguish between **a** 'that' and **gun** 'that' in
Gaelic. Both **a** and **gun** correspond to different functions of 'that'
in English and there can be some confusion amongst learners about
when to use **a** and when to use **gun**. The difference between them
is this: **a** is a relative pronoun and **gun** is a conjunction. **A** is used
following nouns, adverbs and independent particles and is followed
by an independent verbal form. **Gun** always follows verbs, usually
verbs meaning 'to say, to tell, to hear, to think, etc.' (i.e. in
reported speech), and is followed by a dependent verbal form.
Consider the following examples:

Có a rinn seo?	Who did this?
Dé a dh'òl thu?	What did you drink?
an t-òran a sheinn Seumas.	the song that James sang.
am bàta a thàinig a-steach.	the boat that came in.
Sann fliuch a tha an latha.	It is wet that the day is.
Sann an-dé a chaidh Iain a Ghlaschu.	It is yesterday that John went to Glasgow.
Thuirt Iain gun robh sneachda an Glaschu.	John said that there was snow in Glasgow.
Chuala mi gun do dh'fhalbh Anna.	I heard that Ann left.

Dh'innis iad dhomh <u>gun</u> digeadh iad.	They told me that they would come.
Gheall Màiri <u>gun</u> tilleadh i a dh'aithghearr.	Mary promised that she would return soon.
Tha mi a' smaoineachadh <u>gun</u> dàinig Iain.	I think that John came.

Note: 'that' may be left out in English but never in Gaelic, e.g.:

an t-òran a sheinn Iain	the song (that) John sang
chuala mi gun dàinig Anna	I heard (that) Ann came

Note also that **nach** serves as the negative form of both **a** and **gun**, e.g.:

an t-òran nach do sheinn Seumas (*rel*)
the song that James didn't sing

chuala mi nach do dh'fhalbh Anna (*conj*)
I heard that Ann didn't leave

91a *'Gun'*: linking *'is'* sentences

We have seen that all sentences involving 'is' can begin with **se = is + e**. When **gun** is used to link an **is** sentence to a verb phrase preceding it, **gun** and **is** combine to give **gur** which prefixes **h** to **e** as follows: (note that some dialects use **gun** and do not prefix **h-** to **e**).

Thuirt Iain + se tidsear a tha ann an Anna becomes:

Thuirt Iain gur h-e tidsear a tha ann an Anna.
John said that Ann is a teacher.

Here are some other examples:

Tha mi a' smaoineachadh gur h-e damhan-allaidh a tha ann.
I think that it is a spider.

Dh'innis Iain dhomh gur h-e Màiri a sheinn aig a' chéilidh.
John told me that it was Mary who sang at the ceilidh.

Chuala mi gur h-e co-latha breith Sìle a tha ann an-diugh.
I heard that it is Sheila's birthday today.

91b Linking *'sann'* sentences

As before, **gun** combines with **is** to give **gur** which prefixes **h-** to **ann**. Some dialects use **gun** and do not prefix **h-** to **ann**.

Dh'innis Iain dhomh + sann air a' bhus a chunnaic e Catrìona
becomes:

Dh'innis Iain dhomh gur h-ann air a' bhus a chunnaic e Catrìona.
John told me that it was on the bus that he saw Catherine.

Here are some other examples:

Chuala mi gur h-ann an-diugh a tha an clas.
I heard that it is today that the class is i.e. that the class is
    (on) today.

**Leugh mi gur h-ann ann an Dùn Éideann a bha Donnchadh
    Bàn a' fuireach.**
I read that it was in Edinburgh that Duncan Bàn lived.
(See page 202.)

Exercise 3

Link the following clauses using **gun (gur)** *or* **a** *where appropriate and
translate:*

1 Thuirt Iain + bha e a-muigh an-raoir
2 Chuala mi + thàinig Seumas
3 An rud + chunnaic mi
4 An naidheachd + chuala tu
5 Thuirt Anna + se ministear a tha ann
6 Tha mi a' smaoineachadh + se co-latha breith Sheumais a tha
    ann an-diugh
7 Leugh mi + sann an-diugh a thachair e
8 Tha iad a' ràdh + sann an Glaschu a bha iad a' fuireach

92 Adjectives: plural

Only adjectives with one syllable have plural forms. Adjectives
with more than one syllable do not change form in the plural.
Nominative, prepositional and genitive plural forms are identical.
To form the plural of adjectives, we add **-a** or **-e** to final
consonants; **-a** is added to adjectives which end in broad
consonants; **-e** is added to adjectives which end in slender
consonants. Consider the following examples:

SINGULAR	PLURAL	
mór	**móra**	big
beag	**beaga**	small
dubh	**dubha**	black

math	matha	good
glic	glice	clever
mìn	mìne	smooth
tinn	tinne	sick

Plural adjectives are lenited if they follow a plural noun which ends in a slender consonant (i.e. Type B plurals; see Lesson 8, **Section 68**). Consider the following examples:

TYPE A PLURALS

na caileagan òga	the young girls
na bùthan ùra	the new shops
na leabhraichean matha	the good books

TYPE B PLURALS

na balaich bheaga	the small boys
na cait dhubha	the black cats
na boireannaich ghlice	the clever/wise women

Note that the lenited plural form of adjectives is used with the indefinite pronoun **feadhain** 'some', e.g.:

| **an fheadhain bheaga** | the small ones |
| **an fheadhain mhóra** | the big ones |

Vocabulary

| **inntinneach** | /iːɲdʲiɲəx/ | interesting |

Exercise 4

Remove the brackets and make the necessary adjustments and translate the following phrases:

1 caileagan (òg)
2 an fheadhain (geal)
3 cait (dubh)
4 clasaichean (mór)
5 balaich (modhail)
6 daoine (làidir)
7 bùird (glan)
8 pàistean (math)
9 leabhraichean (inntinneach)
10 boireannaich (beairteach)

93 Personal numerals

When referring to people, the following numerals are used:

dithis	two people
triùir	three people
ceathrar	four people
cóignear	five people
sianar	six people
seachdnar	seven people
ochdnar	eight people
naonar	nine people
deichnear	ten people

These numerals, unlike the other numerals we have met so far, are nouns and may be used on their own without a following noun, e.g.:

bha dithist aca ann	there were two of them there
thàinig ceathrar a-steach	four (people) came into the room
dhan an t-seòmar	

All are masculine except dithis and triùir which are feminine. The lenited plural form of adjectives is generally used with the personal numbers, e.g.:

an dithis mhóra	the two big people
an triùir bheaga	the three small people

Qualifying nouns may follow these numerals, in which case they appear in the genitive plural. Recall that genitive plurals are automatically lenited when the definite article does not precede. Here are some examples:

dithis dhaoine	two people	dithis ghillean	two boys
triùir dhaoine	three people	triùir ghillean	three boys
ceathrar dhaoine	four people	ceathrar ghillean	four boys
cóignear dhaoine	five people	cóignear ghillean	five boys
sianar dhaoine	six people	sianar ghillean	six boys
seachdnar dhaoine	seven people	seachdnar ghillean	seven boys
ochdnar dhaoine	eight people	ochdnar ghillean	eight boys
naonar dhaoine	nine people	naonar ghillean	nine boys
deichnear dhaoine	ten people	deichnear ghillean	ten boys

In each case it is possible to translate as 'a twosome of . . .', 'a threesome of . . .', etc.

Vocabulary

có dhiubh?	/ko: ju:/	which of?
tì (*f*)	/ti:/	tea
tairg (*vb*)	/t̪[ɛrʲɛ]gʲ/	offer
plana (*m*),	/planə/,	plan, plans
planaichean (*pl*)	/planiçən/	
luchd-ionnsachaidh (*m*)	/ɬuxg jũːn̥səxi/	learners
Alba (*f*)	/[aɫa]bə/	Scotland
an toiseach	/ən̪ t̪ɔʃəx/	firstly
cuir air dòigh (*vb*)	/kurʲ ɛrʲ d̪ɔːj/	arrange, set up, organise
dian-chùrsa (*m*)	/dʲian xuːr̥sə/,	intensive course
	/dʲiən xuːr̥sə/	
labhairt (*f*)	/ɫavər̥tʲ/	speaking
mìos (*f*)	/mĩãs/, /mĩə̃s/	month
mair (*vb*)	/marʲ/	live, last
dealbh (*vb*)	/dʲ[aɫa]v/	create, shape, construct, design
an uair sin	/ən̪ uərʲ ʃin/	that time, then
an lorg sin	/ən̪ ɫ[ɔrɔ]g ʃin/	after that, following that
cùrsa-taic (*m*)	/kuːr̥sə taçgʲ/	support-course, back-up course
clas-oidhche (*m*)	/klas ɤiçə/	night-class, evening-class
air neo	/ər̥ n̪ɔː/	or, alternatively
sgoil (*f*)	/sgɔl/	school
deireadh-sheachdain (*m*)	/dʲɛrʲə hɛxgɛn/	weekend
cum (*vb*)	/ku:m/	keep
fileanta	/filan̪d̪ə/	fluent
fuasgailte	/fuəsgiʎdʲə/	fluent, active
suidhich (*vb*)	/suɪ-iç/	situate
Gàidhealdachd (*f*)	/gɛː-əɫd̪axg/	Highlands, Gaelic-speaking area
Galldachd (*f*)	/gauɫd̪axg/	Lowlands
an dà chuid	/ən̪ d̪aː xudʲ/	both
leudaich (*vb*)	/ʎiad̪iç/	expand
iarr (*vb*)	/iər̥/	want, ask
beò	/bjɔː/	alive
seòrsa	/ʃɔːr̥sə/	type
cuir air bhonn (*vb*)	/kurʲ ɛrʲ voun̪/	set up, found
boin (*vb*)	/bɔɲ/	belong to, relate to
teagasg (*vn*)	/tʲegəsg/	teaching
fa leth	/fa le/	particular
is dòcha	/əs d̪ɔːxə/	probably, perhaps
lean (*vb*)	/ʎɛn/	follow
dualchainnt (*f*)	/d̪uəɫxaiɲdʲ/	dialect
modh (*m*) cainnte	/mɤɣ kaiɲdʲə/	mode of speaking, speech
cuingichte	/kuiɲʲgiçdʲə/	restricted, limited to
beachd (*m*)	/bɛxg/, /bjaxg/	opinion
leig fios gu (*vb*)	/ʎegʲ fis gɔ/	inform

COMHRADH

Iain a' dèanamh agallamh airson obair mar oifigeach cànain le Comann Luchd Ionnsachaidh

Màiri   Thig a-staigh agus suidh an-seo. Có dhiubh a b'fheàrr leat tì no cofaidh?

Iain   Cofaidh as fheàrr leamsa, gun bhainne, gun siùcar.

Màiri   Ceart gu leòr. A-nis, nan gabhadh tu an obair seo – nan tairgeamaid dhut i – dé na planaichean a bhiodh agad airson luchd-ionnsachaidh na Gàidhlig ann an Alba an-diugh?

Iain   An toiseach, chuirinn air dòigh dian-chùrsa labhairt a mhaireadh mìos no dà mhìos. Dhealbhainn an uair sin, an lorg sin, cùrsaichean-taic a bhiodh na bu ghiorra a ghabhadh iad ann an clasaichean-oidhche air neo ann an sgoiltean deireadh-sheachdain. Chumadh sin a' Ghàidhlig aca fileanta fuasgailte.

Màiri   Càite an suidhicheadh tu na cùrsaichean sin? An ann air a' Ghàidhealdachd air neo air a' Ghalldachd a chuireadh tu iad?

Iain   An dà chuid. Anns an dà àite.

Màiri   An leudaicheadh tu air sin dhuinn?

Iain   Dh'iarrainn gum biodh cuid aca air a' Ghàidhealdachd a chionn is gur h-ann an-sin as motha a tha a' Ghàidhlig beò. Ach air an làimh eile, bhiodh e na b'fhasa do mhóran luchd-ionnsachaidh air a' Ghalldachd nam biodh cothrom aca air cùrsaichean a bhiodh na b'fhaisge orra.

Màiri   Nan cuireadh tu na cùrsaichean sin air bhonn, am boineadh an seòrsa Gàidhlig a bhiodh tu a' teagasg do dh'àite sam bith fa leth?

Iain   Air a' Ghàidhealdachd, is dòcha gum biodh e na b'fheàrr nan leanamaid ri dualchainnt an àite. Ach air a' Ghalldachd, chanainn gum biodh e na b'fhasa nan taghamaid modh cainnte nach robh cho cuingichte.

Màiri   Tapadh leat airson do bheachdan. Leigidh sinn fios thugad uair-eigin air an ath sheachdain ciamar a chaidh dhut anns an agallamh. Beannachd leat.

Iain   Mar sin leibh.

TRANSLATION

John doing an interview for a job as a language officer with Comann Luchd Ionnsachaidh (Learners' Society)

Mary   Come in and sit here. Which do you prefer, tea or coffee?

John   I prefer coffee, without milk or sugar.

Mary   Very well. Now, if you should accept this job – if we were to offer it to you – what plans would you have for Gaelic learners in Scotland today?

John   First, I would set up an intensive course of speaking that would last for a month or two months. Then, after that, I would design back-up courses that were shorter that they could take in night-classes or in weekend-schools. That would keep their Gaelic fluent and active.

Mary   Where would you situate these courses? Is it in the Gaelic-speaking areas you would put them or in the Lowlands?

John   Both. In the two places.

Mary   Would you expand on that for us?

John   I would want some of them to be in the Gaelic speaking area since that is where Gaelic is most alive. But on the other hand, it would be easier for most of the learners in the Lowlands if they had an opportunity to have courses that were nearer them.

Mary   If you should set up these courses, would the kind of Gaelic you would be teaching belong to any particular place?

John   In the Gaelic-speaking areas, perhaps it would be better if we followed the dialect of the place. But in the Lowlands, I would say it would be easier if we selected a mode of speech that wasn't so restricted.

Mary   Thank you for your opinions. We'll let you know sometime next week how you fared in the interview. Good-bye.

John   Goodbye.

Lesson 11

94 Modal verbs

The modal verbs **feum** 'must' and **faod** 'may' are defective verbs, which usually appear in the future and conditional only.

Future:

feumaidh mi	I must
faodaidh tu	you may

Conditional:

dh'fheumadh Iain	John would have to
dh'fhaodadh Anna	Ann could

95 Infinitives

The infinitive form of a verb in Gaelic is the verbal noun. See **Section 17**. The infinitive forms of the irregular verbs **rach** and **thig** are normally **a dhol** and **a thighinn**, although **dol** and **tighinn** are also used respectively. Infinitives are used with the following auxiliary verbs and idioms:

(a) the modal verbs **feum** and **faod**
(b) modal idioms expressing obligation
(c) a number of idioms expressing 'wanting, liking, hoping, capability, remembering'
(d) verbs expressing motion or intent
(e) the verb **sguir** 'cease'

Consider the following examples:

	VERBAL NOUN/INFINITIVE	
(a)		
feumaidh tu	**falbh**	you must leave
faodaidh tu	**a thighinn**	you may come
dh'fheumadh Anna	**tilleadh**	Ann would have to return
dh'fhaodainn	**a dhol**	I could go
(b)		
is fheàrr dhut	**sguir**	you had better stop, cease

| bu chòir dhut | seinn | you should sing |
| tha còir agad | falbh | you should leave |

(c)

tha mi airson	seinn	I want to sing
tha mi ag iarraidh	tilleadh	I want to return
bu toil le Iain	suidhe	John would like to sit
tha dùil aig Màiri	siubhal	Mary expects to travel
is urrainn do Sheumas	draibheadh	James can drive
tha cuimhne agam air	dùsgadh	I remember wakening

(d)

chaidh Iain	a cheannach	John went to buy
tha Seumas a' dol	a bhruidhinn	James is going to speak
thàinig Anna	a dh'fhaicinn	Ann came to see

(e)

| sguir iad | a chaoineadh | they stopped crying |

You will see from the above examples that 'to' is only translated before an infinitive when the auxiliary verb is a verb of motion or a verb implying intent and after the verb **sguir** 'cease'. 'To' is translated in such instances as:

a* before consonants
a dh' before vowels and **f** + vowel

95a Indirect objects of infinitives

Objects (nouns and pronouns) of verbs complemented by prepositions simply follow the preposition, e.g.:

Bu toil leam bruidhinn ri Seumas.
I would like to speak to James.

An urrainn dhut faighneachd de dh'Anna?
Are you able to ask Ann?

Bu chòir dhut fuireach ruinn.
You should stay with us.

Thàinig Iain a bhruidhinn ris a' chlas.
John came to talk to the class.

Chaidh Anna a dh'fhuireach comhla ri Peigi.
Ann went to stay with Peggy.

Tha Ailean a' dol a dh'innse dhuinn.
Alan is going to tell (to) us.

Vocabulary

ithe (*vn*)	/i-ə/, /içə/	eating
duilich	/d̪uliç/	sorry
falbh (*vn*)	/f[aɫa]v]	leaving
cuideachadh (*vn*)	/kudʲəxəɣ/	helping
a-nis	/ə niʃ/	now
tighinn (*vn*)	/tʲi-iɲ/, tʲi-ən/	coming
coimhead (*vn*)	/kɔ̃jəd̪/, /kɛ̃-əd̪/	watching
fuireach (*vn*)	/furʲəx/	living
dol (*vn*)	/d̪ɔɫ/	going
Baile Àtha Cliath	/bal a kliə/	Dublin
éisteachd (*vn*)	/eːʃdʲaxg/	listening
snàmh (*vn*)	/sn̪ãːv/	swimming

Exercise 1

Translate

1 I like to eat
2 I have to leave
3 he would like to help
4 she wants to speak
5 he was going to come
6 she came to watch
7 they expect to live in Oban
8 you should go to Dublin
9 Aren't you going to listen?
10 Peggy can swim

95b Direct objects of infinitives: nouns

When the infinitive is preceded by **a***/**a dh'** 'to', noun objects follow the infinitive directly.

Thàinig Seumas a dh'ithe biadh.
James came to eat food.

Chaidh iad a cheannach leabhraichean.
They went to buy books.

Dh'fhalbh na gillean a chluich ball-coise.
The boys went off to play football.

Thàinig Anna a dhèanamh na h-obrach. (G)
Ann came to do the work.

Tha Peigi a' dol a leughadh <u>a' phàipeir</u>. (G)
Peggy is going to read the paper.

(G): A following noun object usually appears in the genitive only when the object is a definite noun. See **Section 20**.

95c Inversion

When the infinitive is not preceded by **a**★/**a dh'**, i.e. when 'to' is not translated, the object of the infinitive comes before the infinitive i.e. the normal order is inverted, and **a**★ is inserted between the object and the infinitive. When this **a**★ precedes a vowel or **fh-** it is usually not written in order to reflect pronunciation but it is retained here for reasons of clarity. Here are some examples:

bu toil leam <u>bruidhinn</u>	I would like to speak
bu toil leam <u>Gàidhlig a bhruidhinn</u>	I would like to speak Gaelic
bu chòir dhut <u>ionnsachadh</u>	you should learn
bu chòir dhut <u>Gàidhlig a ionnsachadh</u>	you should learn Gaelic

Some other examples:

Tha Alasdair ag iarraidh <u>leabhar a cheannach</u>.
Alasdair wants to buy a book.

Bha dùil aig Anna <u>Iain a fhaicinn</u> a-màireach.
Ann hoped to see John tomorrow.

Dh'iarr an tidsear orm <u>an doras a fhosgladh</u>.
The teacher asked me to open the door.

An urrainn dhut <u>Gàidhlig a bhruidhinn</u>.
Can you speak Gaelic?

Note: **a** is normally omitted when it appears before vowels and **fh** but is written here for reasons of clarity.

Vocabulary

obair (*f*)	/obər^j/	work
dotair (*m*)	/dɔhtɛr^j/	doctor
pàigheadh (*vn*)	/pɛ:-əɣ/	paying
faighinn (*vn*)	/fɛ-iɲ/, /fɛ-in/, /fajiɲ/	getting
bainne (*m*)	/baɲə/	milk

Exercise 2

Translate

1 I must do my work
2 she can speak Gaelic
3 you should buy a new car
4 John wants to write a book
5 you had better close the door after you
6 we couldn't pay the doctor
7 we are going to get milk
8 Ann came to pick up her son
9 Donald remembers reading that book
10 Peggy could speak Gaelic

96 Direct objects of infinitives: pronouns

Direct object pronouns of infinitives do not follow the infinitive.
Possessive pronouns are used instead of the ordinary pronouns to
denote the objects of infinitives; they precede the infinitive. 'I
would like to do it' becomes in Gaelic 'I would like its doing': **bu
toil leam a dhèanamh**.

Here are other examples:

Bu toil leam a faicinn.	I would like to see her.
Tha Iain ag iarraidh a cheannach.	John wants to buy it.
Tha dùil aig Seumas mo phòsadh.	James hopes to marry me.
Dh'iarr iad orm an dùnadh.	They asked me to close them.
Tha mi airson ur coinneachadh.	I would like to meet you.
An urrainn dhuibh ar faicinn an-diugh?	Can you see us today?

When **a*/a dh'** precedes the infinitive, the possessive pronouns
combine with it to give the following forms:

gam*	**gar**
gad*	**gur**
ga*	**gan/gam**
ga	

Examples:

Tha sinn a' dol ga choimhead.	We are going to watch it.
Thàinig na caileagan ga dùsgadh.	The girls came to wake her.
Chaidh Iain gan iarraidh.	John went to get them.

96a Demonstrative pronouns as objects of infinitives

The demonstrative pronouns **seo, sin, siud** are treated like nouns, e.g.:

Thàinig Anna a dhèanamh <u>sin</u>.	Ann came to do that.
Bu toil leam <u>sin a dhèanamh</u>.	I would like to do that.
Feumaidh mi <u>seo a ràdh</u>.	I must say this.

97 'A bhith', 'to be'

The infinitive form of the verb **tha** is a **bhith**. It cannot be used with the periphrastic construction involving **tha**, unlike other infinitives/verbal nouns. Here are some examples:

Bu toigh leam a bhith an Glaschu.	I would like to be in Glasgow.
Tha mi a' dol a bhith an Dùn Éideann.	I am going to be in Edinburgh.
Tha dùil aca a bhith a' falbh.	They expect to be leaving.
Bu chòir dhut a bhith modhail.	You should be well behaved.
Tha Domhnall a' dol a bhith ag obair.	Donald is going to be working.

Vocabulary

iasg (*m*, 1)	/iəsg/	fish
tha eagal air Iain	/ha egəɫ ɛrʲ i-aɲ/	John is afraid
tarraing (*vn*)	/ṭaɾiɲ/	pull
ròpa (*f*, 5)	/ʀɔːhpə/	rope
coimhead (*vn*)	/kɔ̃jəḍ/, /kɛ̃-əḍ/	watching, seeing (of visit)
glanadh (*vn*)	/gɫanəɣ/	cleaning
bòrd (*m*), **bùird** (*pl*)	/bɔːʀsḍ/, /buːʀsdʲ/	table, tables
is fheàrr le Màiri	/ʃaːʀ lɛ maːrʲi/	Mary prefers
creidsinn (*vn*)	/krʲedʲ ʃiɲ/	believing
dùsgadh (*vn*)	/ḍuːsgəɣ/	wakening
cuideachadh (*vn*)	/kudʲəxəɣ/	helping
òran (*m*, 1)	/ɔːran/	song
ràdh (*vn*)	/ʀaː(ɣ)/	saying

Exercise 3

Translate

1 He likes to eat it (*m*).
2 Ann hoped to sing it (*m*) at the ceilidh.

3 John was afraid to pull it (*f*).
4 The young boys have to clean them.
5 Calum went to watch her.
6 Mary prefers to teach it (*f*).
7 You should believe us.
8 Ann is going to waken them.
9 We would like to help you.
10 James remembers saying that.

98 Perfect

A periphrastic construction is used to form the perfect in Gaelic. It is similar to that which we learnt for the present tense except that **air** 'after' replaces **aig** 'at'. Compare:

Tha Iain a' tighinn.	John is coming.
Tha Iain air tighinn.	John has come, *lit* 'John is after coming'.

Here are some other examples:

Tha Anna air falbh.	Ann has left.
Tha Uilleam air tilleadh.	William has returned.
Tha iad air a dhol a-mach.	They have gone out.
Tha Màiri air seinn.	Mary has sung.

Direct objects are inverted and placed before the verbal noun as before (see **Section 95c**):

Tha Calum air leabhar a cheannach.	Calum has bought a book.
Tha Niall air Gàidhlig a ionnsachadh.	Neil has learnt Gaelic.
Tha Dàibhidh air an doras a pheantadh.	David has painted the door.

Note that when the object is preceded by the definite article, it does not take the prepositional form after the preposition **air**, e.g.:

Tha Raibeart air an cù a bhiadhadh mar-thà.
Robert has fed the dog already.

Tha Anna air am borbair a phàigheadh.
Ann has paid the hairdresser.

98a Pluperfect

The pluperfect is formed by replacing **tha** with the past form, **bha** in the periphrastic perfect construction:

bha Anna air tighinn   Ann had come

bha Uilleam air tilleadh	William had returned
bha iad air a dhol a-mach	they had gone out
bha Màiri air seinn	Mary had sung

bha Calum air leabhar a cheannach
Calum had bought a book
bha Niall air Gàidhlig a ionnsachadh
Neil had learnt Gaelic
bha Dàibhidh air an doras a pheantadh
David had painted the door

98b Future perfect

The future perfect is formed by replacing **tha** with the future form **bidh** in the periphrastic perfect construction:

bidh Anna air falbh	Ann will have left
bidh Uilleam air tilleadh	William will have returned
bidh iad air a dhol a-mach	they will have gone out
bidh Màiri air seinn	Mary will have sung

bidh Calum air leabhar a cheannach
Calum will have bought a book
bidh Niall air Gàidhlig a ionnsachadh
Neil will have learnt Gaelic
bidh Dàibhidh air an doras a pheantadh
David will have painted the door

98c Conditional perfect

The conditional perfect is formed by replacing **tha** with the conditional form **bhiodh** in the periphrastic perfect construction:

bhiodh Anna air falbh	Ann would have left
bhiodh Uilleam air tilleadh	William would have returned
bhiodh iad air a dhol a-mach	they would have gone out
bhiodh Màiri air seinn	Mary would have sung
bhiodh Calum air leabhar a cheannach	Calum would have bought a book
bhiodh Niall air Gàidhlig a ionnsachadh	Neil would have learnt Gaelic
bhiodh Dàibhidh air an doras a pheantadh	David would have painted the door

The pluperfect is also formed with **an deidh** and the infinitive as follows:

an deidh do Sheumas tilleadh
after/when James had returned (*lit* 'after returning by James')

an deidh do Chatrìona an cat a chur a-mach
after/when Catherine had put out the cat

an deidh dhomh mo bhracaist a ghabhail
after/when I had had my breakfast

an deidh dhi an sgoil a fhàgail
after/when she had left the school

an deidh dhuinn an obair againn a dhèanamh
after/when we had done our work

98d The immediate perfect

The immediate perfect is formed by inserting **dìreach** 'just' before **air** in the ordinary perfect construction.

tha Màiri dìreach air tighinn   Mary has just arrived
tha iad dìreach air falbh   they have just left
tha mi dìreach air an doras a dhùnadh I have just closed the door

Vocabulary

litir (*f*)	/ʎihtʲərʲ/	letter
cuideam (*m*)	/kudʲəm/	weight
cuir air (*vb*)	/kurʲ erʲ/	to put on (of weight)
tòisich (*vb*)	/tɔːʃiç/	begin, start
oilthigh (*m*)	/ɔlɣj/	university
an t-seachdain seo tighinn	/ən tʲɛxkɛn ʃɔ tʲi-iɲ/	next week
reic (*vb*)	/ʀeçkʲ/	selling
ionnsaich (*vb*)	/jũːn̪siç/	learn
cruinneachadh (*vn*)	/krɯɲəxəɣ/	gathering
fiosrachadh (*m*, 1)	/fisrəxəɣ/	information

Exercise 4

Translate

1 Robert has just gone.
2 Joan has come.
3 John has written the letter.
4 He has put on weight.
5 They have gone out.

6 Mary will have started in the university next week.
7 Ann has sold the old house at last.
8 James would have learnt Gaelic.
9 John has eaten too much already.
10 After Neil had gathered all of the information.

99 'Ri' + noun

Ri followed by a noun (mostly verbal nouns) can imply:

(i) being engaged in something
(ii) that something is to be done

Consider the following examples:

(i) being engaged in something

bha na balaich ri eughachd	the boys were screaming
bha a' chlann ri caoineadh	the boys were crying
tha Iain ri sgrìobhadh an comhnaidh	John is writing always
bha Anna ri ceòl fad a beatha	Ann was at music all her life
bidh iad ri iasgach as t-earrach	they will be at fishing in the Spring time

(ii) something is to be done

The formula is:

THA + SUBJECT + RI + POSSESSIVE PRONOUN A* + VERBAL NOUN
tha   obair   ri   a   dhèanamh
there is work to be done

Here are some further examples:

tha gu leòr ri a ràdh	there is much to be said
bha cus ri a ithe	there was too much to eat
tha Iain ri a mholadh	John is to be praised

Note: **ri a** is pronounced **ri** here.

100 'Gu' + verbal noun

Gu followed by a verbal noun implies 'about to, on the point of, almost':

tha mi gu spreadhadh	I am almost bursting
tha e gu bristeadh	it is about to break
tha iad gu bhith deiseil	they are almost ready (*lit* 'about to be ready')

Vocabulary

Colours

The colour systems used in Gaelic are slightly different to those used in English, most notably with the colours grey, green, and blue.

geal	/gʲal̪/	white, bright
dubh	/d̪u/	black
gorm	/g[ɔrɔ]m/	(dark) blue, green
uaine	/uəɲə/	green
glas	/gl̪as/	grey, grey-green
liath	/ʎiə/	(light) blue, grey
dearg	/dʲ[ara]g/	(bright) red
ruadh	/ʀuəɣ/	(darker) red
buidhe	/buɪjə/	yellow
orains	/ɔrəɲʃ/	orange
donn	/d̪ouɲ/	brown
bàn	/ba:n/	fair (of hair), pale
pinc	/piŋʲgʲ/	pink

101 Ordinal numbers (first, second . . .)

Most ordinal numbers are formed by adding **-th(e)amh** or **-(e)amh** to the basic numeral except in the case of 'first, second, third' which have special forms. The ordinal numbers are normally preceded by the article. The following examples are illustrated with the word **fear**, here meaning 'one':

1st	**a' cheud* fhear**	the first one
2nd	**an dàrna/dara fear**	the second one
3rd	**an treas/trìtheamh fear**	
4th	**an ceathramh fear**	
5th	**an cóigeamh fear**	
6th	**an siathamh fear**	
7th	**an seachdamh fear**	
8th	**an t-ochdamh fear**	
9th	**an naoitheamh fear**	
10th	**an deicheamh fear**	
11th	**an t-aonamh fear deug**	
12th	**an dàrna/dara fear deug**	
13th	**an treas/trìtheamh fear deug**	
18th	**an t-ochdamh fear deug**	
20th	**am ficheadamh fear**	

VIGESIMAL	DECIMAL
21st **an t-aonamh fear ar fhichead**	**am ficheadamh fear is a h-aon**
22nd **an dàrna/dara fear ar fhichead**	**am ficheadamh fear is a dhà**

29th	an naoitheamh fear ar fhichead	am ficheadamh fear is a naoi
30th	an deicheamh fear ar fhichead	an tritheadamh fear
31st	an t-aonamh fear deug ar fhichead	an tritheadamh fear is a h-aon
35th	an cóigeamh fear deug ar fhichead	an tritheadamh fear is a cóig
40th	an dà fhicheadamh fear	an ceathradamh fear
41st	an dà fhicheadamh fear is a h-aon	an ceathradamh fear is a h-aon
42nd	an dà fhicheadamh fear is a dhà	an ceathradamh fear is a dhà
49th	an dà fhicheadamh fear is a naoi	an ceathradamh fear is a naoi
50th	an dà fhicheadamh fear is a deich	an caogadamh fear
55th	an dà fhicheadamh fear is a cóig deug	an caogadamh fear is a cóig
60th	an trì ficheadamh fear	an seasgadamh fear
61st	an trì ficheadamh fear is a h-aon	an seasgadamh fear is a h-aon

100th	an ceudamh fear
1,000th	an mìleamh fear
1,000,000th	an muilleanamh fear

Here are some examples involving **latha** 'day':

8th	an t-ochdamh latha
12th	an dàrna/dara latha deug
27th	an seachdamh latha ar fhichead
31st	an t-aonamh latha deug ar fhichead or a' cheud latha deug ar fhichead

Vocabulary

Oidhche na Bliadhna Ùire	/xiçə nə bləᶇ u:rʲə/	Hogmanay, New Year's Eve
Bliadhna Mhath Ùr	/bliəᶇə vã u:r/	Happy New Year
a leithid	/a lehidʲ/	its like, the same
drama (*m*)	/ḍramə/	a dram, a drink of whisky
dòirt (*vb*)	/ḍɔːɾsdʲ/	pour
tog (*vb*)	/ṭog/	raise, lift
foghain (*vb*)	/fo-iɲ/	suffice
foghnaidh sin	/foːni ʃin/	that will suffice
céilidh (*vn*)	/kʲeːli/	visit, visiting
a' cheud ★	/ə çiəḍ/	the first
céiliche (*m*)	/kʲeːliçə/	visitor
nochdadh (*vn*)	/ᶇɔxgəɣ/	appearing, showing up
ruigheachd (*vn*)	/ɾuijəxg/	reaching, getting to
fàs (*vb*)	/faːs/	growing
mear	/mɛr/	merry
ceann (*m*)	/kʲauᶇ/	head, end
stiall ort (*vb*)	/sdʲiəɫ ɔɾsḍ/	on you go, continue
làn dì do bheatha	/ɫaːn dʲiː ḍə vɛhə/	you are very welcome
ged-ta	/gə ṭaː/	however
tadhal (*vn*)	/ṭɤ-əɫ/	visiting
grunn	/gruːᶇ/	a good deal, a lot
grian (*f*)	/grʲiən/	sun
sgrìob (*f*)	/sgrʲiːb/	trip
di-beathte	/dʲə bɛhtʲə/	welcome

174

togail (*vn*)	/ʈogal/	raising, taking
fairich (*vb*)	/farʲiç/	perceive, feel
seachad	/ʃɛxad̪/	past
feuch (*vb*)	/fiax/	see, make sure

COMHRADH

Oidhche na Bliadhna Ùire

Donnchadh Thig a-staigh a Theàrlaich. Is math d'fhaicinn.

Teàrlach Bliadhna Mhath Ùr a Dhonnchaidh. Bliadhna Mhath Ùr a Mhàiri.

Donnchadh A leithid eile dhuibh fhéin is móran dhiubh.

Teàrlach Feumaidh tu drama a ghabhail. Seo agad uisge-beatha math. Gloine dhut an-seo.

Donnchadh Tog, tog. Foghnaidh sin.

Teàrlach Do dheagh shlàinte. 'A h-uile latha a chì is nach fhaic.'[1] An dàinig duine eile a chéilidh oirbh mar-tha?

Donnchadh Cha dàinig. Is tu fhéin a' cheud chéiliche a tha air nochdadh gu ruige seo. Nach e a Mhàiri?

Màiri Se. Chan fhaca sinn duine eile fhathast.

Teàrlach Seo an treas taigh a tha mise air a ruigheachd a-nochd.

Donnchadh Sann a bhios tu a' fàs mear a Theàrlaich. Is dòcha gum bu chòir dhut beagan uisge a chur 'na cheann.

Teàrlach B'fheàrr leamsa a ghabhail dìreach mar a tha e.

Donnchadh Nach tusa a dh'fhaodas a bhalaich. Stiall ort – agus làn dì do bheatha.

Teàrlach Chan fheum mi cus a òl ged-ta. Tha dùil agamsa tadhal ann an grunn thaighean eile mus éirich a' ghrian.

Donnchadh Sann a dh'fhaodainn fhìn a dhol comhla riut. Tha mi air a bhith aig baile fad na h-oidhche. Is bu toil leam sgrìob a ghabhail a-mach.

Teàrlach Dèan sin gu dearbh. Chan eil an oidhche ach òg fhathast. Ach aon drama eile mus fhalbh sinn, ma-tha.

Donnchadh Tapadh leat fhéin a Theàrlaich.

Teàrlach Tha thu di-beathte – glé dhi-bheathte. Slàinte mhath.

Donnchadh Tha còir againn a bhith a' togail oirnn. Seall an uair a tha e.

[1]'Every day that (we) see (one another) or not.' The expression wishes good health at all times.

Teàrlach   Oidhche mhath a bhean an taighe.

Màiri   Oidhche mhath a Theàrlaich agus tapadh leat airson
do chéilidh. Cha do dh'fhairich sinn an oidhche a' dol
seachad. A Dhonnchaidh, feuch nach bi thu ro
anmoch a' tighinn dhachaigh!

TRANSLATION

Hogmanay

Duncan   Come in Charles. It's good to see you.

Charles   Happy New Year Duncan. Happy New Year Mary.

Duncan   The same to you and many of them.

Charles   You'll have to take a dram. Here's a good whisky for
you. A glass for you here.

Duncan   Stop, stop.[2] That will do.

Charles   Your good health. 'Every day we see and don't.' Has
anyone else visited you already?

Duncan   No one. You're the first visitor who has appeared
until now. Isn't he Mary?

Mary   He is. We haven't seen anybody else yet.

Charles   This is the third house I've got to tonight.

Duncan   Then you will be getting merry, Charles. Perhaps you
should put a little water in it.

Charles   I would rather take it just as it is.

Duncan   And well you may boy. On you go – and very
welcome you are!

Charles   I mustn't drink too much, though. I expect to call in a
number of other houses before the sun rises!

Duncan   Indeed, I could go with you myself. I've been at home
all night. And I'd like to take a trip out.

Charles   Do that indeed. The night is but young yet. But one
more dram before we go, then.

Duncan   Thank you, Charles.

Charles   You're welcome, very welcome. Good health.

Duncan   We ought to be setting off. Look at the time.

Charles   Good night, lady of the house!

Mary   Good night, Charles and thank you for your visit. We
didn't feel the night passing. Make sure you're not too
late coming home, Duncan.

[2] *lit* lift (stop pouring).

Lesson 12

102 Irregular verbs: conditional/past habitual

It is possible to group conditional/past habitual formation into two groups:

(i) Verbs whose formation is regular:

INDEPENDENT	DEPENDENT	
bheireadh	beireadh	would catch
chluinneadh	cluinneadh	would hear
dhèanadh	dèanadh	would do/make
rachadh	rachadh	would go
ruigeadh	ruigeadh	would reach

(ii) Verbs whose independent and dependent forms are different:

INDEPENDENT	DEPENDENT	
theireadh	abradh	would say
chitheadh	faiceadh	would see
gheibheadh	faigheadh	would get, find
thigeadh	digeadh	would come
bheireadh	doireadh	would give

Note: some prefer to spell the dependent forms of the last two verbs with an initial **t-** or even **d'th-**.

Note: the endings we learnt for the regular verbs are also used with the irregular verbs. Consider the following example:

chluinninn	I would hear
chluinneadh tu	you would hear
chluinneadh e/i	he/she would hear
chluinneamaid	we would hear
chluinneadh sibh	you would hear
chluinneadh iad	they would hear

The conditional/past habitual forms of the verbs **cluinn** and **faic** can imply 'capability' as with the future forms:

Chluinneadh tu na h-eòin a' seinn.
You could hear the birds singing.

Chitheadh tu na reultan anns an adhar.
You could see the stars in the sky.

Note: the regular verb **can** may be used for **abair** in the conditional/past habitual as in the future tense and imperative.

Examples

Theirinn ris gun robh e gòrach sin a dhèanamh.
I would say to him that he was silly to do that.

Bheireadh i air a' chupa mus ruigeadh e an làr.
She would catch the cup before it reached the floor.

Dé chluinneadh a' chlann nuair a bhiodh iad a-muigh?
What would the children hear when they were out?

Dhèanadh iad an obair sin gun teagamh.
They would do that work without doubt.

Chitheamid a' mhuir a-mach romhainn.
We could see the sea before us.

Chan fhaigheadh tu móran airgid air a shon.
You wouldn't get much money for it.

Rachainn ann nan digeadh tusa còmhla rium.
I would go there if you came along with me.

Thigeadh Anna gam choimhead nam biodh an ùine aice.
Ann would come to see me if she had the time.

Cha doireadh iad sgilling dhut.
They wouldn't give you a penny.

102a Answering questions

As usual, the verb is echoed:

An digeadh tu comhla rium?	Would you come with me?
Thigeadh.	Yes.
Cha digeadh.	No.
An doireadh Anna an leabhar do Pheigi?	Would Ann give the book to Peggy?
Bheireadh.	Yes.
Cha doireadh.	No.

Vocabulary

toilichte	/ʈɔliçdʲə/	pleased
uabhasach toilichte	/ūavasəx ʈɔliçdʲə/	very, terribly pleased
balgam (*m*) **tea**	/b[aʈa]gəm ti:/	some tea (*lit* 'a mouthful')
ceart gu leòr	/kʲaɾsd gə ʎɔ:r/	right enough, OK
càirdean, companaich (*m, pl*)	/ka:ɾsdʲən/, /koumbaniç/	friends

178

taigh-tasgaidh (*m*)	/ʈɤj ʈasgi/	museum
mìos (*f*)	/mĩãs/, /mĩə̃s/	month
suidheachan (*m*, 1)	/suɪjəxan/	seat
plèan (*m*)	/plɛ:n/	aeroplane
uisge (*m*)	/uɪʃgʲə/	rain
dràma	/ɖra:ma/	drama (play)
cùil (*f*)	/ku:l/	corner
aiseag (*m*)	/aʃəg/	ferry
mu dheireadh	/ma jerʲəɣ/	last
a leithid sin	/ə lehidʲ ʃin/	the likes of that
àite sam bith	/a:htʲə səm bi/	anywhere
eile	/elə/	other, else
cead (*m*)	/kʲeɖ/	permission

Exercise 1

Translate

1 I would be very pleased if they came.
2 He would drink some tea right enough.
3 They would see their friends at school.
4 We used to go to the museum every month.
5 You would not get a seat on the aeroplane now.
6 Would you say that John would go out to the drama?
7 Would you get the bus from that corner?
8 You would catch the last ferry at nine o'clock.
9 You would not hear the likes of that anywhere else.
10 Donald's mother would not give him permission to go out.

103 'Usually'

If we want to say someone usually or frequently does something, we use the idiom **is àbhaist do** which means literally 'it is customary for' as follows:

IS + ÀBHAIST + DO* + SUBJECT + A BHITH + VERBAL NOUN + ADVERB

is   àbhaist   do   Sheumas   a bhith   a' seinn
James usually sings

Here are some more examples:

Is àbhaist do Mhàiri a bhith a' dùsgadh tràth.
Mary usually wakes up early.

Is àbhaist dhomh a bhith a' dol a dh'Eirinn as t-samhradh.
I usually go to Ireland in the summer.

Negative forms:

Chan àbhaist do Mhórag a bhith a' smocadh.
Morag doesn't usually smoke.

Chan àbhaist dhut a bhith a' draibheadh.
You don't usually drive.

Interrogative (positive) forms:

An àbhaist do Dhomhnall a bhith a' cluich ball-coise?
Does Donald usually play football?

An àbhaist dha a bhith a' dol a dh'Uibhist?
Does he usually go to Uist?

Interrogative (negative) forms:

Nach àbhaist do Ruairi a bhith ag ithe feòil?
Doesn't Ruairi usually eat meat?

Nach àbhaist dhi a bhith a' dol a-mach feasgar?
Does she not usually go out in the evening?

In reply to these positive and negative interrogative forms **An/nach àbhaist . . .?**, we find:

| **Is àbhaist** | Yes |
| **Chan àbhaist** | No |

104 'Used to'

Is àbhaist do becomes **b'àbhaist do** in the past tense and means 'used to'. It is frequently used instead of the past habitual.
Here are some examples:

B'àbhaist do Mhàiri a bhith ag obair ann an Glaschu.
Mary used to work in Glasgow.

Cha b'àbhaist dha a bhith ag obair cho dian.
He didn't use to work so hard.

Nach b'àbhaist dhut a bhith ag ionnsachadh Gàidhlig? Cha b'àbhaist.
Didn't you use to learn Gaelic? No.

Nach b'àbhaist do Chatrìona a bhith a' teagasg? B'àbhaist.
Didn't Catherine use to be teaching? Yes.

105 Past particles and the perfective

Gaelic uses a small number of past participles. Here is a list of those which are most commonly used:

pòsta	married
sgrìobhte	written
reòite	frozen
stéidhichte	established
foghlaimte	learned, educated

Some past participles have developed 'new' meanings:

seòlta	cunning, clever
sgiobalta	tidy, neat
gleusta	canny, prudent
do-dhèante	impossible

The perfective is normally formed in a similar way as the perfect. See Lesson 11, **Section 98**. The pattern is as follows:

THA + SUBJECT + AIR + POSS PRON + VERBAL NOUN
(AGREEING WITH SUBJ)

tha   am feur   air   a*   ghearradh
the grass is cut

Here are some further examples:

bha am fiadh air a mharbhadh	the deer was killed
an robh Niall air a bhualadh?	was Neil hit?
bha an t-uisge beatha air a òl uile gu léir	the whisky was all drunk
cha robh na bàtaichean air an càrachadh	the boats were not fixed
an robh Mórag air a taghadh?	was Morag (s)elected?

Note that these perfectives can also have passive meaning. See below.

106 Passive

In Gaelic a passive sentence like 'the door was closed' can be expressed in three ways:

(a) by using the auxiliary verb **rach** 'go' + subject + **a*** + verbal noun:

chaidh an doras a dhùnadh   the door was closed

(b) by using the perfective construction introduced above: THA+ SUBJECT+AIR+POSS PRON (AGREEING WITH SUBJ)+VERBAL NOUN

bha Niall air a bhualadh   Neil was hit

(c) by using special impersonal forms of the verb:

dhùineadh an doras   the door was closed

Type (a) is the most commonly used in modern Gaelic. Type (c) is frequently used in literary Gaelic although it also occurs in ordinary spoken Gaelic.

Here are some more examples of type (a):

chaidh Iain a bhualadh	John was hit
cha deach an telebhisean a ghoid	the television was not stolen
An deach am biadh a ithe?	Was the food eaten?
théid an càr a reic	the car will be sold

If the subject of a passive sentence of type (a) is a pronoun, possessive pronouns are used with the verb **rach** and the verbal noun as follows:

chaidh mo bhualadh	I was hit
	(*lit* 'my hitting went/passed')
chaidh do mholadh	you were recommended/praised
chaidh a dhèanamh	it was done
chaidh a pòsadh	she was married
chaidh ar stiùireadh	we were directed
an deach ur leantainn?	were you followed?
cha deach an clò-bhualadh fhathast	they were not printed yet

Here are some examples of type (b):

bha an càr air a ghoid	the car was stolen
bha an t-àite air a lìonadh le uisge	the place was filled with water

The following phrase using type (c) is used in all dialects.

rugadh is thogadh mi ann an Alba
I was born and brought up in Scotland

The agent of a passive sentence is introduced by the preposition **le** 'with' or in some cases by the preposition **aig** 'at' as follows:

chaidh a' bhùth a cheannach le Iain
the shop was bought by John

chaidh a' chaora a leagail le càr
the sheep was knocked down by a car

an deach Anna a bhreabadh leis an each?
was Ann kicked by the horse?

bha Iain air a bhualadh aca
John was hit by them

107 Impersonal verbal forms

Type C

The past, future and conditional/past habitual all have impersonal forms. In each case, the impersonal forms consist of endings which are attached to the relevant tense form of the verb. Here are the impersonal forms illustrated with the verb **dùin** 'close' and **buail** 'hit':

dhùineadh an doras the door was closed, someone closed the door

dùinear an doras the door will be closed, someone closes the door

dhùinte an doras the door would be closed, the door used to be closed, someone would close the door, someone used to close the door

bhuaileadh mi I was struck, someone struck me

buailear e he will be struck, someone will strike him

bhuailte iad they would be struck, they used to be struck, someone would strike them, someone used to strike them

The impersonal use of these forms is clearly seen with intransitive verbs, i.e. verbs which do not have objects, e.g.:

thathar a' dol ann a h-uile bliadhna
one is/people are going there every year

thigear an-seo a h-uile madainn
one comes/people come here every morning

chan urrainnear tiocaid a cheannach an-seo
one cannot buy a ticket here

dh'fheumte a dhol ann
one had to go there/people had to go there

108 Independent and dependent impersonal forms

Independent and dependent forms are identical in the future. In the past the distinction between both forms is as with other forms of the past: dependent form = **do** + independent form. The difference in the conditional/past habitual is as with other forms: the independent forms are lenited; the dependent forms are not lenited. This may be summarised as follows:

IMPERSONAL FORMS:

TENSE	INDEPENDENT	DEPENDENT
PAST	lenition + **(e)adh**	**do** + independent forms
	dh'+**(f)** vowel+**(e)adh**	
PRESENT	**(e)ar**	**(e)ar**
COND/PAST HAB	lenition + **te**	**te**
	dh' + vowel/**f** +	
	vowel + **te**	

Note: some dialects use **(a)ist** for **te** in the conditional/past habitual.

Examples:

dhùineadh an uinneag
the window was closed,
someone closed the window

cha do dh'fhosgladh an uinneag
the window was not opened,
no one opened the window

seinnear an t-òran sin a h-uile bliadhna
that song will be sung every year,
someone will sing that song every year

an leughar e?
will it be read?,
will someone read it?

cheannaichte gu leòr salainn an uair ud
a lot of salt used to be bought at that time,
people used to buy a lot of salt at that time

an cante sin an da-rìribh?
was that said seriously?,
did people say that seriously?

Here is a list of the most commonly used impersonal forms of irregular verbs:

VERB	PAST		FUTURE		COND/PAST HAB	
	INDEP	DEP	INDEP	DEP	INDEP	DEP
abair	thuirteadh	duirteadh	theirear	deirear	theirte	deirte
beir	rugadh	do rugadh	beirear	beirear	bheirte	beirte
cluinn	chualas	cualas	cluinnear	cluinnear	chluinnte	cluinnte
dèan	rinneadh	do rinneadh	nithear	dèanar	dhèante	dèante
faic	chunncas	facas	chithear	faicear	chìte	faicte
faigh	fhuaradh fhuaras	d'fhuaradh d'fhuaras	gheibhear	faighear	gheibhte	faighte
thoir	thugadh	dugadh	bheirear	doirear	bheirte	doirte

The impersonal forms of the verb **tha** are as follows:

PAST		PRESENT		FUTURE		COND/PAST HAB	
INDEP	DEP	INDEP	DEP	INDEP	DEP	INDEP	DEP
bhathar bhathas	robhar robhas	thathar thathas	(bh)eilear (bh)eileas	bithear	bithear	bhite	bite

109 Another passive construction

The periphrastic (long) construction involving the verb **tha** and the preposition **aig** can be used passively. The formula is as follows:

THA + SUBJECT + (AG + POSS PRON, AGREEING IN NUMBER AND GENDER WITH THE SUBJECT) + VERBAL NOUN

Recall from Lesson 8, **Section 72** that **ag** combines with the possessive pronouns as follows:

gam*	gar
gad*	gur
ga*	gan/gam
ga	

Here are some examples:

Bha Gàidhlig 'ga bruidhinn air feadh Alba.
Gaelic was spoken all over Scotland.

Tha leabhraichean gan reic anns a' bhùth sin.
Books are being sold in that shop.

Bhiodh an t-òran sin ga ghabhail gu math tric air an rèidio.
That song used to be sung fairly often on the radio.

Vocabulary

leag (*vb*)	/ʎeg/	knock down
caill (*vb*)	/kaiʎ/	lose
airgead (*m*)	/[ɛrʲɛ]gʲəd̪/	money
lean (*vb*)	/ʎɛn/	follow
nigh (*vb*)	/ɲi/	wash
bho	/ɔ/, /vɔ/	since
marbh (*vb*)	/m[ara]v/	kill
feadh (+*G*)	/fjɣɣ/	(at some point) during

Exercise 2

Translate the following using the impersonal forms of the verbs:

1 The song will be sung.
2 The window was opened.
3 The old house was pulled down/demolished.
4 Money is lost every year.
5 John was followed home yesterday.
6 It used to be washed every day.
7 The bird has not been seen or heard since last week.
8 It is said that he lived in Edinburgh when he was younger.
9 He was killed during the night.
10 I was born and brought up in Ireland.

110 Subjunctive

Scottish Gaelic does not have special subjunctive verbal forms which express desire or uncertainty. Normally the conditional form corresponds to the subjunctive in other languages.

Rachainn a Ghlaschu nan digeadh Anna comhla rium.
I would go to Glasgow if Ann came with me.

Subjunctive forms do survive, however, in higher registers of the language, particularly in the Bible, e.g.:

Tog do shùil is gum faic thu a-nis am mùthadh mór.
Lift thine eye that thou may now see the great change.

Gun dige do rìoghachd.
May Thy kingdom come.

Special 'wish' forms once common also survive in some phrases. These 'wish' forms are preceded by **gun** and **guma** '(would) that', '(wish) that', 'may'. Here are some examples:

gun robh math agad
lit 'may you have good', which is used in some south-western dialects for 'thank you' as in Irish Gaelic

gun déid (gu math) leat!
may it go (well) with you, good luck!

guma math a théid leat!
may it go well with you, good luck!

guma fada beò thu is ceò as ur taigh
long may you live and may there be smoke from your house!

111 Defective verbs

Defective verbs are verbs which do not appear in all tenses. We've already met some defective verbs, e.g.: **faod** 'may', **feum** 'must', **is** 'be'. Here are some more:

(a) **Arsa** 'says, said'

Arsa means 'says' or 'said' and is used in quotative speech. When pronouns are used with **arsa**, they appear in the emphatic form:

"Dé a tha a' dol?" arsa Iain. "What's doing?" says/said John.
"Ciamar a tha sibh?" arsa esan. "How are you?" says/said he.

(b) **Theab** 'almost'

Theab is used in the past tense. It is always followed by an infinitive noun:

Theab mi tuiteam. I almost fell.
Theab i a dhol ás a ciall. She almost went out of her mind.

(c) Dh'fhidir 'know'

Dh'fhidir is used in the past tense and present/future.

Dh'fhidir mi.	I know, I have heard.
Ma dh'fhidireas mi.	If I know
Fidiridh an cù sin.	The dog will sense that.

(d) Trobhad 'come along'; thugainn 'let's go'; siubhad 'go on, continue'

Trobhad, thugainn (with dialect variants) and **siubhad** are only used in the imperative (singular and plural):

Trobhad a Sheumais!	Come along, James!
Trobhadaibh an-seo!	Come here!
Thugainn a Mhàiri!	Let's go, Mary!
Thugnaibh a ghillean!	Let's go, boys!
Siubhad a Dhomhnaill!	Go on, Donald!
Siubhdaibh a nigheanan!	Continue, girls!

112 Interjections

Here is a list of some commonly used interjections:

a chiall!	/ə çiəɫ/	Oh dear!
a thiarna!	/ə hiərn̪(ə)/	Oh lord!
a dhiamh!	/ə jĩã/	yuck!
a dhuine!	/ə ɣuɲə/	dear man!
a thiarcais fhéin!	/ə hiərkiʃ heːn/	goodness me!
mo chreach!	/mə xrɛx/	alas!
obh obh!	/o vo-əv/	dear me!
(dé) b'àill leibh!	/(dʲeː) baːʎ lu/	excuse me! (I didn't hear)

188

Remaining prepositional pronouns

gu 'to'	bho 'from'	fo 'under'	á 'out of'
thugam	bhuam	fodham	asam
thugad	bhuat	fodhad	asad
thuige	bhuaidhe	fodha	as
thuice	bhuaipe	foidhpe	aiste
thugainn	bhuainn	fodhainn	asainn
thugaibh	bhuaibh	fodhaibh	asaibh
thuca	bhuapa	fodhpa	asta

de 'of'	ro 'before'	tro 'through'	mu 'about'
dhiom	romham	tromham	umam
dhiot	romhad	tromhad	umad
dhe	roimhe	troimhe	uime
dhi	roimpe	troimpe	uimpe
dhinn	romhainn	tromhainn	umainn
dhibh	romhaibh	tromhaibh	umaibh
dhiubh	rompa	trompa	umpa

Vocabulary

ceasnaiche (m)	/kʲesn̪ʲiçə/	interviewer
fàilte air	/faːʎtʲə ɛrʲ/	welcome to
bàrd (m)	/baːr̪sd̪/	poet
ainmeil	/[ɛnɛ]mɛl/	famous
Ratharsair	/r̪a-ərsɛrʲ/	Isle of Raasay
tìr-mór (m)	/tʲirʲ moːr/	mainland
fad an t-siubhail	/fad̪ ən tʲu-əl/	all the time
foghlam (m)	/fɤːɫəm/	education
gun teagamh	/ɡən tʲegu/	without a doubt, of course
Port Rìgh	/por̪sd̪ r̪iː/	Portree
cuspair (m)	/kusberʲ/	subject
builich (vb)	/buliç/	grant, bestow, confer
ceum (m)	/kʲeːm/	degree
dreuchd (f)	/driaxg/	post, job
teagasg (m)	/tʲegəsg/	teaching
àrd-sgoil (f)	/aːr̪sd̪ sgɔl/	secondary school
taghadh (vn)	/tɤ-əɣ/	electing, choosing
thoir air (vb)	/hɔrʲ ɛrʲ/	cause
bàrdachd (f)	/baːr̪sd̪axg/	poetry
fhathast	/ha-əsd̪/	still
adhbhar (m)	/ɤːvər/	reason
céilidh (vn)	/kʲeːli/	visiting
gu h-àraid	/ɡə haːrɛdʲ/	especially
miosail air	/misal ɛrʲ/	fond of
sin as coireach	/ʃin əs kɤrʲəx/	that (which) is the reason

litreachas (*m*)	/ʎiht̪rəxəs/	literature
ùr-nodha	/u:r n̪ɔ-ə/	brand new
foillsich (*vb*)	/fɤiʎ∫iç/	publish
comharradh (*m*)	/kɔ̃həɾəɣ/	sign
feadhain (*f*)	/fjo:-iɲ/	some
ginealach (*m*)	/gʲinət̪əx/	generation
seadh	/∫ɤɣ/	yes, indeed
am bheil thu an dùil?	/ə vɛl u əɳ d̪u:l/	do you think (so)?

COMHRADH

Bàrd ainmeil a' bruidhinn air prògram rèdio

Ceasnaiche Fàilte oirbh do phrògram na seachdain seo. Tha am
bàrd ainmeil Niall MacLeòid a-staigh comhla rium
an-diugh. Feasgar math dhuibh a Nèill. Ciamar a tha
sibh?

Niall Tha gu dòigheil. Tha mi fìor thoilichte a bhith an-seo
'nur cuideachd feasgar an-diugh.

Ceasnaiche A-nis, innsibh beagan dhuinn mu ur deidhinn fhéin
an toiseach. Càite an do rugadh sibh?

Niall Rugadh is thogadh mi ann an Ratharsair. Àite
brèagha. Tha mi a-nis a' fuireach air tìr-mór ged-ta.
Bha m'athair ri iasgach. Bha e air a chumail a' dol.
Bhiodh e aig muir fad an t-siubhail. Dh'fheumadh e
sin a chionn bha teaghlach mór aige. Bha ceathrar
bhràithrean agam agus triùir pheathraichean.

Ceasnaiche Càite an d'fhuair sibh ur foghlam?

Niall Fhuair an toiseach ann an Ratharsair gun teagamh
agus an deidh sin ann am Port Rìgh. Nuair a dh'fhàg
mi an sgoil, chaidh mi dhan an oilthigh an Dùn
Éideann. Chuir mi seachad ceithir bliadhna an-sin. Se
Gàidhlig agus Beurla a rinn mi ann. Chòrd an dà
chuspair sin rium glan – le chéile. Bhuilicheadh ceum
MA orm ann an naoi deug trì fichead is a dhà.

Ceasnaiche Dé a rinn sibh an deidh dhuibh a bhith anns an
oilthigh?

Niall Chuir mi a-staigh airson dreuchd teagaisg ann an
àrd-sgoil is chaidh mo thaghadh airson na h-obrach.
Bha mi a' teagasg an dà chuid Gàidhlig is Beurla is
beagan Fraingeis cuideachd.

Ceasnaiche Dé a thug oirbh tòiseachadh air sgrìobhadh agus cuine
a thòisich sibh air sgrìobhadh?

Niall   B'àbhaist dhomh a bhith a' sgrìobhadh tric nuair a
            bha mi òg. Tha cuimhne agam gun do sgrìobh mi pìos
            bàrdachd nuair a bha mi sia bliadhna a dh'aois. Tha e
            agam fhathast.

Ceasnaiche An ann anns a' Ghàidhlig as motha a bha sibh a'
              sgrìobhadh?

Niall   Sann, sann anns a' Ghàidhlig a bha mi a' sgrìobhadh
            mar bu trice. Cha b'urrainn dhomh an aon rud a
            dhèanamh anns a' Bheurla airson adhbhar air
            choireigin, tha fhios agaibh. Nuair a bha mi òg, bhinn
            a' cluinntinn tòrr òrain bho na seann daoine a
            thigeadh a-steach a chéilidh oirnn. Bhinn gan
            ionnsachadh. Tha mi cinnteach gun robh sin 'na
            chuideachadh mór dhomh mar bhàrd. Ghabhte òrain
            is dh'innste sgeulachdan a h-uile h-oidhche anns an
            taigh againne, gu h-àraid anns a' gheamhradh. Bha
            fìor dheagh bhàrdachd anns na h-òrain sin is anns na
            sgeulachdan cuideachd. Bha mi eagalach miosail air na
            h-òrain. Is dòcha gur h-e sin as coireach gur h-e
            Gàidhlig a thagh mi seach Beurla nuair a thòisich mi
            air sgrìobhadh an toiseach.

Ceasnaiche Dé ur beachd air na thathar a' sgrìobhadh anns a'
              Ghàidhlig an-diugh?

Niall   Deagh bheachd air a' chuid as motha dhe, feumaidh
            mi a ràdh. Feumar a ràdh ged-ta gum bheil cuid dhen
            an litreachas ùr-nodha nas fheàrr na chéile.
            Foillsichear móran leabhraichean Gàidhlig a h-uile
            bliadhna seach mar a b'àbhaist. Se comharradh math a
            tha sin. Tha feadhain dhen a' ghinealach òg air leth
            math.

Ceasnaiche O, seadh, am bheil sibh an dùil? Tha mi duilich ach
              chan eil an còrr ùine againn. Tha an ùine air ruith
              agus feumaidh sinn a fhàgail mar sin an-dràsta chun
              na seachdain seo a' tighinn. Sin agaibh e. Tapadh
              leibh a Nèill airson tighinn a-steach a bhruidhinn
              ruinn. Tha sinn fada 'nur comain. Beannachd leibh.

Niall   Mar sin leibh.

TRANSLATION

A famous poet speaking on a radio programme

Interviewer Welcome to this week's programme. The famous poet Neil Macleod is here with me today. Good evening Neil. How are you?

Neil Fine. I am very happy to be here in your company this evening.

Interviewer Now, tell us a bit about yourself first. Where were you born?

Neil I was born and brought up in Raasay. A beautiful place. I now live on the mainland however. My father was at the fishing. He was kept going (i.e. busy). He used to be at sea all the time. He had to be because he had a big family. I had four brothers and three sisters.

Interviewer Where were you educated?

Neil In Raasay at first of course and after that in Portree. When I left school, I went to the university in Edinburgh. I spent four years there. It was Gaelic and English that I did there. I enjoyed those two subjects a lot – both of them. I was granted an MA degree in the year nineteen sixty two.

Interviewer What did you do after being in the university?

Neil I applied for a teaching post in a secondary school and I was chosen for the work. I was teaching both Gaelic and English and a bit of French too.

Interviewer What caused you to begin writing and when did you start to write?

Neil I used to write often when I was young. I remember that I wrote a piece of poetry when I was six years of age. I still have it.

Interviewer Was it in Gaelic that you wrote mostly?

Neil Yes, it was in Gaelic that I most often wrote. I couldn't do the same thing in English for some reason or other, you know. When I was young, I used to hear lots of songs from the old people that would come in to visit us. I used to learn them. I am certain that that was a great help to me as a poet. Songs were sung and stories were told every night in our house, especially in the winter. There was really good poetry in those songs and in the stories too. I was terribly fond of the songs. I suppose that is the reason that it was Gaelic rather than English that I chose when I started writing at first.

Interviewer What is your opinion of what is being written in Gaelic nowadays?

Neil A good opinion of most of it, I must say. It must be said however that some of the modern literature is better than the rest. Many Gaelic books are published every year compared to the way it used to be. That's a good sign. Some of the young generation are exceptionally good.

Interviewer Oh, indeed, do you think so? I am sorry but we have no more time. The time has run out and we must leave it like that until next week. That's it. Thank you Neil for coming in to speak to us. We are very indebted to you. Goodbye.

Neil Goodbye.

Appendix 1

Vowel changes with slenderisation

The following vowels are affected by slenderisation as follows:

Vowel	Vowel + i	Examples	Examples with slenderisation
ea	ei i	each, caileag fear, cailleach	eich, caileig fir, caillich
ia	éi, èi	fiadh, Niall	féidh, Nèill
eò	iùi	ceòl	ciùil
eu	éi eòi	geug beul	géig beòil
io	i	fionn	finn
ìo	i	sìol	sìl
o ò	ui ùi	cnoc bòrd	cnuic bùird

The following vowels may or may not change form with slenderisation. There are no hard and fast rules to tell us if a particular word will change form or not; the vowel changes must be learnt for each noun in question:

Vowel	Vowel + i	Examples	Examples with slenderisation
a	ai	cat	cait
	oi	cas	cois
	ui	falt	fuilt
	i	mac	mic
ò	òi	sròn	sròin
	ùi	bòrd	bùird

Appendix 2

Prepositions and prepositional pronouns

aig 'at'	*air 'on'*	*do 'to, for'*	*gu 'to'*
agam	orm	dhomh	thugam
agad	ort	dhut	thugad
aige	air	dha	thuige
aice	oirre	dhi	thuice
againn	oirnn	dhuinn	thugainn
agaibh	oirbh	dhuibh	thugaibh
aca	orra	dhaibh	thuca

bho 'from'	*fo 'under'*	*le 'with'*	*ri 'with, to'*
bhuam	fodham	leam	rium
bhuat	fodhad	leat	riut
bhuaidhe	fodha	leis	ris
bhuaipe	foidhpe	leatha	rithe
bhuainn	fodhainn	leinn	ruinn
bhuaibh	fodhaibh	leibh	ruibh
bhuapa	fodhpa	leotha	riutha

de 'of'	*ro 'before'*	*tro 'through'*	*ann an 'in'*
dhiom	romham	tromham	annam
dhiot	romhad	tromhad	annad
dhe	roimhe	troimhe	ann
dhi	roimpe	troimpe	innte
dhinn	romhainn	tromhainn	annainn
dhibh	romhaibh	tromhaibh	annaibh
dhiubh	rompa	trompa	annta

mu 'about'	*á 'out of'*
umam	asam
umad	asad
uime	ás
uimpe	aiste
umainn	asainn
umaibh	asaibh
umpa	asta

Appendix 3

Forms of the article

The article may be grouped into four main varieties: **an**, **an★**, **na**, **nam**. These are as follows:

ARTICLE	FORMS	ENVIRONMENT	FUNCTION
an	am an t- an	before labials **b p f m** before vowels otherwise	nom. sing. masculine
an★	a'★ an t- an an★	before lenitable consonants except **d t s f** before **s sl sn sr** before **d t** before **f**	nom. sing. feminine prepositional sing. genitive sing. masculine
na	na h- na	before vowels otherwise	genitive sing. feminine nominative plural
nan	nam nan	before labials **b p f m** otherwise	genitive plural

Recall that ★ indicates that a form lenites.

Appendix 4

Nasalisation

Forms of the article ending in **-n/-m** can affect the pronunciation of the following consonants: **c t p g d b** to varying degrees in Gaelic dialects. There are two main varieties:

Gaelic orthography	TYPE A	TYPE B
an càr	a(n) gàr [ə(ŋ) g(h)a:ʀ]	ang hàr [əŋ ha:ʀ]
an taigh	a(n) daigh [ə(n̥) d(h)ɣj]	an haigh [ən̥ hɣj]
am pinnt	a(m) binnt [ə(m) b(h)i:ɲdʲ]	am hinnt [əm hi:ɲdʲ]
an gobha	a(n) gobha [ə(ŋ) go-ə]	a ngobha [ə ŋo-ə]
an duine	a(n) duine [ə(n̥) duɲə]	a nuine [ə n̥uɲə]
am baile	a(m) bainne [ə(m) baɲə]	a mainne [ə maɲə]

Both types are localised pronunciations, 'A' belonging, broadly speaking, to most dialects and 'B' to a number of dialects of the north west, e.g. Lewis and parts of Skye.

Appendix 5

Example of the regular verb **mol** 'praise'

PRESENT

tha mi a' moladh	I am praising, I praise
tha thu a' moladh	you are praising, you praise
tha e/i a' moladh	he/she is praising, he/she praises
tha sinn a' moladh	we are praising, we praise
tha sibh a' moladh	you are praising, you praise
tha iad a' moladh	they are praising, they praise

PAST

Independent		*Dependent*	
mhol mi	I praised	**cha do mhol mi**	I did not praise
mhol thu	you praised	**cha do mhol thu**	you did not praise
mhol e/i	he/she praised	**cha do mhol e/i**	he/she did not praise
mhol sinn	we praised	**cha do mhol sinn**	we did not praise
mhol sibh	you praised	**cha do mhol sibh**	you did not praise
mhol iad	they praised	**cha do mhol iad**	they did not praise

FUTURE

Independent (i)	*Relative* (= *Independent* (ii))	
molaidh mi	**mholas mi**	I will praise
molaidh tu	**mholas tu**	you will praise
molaidh e/i	**mholas e/i**	he/she will praise
molaidh sinn	**mholas sinn**	we will praise
molaidh sibh	**mholas sibh**	you will praise
molaidh iad	**mholas iad**	they will praise

Dependent

nach mol mi?	will I not praise?
nach mol thu?	will you not praise?
nach mol e/i?	will he/she not praise?
nach mol sinn?	will we not praise?
nach mol sibh?	will you not praise?
nach mol iad?	will they not praise?

CONDITIONAL/PAST HABITUAL

Independent

mholainn	I would praise, I used to praise
mholadh tu	you would praise, you used to praise
mholadh e/i	he/she would praise, he/she used to praise
mholamaid	we would praise, we used to praise
(mholadh sinn)	
mholadh sibh	you would praise, you used to praise
mholadh iad	they would praise, they used to praise

Dependent
The dependent forms are the same as the independent forms
without the lenition.

IMPERATIVE

mol	praise
moladh e/i	let him/her praise
molamaid	let us praise
molaibh	praise
moladh iad	let them praise

To negate the imperative, the above forms are preceded by **na**.

Reading Practice

Iolaire Loch Tréig

Uair dha robh an saoghal, bha iolaire anns na beanntan a-muigh
taobh Loch Tréig. Bha i a' fuireach ann an coire an-sin ris an can
iad An Coire Meadhain. A' bhliadhna seo thàinig geamhradh fuar
agus móran sneachda, le cur is cathadh. Oidhche dhe na
h-oidhcheannan bha an iolaire a' faireachdainn an fhuachd. 'Cha do
dh'fhairich mi a leithid de dh'fhuachd riamh', thuirt i rithe fhéin.
'Saoil', thuirt i, 'an robh oidhche na b'fhuaire na seo riamh ann?'

Bha dreathann donn a' fuireach faisg oirre is chaidh i far an robh
an dreathann. 'An do dh'fhairich thu oidhche na b'fhuaire na seo
riamh?' thuirt i ris. 'Cha do dh'fhairich', ars an dreathann donn,
'ach dh'fhaodadh e a bhith gun robh a leithid ann. Chan eil fhios
agamsa. Ach tha gobhar dhubh ann am Bun Ruaidh is tha i fada
nas sine na mise. Bidh fhios aicese.'

Chaidh an iolaire chun na goibhre is chuir i an dearbh cheist
oirrese. 'Cha do dh'fhairich', thuirt a' ghobhar, 'ach tha damh
féidh', ars ise, 'ann an Coille Innse a tha fada nas sine na mise agus
bidh fhios aigesan.' Ràinig an iolaire Coille Innse is lorg i an damh
féidh ann an coire fasgach. Se an aon fhreagairt a fhuair i an-sin.
'Thàinig mi', arsa esan, 'an-seo á Inbhir Làire is mi 'nam dhamh
òg is cha do dh'fhairich mi oidhche na b'fhuaire. Ach tha breac
ann an Lochan na Làirig a tha fada nas sine na mise. Bidh fhios
aigesan.'

Chaidh an iolaire chun a' bhric. 'An do dh'fhairich thu oidhche
riamh na b'fhuaire na seo?' thuirt i.

'O dh'fhairich', thuirt am breac, 'fada fada na b'fhuaire. Bha mise
anns an loch seo an oidhche a bha ann is bha an oidhche cho fuar is
gun do chaill mi mo fhradharc leis an fhuachd. Bha an oidhche sin
fada na b'fhuaire na an oidhche a-nochd.'

Bha an iolaire toilichte sin a chluinntinn is thill i dhachaigh.

The Eagle of Loch Treig

Once upon a time there was an Eagle in the mountains out by Loch Treig. She lived in a corry there that they call (the) Middle Corry. One year there came a cold winter and a lot of snow, with fall and drift (blizzard). One particular night the Eagle was feeling the cold. 'I've never known such cold', she said to herself. 'I wonder if there was ever a colder night than this.' There was a Wren living near the Eagle and the Eagle went to the Wren. 'Have you ever known a colder night than this?' she asked. 'No. I haven't', said the Wren, 'but such there might have been. I do not know. But there's a Black Goat in Bun Roy and she's far older than me. She'll know.'

The Eagle went to the Goat and put the very same question to her. 'No, I haven't', said the Goat, 'but there's a Stag in the Wood of Inch who is far older than me and he'll know.' The Eagle reached the Wood of Inch and found the Stag in a sheltered corry. She got the same answer there. 'I came here from Inverlair', said he, 'when I was a young stag and I have not known a colder night. But there is a Salmon in Lochan na Lairig who is far older than me. He'll know.'

The Eagle went to the Salmon. 'Have you ever known a colder night than this?' she asked. 'Oh yes', said the Salmon, 'a far, far colder night. I was in this loch that night and the night was so cold that I lost my sight with the cold. That night was far colder than this night tonight.' The Eagle was glad to hear that and returned home.

Alasdair Mac Mhaighstir Alasdair agus Donnchadh Bàn Mac an t-Saoir

Rinn Donnchadh Bàn òran dhan an té a phòs e, Màiri Bhàn Òg: 'A Mhàiri Bhàn Òg is tu an òigh a tha air m'aire'. Bhathas a' ràdh gun robh seòrsa de dh'fharmad aig Mac Mhaighstir Alasdair ri Donnchadh Bàn. Se duine foghlaimte a bha ann an Alasdair. Cha robh sgoil aig Donnchadh ann. Ach bha Donnchadh chomh miosail aig an t-sluagh fada is farsaing air feadh na Gàidhealdachd, mar dhuine agus mar bhàrd, agus bha fios aig Alasdair gur h-ann mar sin a bha.

An deidh do Dhonnchadh Bàn agus Màiri Bhàn Òg pòsadh, thuirt Mac Mhaighstir Alasdair latha ri Donnchadh: 'Tha mi nis air Màiri fhaicinn agus chan eil i idir cho brèagha is a thuirt thusa a bha i anns an òran'. 'O ged-ta chan fhaca tusa i le mo shùilean-sa', arsa Donnchadh Bàn.

Alasdair Mac Mhaighstir Alasdair (c 1695–1770) and Donnchadh Bàn Mac an t-Saoir (c 1724–1812): two famous poets.

Duncan Bàn (fair-haired) made a song to the girl he married, Màiri Bhàn Òg (Young fair-haired Mary): 'Màiri Bhàn Òg, you are the maiden in my thoughts'. It was said that Alasdair mac Mhaighstir Alasdair was kind of jealous of Duncan Bàn. Alasdair was an educated man. Duncan had no schooling. But Duncan was so popular with people in general, far and wide throughout the Gaidhealdachd as a poet and as a man, and Alasdair knew that that was so.

After Duncan Bàn and Màiri Bhàn Òg married, mac Mhaighstir Alasdair said to Duncan one day: 'I've now seen Màiri and she isn't at all as beautiful as you said she was in the song.' 'Ah, but you didn't see her with my eyes', said Duncan Bàn.

Donnchadh Bàn agus 'Moladh Beinn Dobhrain'

Bhathar ag innse gun robh Donnchadh Bàn Mac an t-Saoir, am bàrd, ag òl comhla ri cuideachd an latha a bha seo ann an taigh-seinnse Chill Fhinn. Có a thachair a bhith an làthair ach Domhnall mac Raghnaill na Sgéithe, Domhnallach á Gleann Comhann. Se bàrd a bha annsan e fhéin.

Bha an dithis bhàrd a' comhdach mu mhaise nam beanntan, gach fear aca a' moladh na dùthcha aige fhéin. Sann a thuirt duine a bha anns an éisteachd: 'Se bàird a tha annaibh le chéile. Carson nach dèan sibh òran am fear mu na beanntan is na sléibhtean sin agus thig sinn cruinn an-seo a-rithist an ceann mìos. Am fear a tha a' chuideachd seo a' meas a rinn an t-òran as fheàrr, faodaidh e a bhith ag òl an asgaidh fad na h-oidhche.'

Sin mar a bha. Bha òran aig Domhnall mac Raghnaill mu bheanntan Ghlinne Comhann. Ach se an t-òran a bha aig Donnchadh Bàn 'Moladh Beinn Dobhrain'.

Duncan Bàn and 'The Praise of Ben Doran'

They used to tell that Duncan Bàn Macintyre the poet was drinking along with a group of companions one day in the tavern of Killin. Who happened to be present but Donald son of Ranald of the Shield, a MacDonald from Glencoe. He was a poet himself. The two poets were arguing about the beauty of the mountains, each of them praising his own district. Then a man who was there listening said: 'You are poets both of you. Why doesn't each of you make a song about those moors and mountains and we'll meet here again in a month's time. The one whom the company here reckons made the better song, he can drink free all night.'

That's how it was. Donald son of Ranald had a song about the mountains of Glencoe. But the song that Duncan had was 'The Praise of Ben Doran'.

Foghlam anns a' Ghàidhlig

Tha cùrsa an Fhoghlaim Ghàidhealaich annasach anns an dà sheagh: tha e a' dùsgadh ùidh agus tha e 'na adhbhar iongantais. Nuair a sheallar air na chaidh a sgrìobhadh ann an Gàidhlig, shaoileadh duine gun deach òigridh na Gàidhealdachd a oideachadh 'nan cànan fhéin ann an sgoiltean an stàit bho shean. Ach cha b'ann mar sin a bha. Bha sgoiltean paraiste thall is a-bhos air feadh na Gàidhealdachd fad ghinealach ach cha robhar a' teagasg Gàidhlig annta ann. Se sgoiltean de ghnè eile a chum taic ri leughadh is sgrìobhadh agus tha ceangaltas ri a lorg a thaobh litearrachd bho linn Chalaim Chille an Eilean Idhe, anns an t-siathamh ceud, a dh'ionnsaigh an latha an-diugh.

Anns na linntean Meadhanach bha sgoiltean nam filidh (is dòcha caochladh sheòrsaichean diubh an àiteachan fa-leth) a' toirt foghlaim ann an Gàidhlig do na sgrìobhadairean agus do theaghlaichean nan uaislean. Mhair a bheag no a mhór dhe a shusbaint gu ruige an t-ochdamh ceud deug. Ach na bu tràithe na sin a-rithist bhathas air modh-litreachaidh na Gàidhlig a leasachadh agus a chur an sàs ann a bhith a' sgrìobhadh cainnt chumanta an t-sluaigh. Rinneadh tomhas dhen obair sin fo sgéith Seanadh Arra Ghàidheal anns an Eaglais Stéite.

Ann an 1709 chaidh Comann a stéidheachadh ann an Dùn Éideann, le barrantas rìoghail, airson sgoiltean a chur air bhonn gus leughadh is sgrìobhadh a ionnsachadh do mhuinntir na Gàidhlig an Alba agus gu sonraichte airson am Bìoball agus leabhraichean cràbhach a chur an eòlas nan Gàidheal. B'e sin an SSPCK (Scottish Society for the Propagation of Christian Knowledge). Aig toiseach tòiseachaidh b'e rùn a' Chomainn foghlam Beurla a thoirt don t-sluagh Ghàidhealach: bha Gàidhlig is Laideann le chéile, uime sin, air an toirmeasg anns na sgoiltean. Ach cha deach leotha. Se buil a bha ann gun dàinig an Comann seo gu bhith 'na chùl-taic don chànan, a' misneachadh agus a' cuideachadh an dà chuid teagasg agus clòbhualadh leabhraichean Gàidhlig.

Bha comainn eile a chuireadh air bhonn gus taic a thoirt do Sgoiltean Gàidhlig. Cha robh ach aon cheann-uidhe anns an amharc aca: fiosrachadh sgriobtaireil a chraobh sgaoileadh. Nuair a thàinig an Dealachadh (1843) agus a dh'fhàg móran dhen t-sluagh an Eaglais Stéite, chuir an Eaglais Shaor a cuid sgoiltean fhéin air chois. A thuilleadh orra sin, bha caochladh chomhlan eile ann, car

dhen aon seòrsa, a chuir ris an obair chèanta. Ma tha laigead ri a
chur as leth ordachadh an fhoghlaim sin air fad, se gun robh e ro
cheangailte ri riaghladh eaglaiseach. Ach a dh'ainneoin sin thug na
sgoiltean litearrachd do ghinealaichean dhe na Gàidheil.

Nuair a thugadh a-mach Achd an Fhoghlaim leis an Stàit, ann an
1872, cha robh àite no cothrom air a thoirt dhan Ghàidhlig. A
chionn is gum feumadh a h-uile leanabh a-nis dol dhan sgoil, agus
leis gur h-e Beurla an aon chainnt ionnsachaidh a bha innte, thug an
t-Achd buille mhairbhteach dhan chànan. Ann an 1918 thàinig achd
a thug inbhe air choireigin dhan Ghàidhlig: chuireadh mar
fhiachaibh air ughdarras an fhoghlaim anns gach sgìreachd
Ghàidhealaich ullachadh freagarrach a dhèanamh as leth an
teagaisg. Ann an 1946 chaidh Gàidhlig a chur air a'
chlàr-oideachaidh ann am beagan sgoiltean anns na bailtean móra,
Glaschu gu h-àraid, airson a' cheud uair. Ann an 1949 stéidhich
Siorrachd Inbhir Nis post fear-eagraidh Gàidhlig ann an sgeama
dà-chànanach. Bhon uair sin thàinig leasachaidhean eile ann an
Roinn na Gàidhealdachd agus ann an Roinn nan Eilean. Tha toradh
na h-obrach sin fhathast ri a mheas.

Education in Gaelic

The course of Gaelic education is remarkable in two senses: it
arouses interest and astonishment. When one considers how much
has been written in Gaelic, one would think that the youth of the
Gaidhealtachd had been instructed in their own language in the
schools of the state from olden times. But that was not the case.
There were parish schools here and there throughout the
Gaidhealtachd for generations but Gaelic was simply not taught in
them. It was schools of another kind that maintained reading and
writing and a continuity of literacy can be traced from the time of
Columba in Iona, in the sixth century, to the present day.

In the Middle Ages the poets' schools (diverse kinds perhaps in
different places) gave instruction in Gaelic to writers and the
families of the aristocracy. The substance of that, to a lesser or
greater degree, survived until the eighteenth century. But earlier
than that again the orthography of Gaelic had been developed and

used in writing to represent the common speech of the people. A certain amount of that work was done under the aegis of the Synod of Argyll in the Established Church.

In 1709 a Society was set up in Edinburgh, under royal charter, to establish schools in order to teach reading and writing to the Gaelic speakers in Scotland and particularly to give Gaels a knowledge of the Bible and books of piety. This was the SSPCK (Scottish Society for the Propagation of Christian Knowledge). At the outset the aim of the Society was to provide education in English to the Gaelic population. Gaelic and Latin together were therefore forbidden in the schools. But they did not succeed in that policy. The result was that this Society came to be a support for the language, encouraging and helping both teaching and publishing Gaelic books.

Other societies were set up to support Gaelic schools. These had the sole aim of disseminating knowledge of the Scriptures. When the Disruption came (1843) and many of the people left the Established Church, the Free Church set up its own schools. In addition to these, there were a variety of other bodies, more or less of the same kind, who supplemented the same work. If there is any weakness to be found in this educational set-up, it is the fact that it was too closely tied to ecclesiastical control. But despite that, the schools made generations of Gaels literate.

When the Education Act of 1872 was passed, no place or opportunity was given to Gaelic. Since every child had now to go to school, and since English was the only language of instruction, the Act gave Gaelic a fatal blow. In 1918, a new act came which gave some status to Gaelic: the educational authority in every Gaelic-speaking district was obliged to make adequate provision for the teaching of Gaelic. In 1946 Gaelic was placed on the curriculum of a few city schools, especially in Glasgow, for the first time. In 1949 Inverness-shire established the post of Gaelic organiser in a scheme for bilingualism. Since then other developments have come in the Highland Region and in the Western Isles. The effects of this work have still to be assessed.

Key to Exercises

LESSON 1

Exercise 1: 1 Tha Màiri toilichte. 2 Tha Iain làidir. 3 Tha mi blàth. 4 Tha iad fuar. 5 Tha sinn an-seo. 6 Tha leabhar aig Anna. 7 Tha càr aig Seumas. 8 Tha deoch agam. 9 Tha taigh againn. 10 Tha balach aice.

Exercise 2: 1 Chan eil Anna sgìth. 2 Chan eil Seumas an-sin. 3 Chan eil cù aig Màiri. 4 Chan eil airgead againn. 5 Am bheil Iain fuar? 6 Am bheil deoch aig Domhnall? 7 Am bheil airgead aca? 8 Chan eil agam ach sgillinn. 9 Nach eil Domhnall toilichte? 10 Nach eil càr aige?

LESSON 2

Exercise 1: 1 Is mise Anna. 2 Is esan Calum. 3 Is ise Peigi. 4 Cha tusa Seumas. 5 Chan iadsan an clas Gàidhlig. 6 Chan ise Màiri. 7 Nach tusa Domhnall? Cha mhi. 8 An tusa Iain? Is mi. 9 Is iadsan Peigi agus Màiri. 10 Is tusa an tidsear.

Exercise 2: 1 an leabhar. 2 an ceòl. 3 a' chraobh. 4 a' phìob. 5 a' bhean. 6 an fheannag. 7 an t-sràid. 8 an sporan. 9 am pàipear. 10 an té.

Exercise 3: 1 mo phiuthar. 2 do mhàthair. 3 a h-athair. 4 am mac. 5 a chas. 6 ar cù; an cù againn. 7 am moncaidh; am moncaidh aca. 8 do bhó; a' bhó agad. 9 a h-obair; an obair aice. 10 a sùil.

Exercise 4: 1 bòrd beag. 2 bó mhór. 3 balach math. 4 oidhche dhorcha. 5 bròg shalach. 6 bàta dearg. 7 seann bhàta. 8 deagh chaileag/caileag mhath. 9 droch shìde. 10 seann chàr gorm.

Translation: 1 a small table. 2 a big cow. 3 a good boy. 4 a dark night. 5 a dirty shoe. 6 a red boat. 7 an old boat. 8 a good girl. 9 bad weather. 10 an old blue car.

LESSON 3

Exercise 1: 1 Dé a tha thu a' smaoineachadh? 2 Tha Anna a' fuireach an Dùn Éideann. 3 Am bheil thu a' tuigsinn Fraingeis? 4 Tha Iain a' sgrìobhadh bàrdachd. 5 Tha Màiri a' dèanamh rannsachadh. 6 Am bheil thu a' tighinn a-mach? 7 Tha iad ag iarraidh cupa cofaidh. 8 Tha Seumas ag obair an Glaschu. 9 Am bheil thu a' faireachdainn ceart gu leòr? 10 Chan eil mi a' tuigsinn.

Exercise 2: 1 Se mise Iain. 2 Se ise Anna. 3 An e esan an tidsear? Se. 4 Chan e Seumas an tidsear agam/mo thidsear. 5 Se Màiri an nurs. 6 Se Domhnall a h-athair. 7 Nach e Uilleam do mhac? Chan e. 8 Se Catrìona a' phiuthar mhór. 9 Se thusa Seòras beag. 10 Se Màiri am ministear ùr aca/am ministear ùr.

Exercise 3: 1 a' chaileag seo. 2 a' bhùth sin. 3 am baile ud. 4 am boireannach sin an-sin. 5 (se) seo mo phiuthar. 6 (se) sin an sgian. 7 tha an t-aran an-siud. 8 (se) sin a' bheinn ud a-rithist. 9 tha seo fuar. 10 tha sin glé mhath.

Exercise 4: 1 a naoi. 2 a cóig. 3 a sia. 4 a h-ochd deug. 5 a seachd. 6 a naoi deug. 7 a h-aon. 8 a cóig deug.

LESSON 4

Exercise 1: **An robh** mi aig an taigh Di-Luain? **An cuala** mi fuaim shuas an staighre? **An deach** mi suas? **Am faca** mi meàirleach? **An do rinn** e bùrach? **An duirt** mi: 'Có thusa?'? **An dàinig** am Poileas agus **an do rug** iad air a' mheàirleach? **An d'fhuair** am meàirleach buille? **An dug** e an t-airgead air ais? **An do ràinig** iad an stèisean? **An robh** e duilich?

Nach robh mi aig an taigh Di-Luain? **Nach cuala** mi fuaim shuas an staighre? **Nach deach** mi suas? **Nach fhaca** mi meàirleach? **Nach do rinn** e bùrach? **Nach duirt** mi: 'Có thusa?'? **Nach dàinig** am Poileas agus **nach do rug** iad air a' mheàirleach? **Nach d'fhuair** am meàirleach buille? **Nach dug** e an t-airgead air ais? **Nach do ràinig** iad an stèisean? **Nach robh** e duilich?

Exercise 2: 1 Bha mi toilichte. 2 Chunnaic mi Anna an-dé. 3 Chaidh Iain a-mach. 4 Thàinig iad a-steach/a-staigh. 5 Chuir sinn seachad bliadhna an-sin. 6 Cha do rinn thu an obair agad. 7 An d'fhuair thu an t-airgead? 8 Nach do ràinig thu Dùn Éideann fhathast? 9 Cha duirt i sìon. 10 Chuala mi Màiri an-raoir.

Exercise 3: 1 Òl an tì agad. 2 Ith an dìnnear agad. 3 Seas (suas). 4 Suidh (sìos). 5 Bi sàmhach. 6 Thigibh a-steach/a-staigh. 7 Thoir sin do Sheumas. 8 Na dèan(aibh) sìon. 9 Faigh e an-diugh. 10 Dùin an doras mas e do thoil e.

Exercise 4: 1 a Dhonnchaidh. 2 a Mhairead. 3 a Mhìcheil. 4 a Mhurchaidh. 5 a Shìne.

LESSON 5

Exercise 1: 1 Tha Iain 'na chadal. 2 Am bheil thu 'nad dhùisg. 3 Tha Màiri 'na laighe/'na sìneadh. 4 Bha e 'na sheasamh an-sin. 5 Tha iad 'nan suidhe.

Exercise 2: 1 Se ministear a tha ann an Iain. 2 Se seinneadair a tha ann an Anna. 3 Se tidsear a tha ann an Seonag. 4 Se croitear a tha ann an Uilleam. 5 Se oileanach a tha ann an Domhnall. 6 Se oileanach a tha annam cuideachd. 7 Se dotair a tha innte. 8 Se borbair a tha annaibh. 9 An e tidsear a tha annaibh/annad? 10 An e ministear a tha ann?

Exercise 3: (a) (Is/)Se sinne a chuala Anna a' seinn aig a' chéilidh an-raoir. (b) Se Anna a chuala sinn a' seinn aig a' chéilidh an-raoir. (c) Sann a' seinn a chuala sinn Anna aig a' chéilidh an-raoir. (d) Sann aig a' chéilidh a chuala sinn Anna a' seinn an-raoir. (e) Sann an-raoir a chuala sinn Anna a' seinn aig a' chéilidh. (f) Sann a chuala sinn Anna a' seinn aig a' chéilidh an-raoir.

Exercise 4: 1 I like Gaelic. 2 She prefers John. 3 Would you prefer beer? 4 Would you like a cup of tea? 5 They don't prefer brown bread. 6 Doesn't Ann like dancing? 7 I don't like meat. 8 I would prefer beer to whisky. 9 Do you like Run Rig? 10 Would you not prefer pibroch?

Exercise 5: 1 ann an taigh. 2 air bòrd. 3 le duine. 4 tro bhaile. 5 ro Sheumas. 6 bho àm gu àm. 7 a dh'Inbhir Nis. 8 á Dùn Éideann/bho Dhùn Éideann. 9 aig geata. 10 fo chàr.

LESSON 6

Exercise 1: 1 aig an doras. 2 anns an t-seòmar. 3 leis a' bhalach. 4 dhan a' chaileig. 5 ron a' chéilidh. 6 leis an airgead. 7 anns a' chàr. 8 anns a' Bheurla. 9 fo chrao(i)bh. 10 tron a' bhaile.

Exercise 2: 1 Dhùin Seumas an uinneag. 2 Choisich Anna dhachaigh. 3 Cheannaich Màiri am pàipear. 4 Dh'òl Catriona an tì aice. 5 Sheinn Iain òran. 6 Leugh Calum am pàipear. 7 Dh'innis e dhomh. 8 Dh'ionnsaich mi (a') G(h)àidhlig. 9 Dh'ith i aran. 10 Ruith Uilleam agus dhùin e an doras.

Exercise 3: 1 Có a dhùin an doras? 2 Cuine a chaidh iad a-mach? 3 Càite an do chuir thu an iuchair? 4 Cha do dh'innis mi dha. 5 An do chòrd an céilidh riut? 6 Leugh mi an leabhar sin nuair a bha mi òg. 7 Fàg e far an d'fhuair thu e. 8 (Se) sin an duine a sheinn aig a' chéilidh. 9 Chan fhaca mi Seumas ma bha e ann. 10 Thàinig e ged a bha e sgìth.

LESSON 7

Exercise 1: 1 mac an t-sagairt. 2 dath an t-sneachd. 3 mullach a' chnuic. 4 doras na sgoile. 5 piuthar mo bhràthar. 6 iuchair an taighe. 7 càr mo pheathar. 8 biadh a' chait. 9 athair Sheumais. 10 leabhar Catriona.

Exercise 2: 1 Tha sinn a' falbh an-diugh. 2 Am bheil iad a' tighinn?
3 Có a tha a' seinn? 4 Chan eil iad ag éisteachd. 5 Bha sinn ag ithe agus
ag òl. 6 An robh thu ag obair an-diugh? 7 Tha i ag òl na tì.
8 Tha iad a' ceannach an leabhair. 9 Tha mi a' fosgladh an dorais.
10 Tha i a' dùnadh na h-uinneig(e).

Exercise 3: 1 air mo chùlaibh. 2 air do bheulaibh. 3 os a chionn. 4
ri a taobh. 5 as ar n-aonais. 6 coltach riutha. 7 comhla rium. 8
timcheall oirnn. 9 seachad air. 10 chun an dorais.

LESSON 8

Exercise 1: 1 Òlaidh Anna an tì aice. 2 Ionnsaichidh mi (a')
G(h)àidhlig. 3 Cuine a sheinneas tu an t-òran? 4 Cha cheannaich i aran
geal uair sam bith. 5 Am falbh iad gu moch anns a' mhadainn?
6 Bruidhnidh mi ris ma thilleas e. 7 Càite am fàg sinn an t-airgead?
8 Có a chuidicheas mi? 9 Leughaidh mi am pàipear nuair a dhùisgeas mi.
10 Ciamar a dhùineas tu an doras?

Exercise 2: 1 na caileagan agus na balaich. 2 anns na bailtean. 3 fo na
bùird. 4 bho na Gàidheil. 5 air na cnuic. 6 tidsearan nan sgoiltean.
7 leabharaichean nam balach. 8 cànan nan Gàidheal. 9 airgead nam
boireannach. 10 an deidh nan oidhcheannan.

Exercise 3: (a) trì uinneagan. (b) deich sgoiltean. (c) seachd
caileagan. (d) dà chlas. (e) ochd craobhan. (f) dà chàr dheug.
(g) cóig pìoban deug. (h) ochd òrain d(h)eug. (i) dà chois. (j) dà
uinneig/uinneag dheug.

Exercise 4: 1 Am bheil thu gam chluinntinn? 2 Am bheil sibh ga
fhaicinn? 3 Tha Iain gan coinneachadh. 4 An robh na balaich gur
bualadh? 5 Có a tha gar n-iarraidh? 6 Bha Anna gad fhaighneachd.
7 Tha mi ga fhreagairt an-dràsta. 8 Am bheil thu gar fàgail an-seo?
9 Am bheil thu ga ceannach? 10 Bha iad ga sheinn.

LESSON 9

Exercise 1: 1 Chan abair (cha chan) mi sìon ris. 2 Dé a bheir thu do
bhean an taighe? 3 An cluinn thu na h-eòin a' seinn? Am bheil thu a'
cluinntinn nan eun a' seinn? 4 An dèan thu an obair air mo
shon/dhomh? 5 Am faigh iad na lathaichean saora aca/an lathaichean
saora a-màireach? 6 Chì sinn iad nuair a ruigeas iad Glaschu. 7 An déid
do bhràthair dhan a' chéilidh? 8 Cha dig iad dhachaigh dìreach an deidh
na sgoile. 9 Gheibh e an trèan nuair a thig e. 10 An dèan thu do
dhìcheall an uair seo a Iain?

Exercise 2: 1 An aithne dhut am balach a thilg a' chlach? 2 Sin am
boireannach a sheinn an t-òran brèagha ud an-raoir. 3 Càite am bheil an
leabhar nach do leugh thu? 4 Seo an seòmar anns an do dh'fhàg mi an

211

iuchair. Seo an seòmar a dh'fhàg mi an iuchair ann. 5 An e sin am boireannach dhan an do dh'innis thu an naidheachd? An e sin am boireannach a dh'innis thu an naidheachd dhi? 6 Is toil leam an sgioba leis an do chluich mi. Is toil leam an sgioba a chluich mi leis. 7 An toil leat an ceòl ris an robh Domhnall ag éisteachd? An toil leat an ceòl a bha Domhnall ag éisteachd ris? 8 An rathad mun an robh sinn a' bruidhinn? An rathad a bha sinn a' bruidhinn mu a dheidhinn? 9 An e sin an duine ris an do thachair thu? An e sin an duine a thachair thu ris? 10 An aithne dhut am fear lagha a fhuair a mhac an ceum aige an-uiridh?

Exercise 3: 1 leis a' chat bheag. 2 air a' bhòrd gheal. 3 dhan a' chaileig mhóir. 4 anns an t-solas gheal. 5 dath na deise ùire. 6 faclan an òrain bhrèagha. 7 ceòl na pìoba-móire. 8 cosgais a' chamara dhaoir. 9 leis a' chàraid laghaich. 10 air an rathad cheàrr.

Exercise 4: *Vigesimal:* (a) dà fhichead leabhar is a cóig. (b) trì fichead each is a sia deug. (c) ceithir fichead séithear is a seachd. (d) naoi bliadhna deug ar fhichead a dh'aois. (e) trì fichead bliadhna is a dhà a dh'aois. (f) trì fichead bliadhna is a deich a dh'aois.

Decimal: (a) ceathrad is a cóig leabhar/ceathrad leabhar is a cóig. (b) seachdad is a sia each/seachdad each is a sia. (c) ochdad is a seachd séithear/ochdad séithear is a seachd. (d) trithead is a naoi bliadhna a dh'aois/trithead bliadhna is a naoi a dh'aois. (e) seasgad is a dhà bliadhna a dh'aois/seasgad bliadhna is a dhà a dh'aois. (f) seachdad bliadhna a dh'aois.

LESSON 10

Exercise 1: 1 Cha chuirinn suas ri sin. 2 Cuine a dhùisgeadh tu anns a' mhadainn? 3 Carson a chreideadh Iain sin? 4 Nigheadh iad iad fhéin anns an abhainn. 5 Lorg/fhuair sinn àite far an gabhadh sinn anail. 6 Chan itheadh/cha ghabhadh iad greim. 7 Cha ghabhainn ach druthag bheag. 8 Am postadh tu an litir seo dhomh/air mo shon? 9 Thuigeadh iad cuid mhath dheth gu dearbh. 10 Dh'fhosglainn an doras dhut/air do shon nam biodh fios agam gun robh thu ann.

Exercise 2: 1 Theirinn/chanainn gum bheil Iain nas sine na Màiri. 2 Nam biodh an t-sìde na b'fheàrr, shuidheadh sinn a-muigh. 3 Dh'innis mi dhut gum buinigeadh tu an duais a bu mhotha. 4 Bha Uilleam ag obair anns an Òban nuair a bha e na b'òige. 5 Se Seumas (an duine) as sine anns an teaghlach. 6 Tha e nas fhasa nuair a tha an sgian nas géire. 7 Tha Peigi nas treasa na Ailean ged a tha i nas lugha na e. 8 Sin a' chraobh as àirde a chunnaic mi riamh. 9 Tha a' Ghàidhlig cho doirbh ris a' Bheurla. 10 Chan eil an tidsear cho beairteach ris an fhear-lagha.

Exercise 3: Thuirt Iain gun robh e a-muigh an-raoir. John said that he was out last night.   2 Chuala mi gun dàinig Seumas. I heard that James came.   3 An rud a chunnaic mi. The thing which I saw.   4 An naidheachd a chuala tu. The news which you heard.   5 Thuirt Anna gur h-e ministear a tha ann. Ann said that he is a minister.   6 Tha mi a' smaoineachadh gur h-e co-latha breith Sheumais a tha ann an-diugh. I think that it is James' birthday today.   7 Leugh mi gur h-ann an-diugh a thachair e. I read that it was today that it happened.   8 Tha iad a' ràdh gur h-ann air a' Ghàidhealdachd a bha iad a' fuireach. They say that it was in the Highlands that they lived.

Exercise 4:   1 caileagan òga. young girls.   2 an fheadhain gheala. the white ones.   3 cait dhubha. black cats.   4 clasaichean móra. big classes.   5 balaich mhodhail. (well-)behaved boys.   6 daoine làidir. strong men/people.   7 bùird ghlana. clean tables.   8 pàistean matha. good children.   9 leabhraichean inntinneach. interesting books.
10 boireannaich bheairteach. rich women.

LESSON 11

Exercise 1:   1 Is toil leam ithe.   2 Feumaidh mi falbh.   3 Bu toil leis cuideachadh.   4 Tha i ag iarraidh bruidhinn.   5 Bha e a' dol a thighinn.   6 Thàinig i a choimhead.   7 Tha dùil aca fuireach anns an Òban.   8 Bu chòir dhut a dhol gu Baile Àtha Cliath. Tha còir agad a dhol gu Baile Àtha Cliath.   9 Nach eil thu a' dol a dh'éisteachd?   10 Is urrainn do Pheigi snàmh.

Exercise 2:   1 Feumaidh mi an obair agam a dhèanamh.   2 Is urrainn dhi Gàidhlig a bhruidhinn.   3 Bu chòir dhut càr ùr a cheannach.   4 Tha Iain ag iarraidh leabhar a sgrìobhadh.   5 Is fheàrr dhut an doras a dhùnadh nad dheidh.   6 Cha b'urrainn dhuinn an dotair a phàigheadh.   7 Tha sinn a' dol a dh'fhaighinn bainne.   8 Thàinig Anna a thogail a mic.   9 Tha cuimhne aig Domhnall air an leabhar sin a leughadh.   10 B'urrainn do Pheigi Gàidhlig a bhruidhinn.

Exercise 3:   1 Is toil leis a ithe.   2 Bha dùil aig Anna a sheinn aig a' chéilidh.   3 Bha an t-eagal air Iain a tarraing.   4 Tha aig na balaich òga ri an glanadh.   5 Chaidh Calum ga coimhead.   6 Is fheàrr le Màiri a teagasg.   7 Bu chòir dhut ar creidsinn.   8 Tha Anna a' dol gan dùsgadh.   9 Bu toil leinn do chuideachadh.   10 Tha cuimhne aig Seumas air sin a ràdh.

Exercise 4:   1 Tha Raibeart dìreach air falbh.   2 Tha Seonag air a thighinn.   3 Tha Iain air an litir a sgrìobhadh.   4 Tha e air cuideam a chur air.   5 Tha iad air a dhol a-mach.   6 Bidh Màiri air tòiseachadh anns an oilthigh an ath sheachdain.   7 Tha Anna air an seann taigh a reic mu dheireadh.   8 Bhiodh Seumas air Gàidhlig a ionnsachadh.   9 Tha Iain air cus a ithe mar-thà.   10 An deidh do Niall an t-eòlas gu léir a chruinneachadh.

LESSON 12

Exercise 1: 1 Bhinn glé thoilichte nan digeadh iad. 2 Dh'òladh e tì ceart gu leòr. 3 Chitheadh iad an càirdean/na càirdean aca aig an sgoil. 4 Rachadh sinn dhan an taigh-t(h)asgaidh a h-uile mìos. 5 Chan fhaigheadh tu suidheachan air a' phlèan a-nis. 6 An abradh tu/an canadh tu gun rachadh Iain dhan an dealbhchluich? 7 Am faigheadh tu am bus aig a' chùil sin? 8 Bheireadh tu air an aiseag mu dheireadh aig naoi uairean. 9 Cha chluinneadh tu a leithid sin ann an àite sam bith eile. 10 Cha doireadh màthair Dhomhnaill cead dha a dhol a-mach.

Exercise 2: 1 Seinnear an t-òran. 2 Dh'fhosgladh an uinneag. 3 Leagadh an seann taigh. 4 Caillear airgead a h-uile bliadhna. 5 Leanadh Iain dhachaigh an-dé. 6 Nighte e a h-uile latha. 7 Chan fhacas is cha chualas an t-eun bhon an t-seachdain seo a chaidh. 8 Theirear/canar gun robh e a' fuireach ann an Dùn Éideann nuair a bha e na b'òige/nas òige. 9 Mharbhadh e feadh na h-oidhche. 10 Rugadh is thogadh mi an Éirinn.

Index

The numbers refer to se**ċ**tions, *not* pages.

Mini-dictionary

Gaelic–English

a *(ppn)* her
á *(prp)* from, out of
a particle used before numerals
  when counting
a *(rel pn)* that, which
a* *(ppn)* his
abair *(vb)* say
abhainn *(f)* river, **aibhne** *(G)*,
  aibhnichean *(pl)*
àbhaist *(f)* customary state
a-bhos *(adv)* over here (location at
  speaker)
ach *(cjn)* but
acras *(m)* hunger
actair *(m)* actor, **actairean** *(pl)*
ad *(f)* hat, **adaichean** *(pl)*
a dh'aithghearr *(adv)* soon
adhar *(m)* sky
adhbhar *(m)* reason, **adhbhair** *(pl)*
agus *(cjn)* and
a h-uile every
aig *(prp)* at
Ailean *(m)* Allan
aimsir *(f)* weather, **aimsirean** *(pl)*
ainm *(m)* name, **ainmean**,
  ainmeannan *(pl)*
ainmeil *(adj)* famous
air *(prp)* on
airgead *(m)* money
airson *(cd prp)* for (the sake of)
  (followed by G)
aiseag *(m)* ferry, **aiseagan** *(pl)*
àite *(m)* place, **àiteachan**,
  àitichean *(pl)*
aithne *(f)* knowledge
aithneachadh *(vn)* recognising,
  knowing
aithnich *(vb)* recognise, know

àlainn *(adj)* beautiful
Alba *(f)* Scotland
àm *(m)* time, **amannan** *(pl)*
a-mach *(adv)* out, outwards
  (motion)
a-màireach *(adv)* tomorrow
am bliadhna *(adv)* this year
a-muigh *(adv)* out (location)
an etc. *(art)* the
an/m *(interr prt pos)*
a-nall *(adv)* over here (motion
  towards speaker)
an comhnaidh *(adv)* always
an-dé *(adv)* yesterday
an-diugh *(adv)* today
an-dràsta *(adv)* now
a-nis, nis *(adv)* now
anmoch *(adv)* late
ann *(adv)* there
ann an *(prp)* in
Anna *(f)* Ann
a-nochd *(adv)* tonight
a-nuas *(adv)* down, downwards; up,
  upwards (towards the speaker)
a-null *(adv)* over there (motion
  away from speaker)
a-null thairis *(adv)* abroad
  (motion to)
an-raoir *(adv)* last night
an-seo *(adv)* here
an-sin *(adv)* there
an-siud *(adv)* there, yonder
an toiseach *(adv)* first
aodach *(m)* cloth, clothes,
  aodaichean *(pl)*
aodann *(m)* face, **aodainnean** *(pl)*
aois *(f)* age, **aoisean** *(pl)*
aon *(num)* one

aon* *(adj)* one, same
aonan *(m)* one
ar *(ppn)* our
aran *(m)* bread, arain *(pl)*
àrd *(adj)* high
àrdsgoil *(f)* secondary school,
   àrdsgoiltean *(pl)*
a-rithist *(adv)* again
arsa *(def vb)* says, said
a-staigh *(adv)* in, inside (location)
a-steach *(adv)* in, inwards (motion)
ath* *(adj)* next
athair *(m, irr)* father, athraichean *(pl)*
atharrachadh *(vn)* changing
atharraich *(vb)* change

baga *(m)* bag, bagaichean *(pl)*
baile *(m)* town(ship), bailtean *(pl)*
bainne *(m)* milk, bainneachan *(pl)*
balach *(m)* boy, balaich *(pl)*
balgam *(m)* mouthful, balgaman *(pl)*
ball-coise *(m)* football
balla *(m)* wall, ballachan *(pl)*
bàn *(adj)* fair (of hair)
banca *(m)* bank, bancaichean *(pl)*
bàrd *(m)* poet, bàird *(pl)*
bàrdachd *(f)* poetry
bas *(f)* palm, boisean *(pl)*
basaidh *(m)* basin, basaidhean *(pl)*
basgaid *(f)* basket, basgaidean *(pl)*
bàta *(m)* boat, bàtaichean *(pl)*
beachd *(m)* opinion, beachdan *(pl)*
beag *(adj)* small
beagan *(m)* a little, a small
   amount/number
beairteach *(adj)* rich
Bealltainn *(f)* May (Day)
bean *(f, irr)* wife, mnathan *(pl)*
beannachd *(m)* blessing,
   beannachdan *(pl)*
beannachd leibh goodbye
   (pl or formal)
beinn *(f, irr)* mountain, beanntan *(pl)*
beir (air) *(vb)* take hold, catch, bear
beò *(adj)* alive
Beurla *(f)* English

(a) bhith *(inf)* being, to be
bho* *(prp)* from; *(cjn)* since
bho chionn *(cjn)* since
bi *(vb)* be
biadh *(m)* food, bidhe *(G)*,
   bidheannan *(pl)*
blas *(m)* taste
blàs *(m)* warmth
blasda *(adj)* tasty
blàth *(adj)* warm
(a') B(h)liadhna Ùr *(f)* New Year
bó *(f)* cow, bà *(pl)* (rare: crodh
   (m, coll), more common as *pl*)
bodach *(m)* old man, bodaich *(pl)*
boin *(vb)* belong to, relate to
boireannach *(m)* woman,
   boireannaich *(pl)*
borbair *(m)* barber, borbairean *(pl)*
bòrd *(m)* table, bùird *(pl)*
bracaist *(m)* breakfast,
   bracaistean *(pl)*
bradan *(m)* salmon, bradain *(pl)*
bràthair *(m, irr)* brother,
   bràithrean *(pl)*
breac *(m)* trout, bric *(pl)*
breac *(adj)* speckled
breith *(vn)* taking hold, catching,
   bearing
brèagha *(adj)* lovely, fine
brist *(vb)* break
bristeadh *(vn)* breaking
bròg *(f)* shoe, brògan *(pl)*
brònach *(adj)* sad
brot *(m)* soup
bruidhinn (ri) *(vb)* speak (to)
bu, b' past & conditional of is
   b'aithne do knows
   bu chaomh le would like
   bu toil le would like
   b'urrainn do could
buail *(vb)* strike
bualadh *(vn)* striking
buidhe *(adj)* yellow
builich *(vb)* grant, bestow, confer
buinig *(vb)* win
buinigeadh *(vn)* winning

bunsgoil *(f)* primary school,
  bunsgoiltean *(pl)*
buntàta *(m, coll)* potatoes
bùrach *(m)* mess
bus *(m)* bus, **busaichean** *(pl)*
bùth *(f)* shop, **bùthan, bùithntean** *(pl)*

cabhag *(f)* hurry
cabhsair *(m)* pavement,
  cabhsairean *(pl)*
cadal *(m)* sleep
(a') C(h)àisg *(f)* Easter
caileag *(f)* girl, **caileagan** *(pl)*
cailleach *(f)* old woman,
  cailleachan *(pl)*
cairteal *(m)* quarter, **cairtealan** *(pl)*
caisteal *(m)* castle, **caistealan** *(pl)*
càite *(interr pn)* where?
call *(m)* loss, pity
Calum *(m)* Calum
can (ri) *(vb)* say to
cànan *(m)* language, **cànanan** *(pl)*
cantainn, cantail *(vn)* saying
caoin *(vb)* cry
caoineadh *(vn)* crying
caora *(f)* sheep, **caoraich** *(pl)*
càr *(m)* car, **càraichean** *(pl)*
caraid *(m)*, friend, relative,
  càirdean *(pl)*
càrn *(m)* cairn, **càirn, cùirn** *(pl)*
cas *(f)* foot, leg, **casan** *(pl)*
cat *(m)* cat, **cait** *(pl)*
cathair *(f)* chair; city **cathraichean** *(pl)*
Catrìona *(f)* Catherine
cead *(m)* permission
ceann *(m)* head, **cinn** *(pl)*
ceann-suidhe *(m)* president,
  cinn-s(h)uidhe *(pl)*
ceannach *(vn)* buying
ceannaich *(vb)* buy
ceàrr *(adj)* wrong
ceart gu leòr *(adv)* all right, OK
ceasnaiche *(m)* interviewer,
  ceasnaichean *(pl)*
ceathrar *(m)* four people
céiliche *(m)* visitor, **céilichean** *(pl)*

céilidh *(m, f)* ceilidh, dance, social
  visit, **céilidhean** *(pl)*
ceist *(f)* question, **ceistean** *(pl)*
Céitean *(m)* May, **Céiteannan** *(pl)*
ceithir *(num)* four
ceòl *(m)* music
ceòl-mór *(m)* pibroch
ceum *(m)* step, degree,
  ceumannan *(pl)*
cha(n) *(neg prt)* not
cho as
chun *(prp)* to (followed by G)
ciamar (a) how?
clach *(f)* stone, **clachan** *(pl)*
cladach *(m)* shore, **cladaichean** *(pl)*
clann *(f, coll)* children
clas *(m)* class, **clasaichean** *(pl)*
clì *(adj)* left
cluas *(f)* ear, **cluasan** *(pl)*
cluich *(vb, vn)* play(ing)
cluinn *(vb)* hear
cluinntinn *(vn)* hearing
cnoc *(m)* hill, **cnuic** *(pl)*
có (a) who?
cùil *(f)* corner, **cùiltean** *(pl)*
co-dhiubh *(adv)* anyway, however
co-dhiubh *(cjn)* whether
cofaidh *(m)* coffee
coibhneil *(adj)* kind
cóig *(num)* five
cóignear *(m)* five people
coille *(f)* wood, **coilltean** *(pl)*
coinneachadh *(vn)* meeting
coinneamh *(m)* meeting,
  coinneamhan *(pl)*
coinnich *(vb)* meet
còir *(f)* right
coiseachd *(vn)* walking
coisich *(vb)* walk
colaiste *(f)* college, **colaistean** *(pl)*
co-latha breith *(m)* birthday
có mheud how many?
coltach ri *(cd prp)* like
coltas *(m)* appearance, **coltais** *(pl)*
comharradh *(m)* sign,
  comharraidhean *(pl)*

comhfhurtail *(adj)* comfortable
comhla ri *(cd prp)* along with
comhlan ciùil *(m)* band (of music)
companach *(m)* companion,
  companaich *(pl)*
còrd ri *(vb)* enjoy (accord with)
còrdadh ri *(vn)* enjoying,
  (according with)
cosgais *(f)* cost, **cosgaisean** *(pl)*
còta *(m)* coat, **còtaichean** *(pl)*
cothrom *(m)* chance,
  cothroman *(pl)*
craobh *(f)* tree, **craobhan** *(pl)*
creach *(f)* plunder, ruin, ruination,
  creachan *(pl)*
  mo chreach *(interj)* alas
creid *(vb)* believe
creidsinn *(vn)* believing
croitear *(m)* crofter, **croitearan** *(pl)*
cruaidh *(adj)* hard
cruinneachadh *(vn)* gathering
cruinnich *(vb)* gather
cù *(m, irr)* dog, **coin** *(pl)*
cuideachadh *(vn)* helping
cuideachd *(adv)* also
cuid-eiginn *(m)* somebody, someone
cuidich *(vb)* help
cuimhne *(f)* memory
cuine (a) when?
cuingichte *(adv)* restricted, limited to
cuir *(vb)* put, send
cùirt *(f)* court, **cùirtean** *(pl)*
cum *(vb)* keep
cumail *(vn)* keeping
cupa *(m)* cup, **cupannan** *(pl)*
cur *(vn)* putting, sending
cùrsa *(m)* course, **cùrsaichean** *(pl)*
cus *(adv)* too much, too many
  (very many)
cuspair *(m)* subject, **cuspairean** *(pl)*

dà* *(num)* two, **a dhà**
  (when counting)
dachaigh *(f)* home, **dachaighean** *(pl)*
dad nothing (in *neg* and *interr*
  sentences)

Damhair *(m)* October,
  Damhairean *(pl)*
damhan-allaidh *(m)* spider,
  damhain-allaidh *(pl)*
dannsa *(m)* dance, **dannsaichean** *(pl)*
dannsa *(vn)* dancing
dath *(m)* colour, **dathan** *(pl)*
de *(prp)* of
dé (a) *(interr pn)* what?
deagh* *(adj)* good (precedes noun)
dealbh *(f, m)* picture, **dealbhannan,**
  deilbh *(pl)*
dealbhchluich *(f)* drama,
  dealbhchluichean *(pl)*
dèan *(vb)* do, make
dèanamh *(vn)* doing, making
dearbh* *(adj)* very
dearg *(adj)* (bright) red
deas *(adj)* right, south
deich *(num)* ten
deichnear *(m)* ten people
deigh *(f)* ice
deireadh *(m)* end
deise *(f)* suit, **deiseachan** *(pl)*
dhachaigh *(adv)* home(wards)
deiseil *(adj)* ready
deoch *(f)* drink, **dighe** *(G, irr)*,
  deochannan *(pl)*
dian *(adj)* intense, hard
Diar-Daoin Thursday
Di-Ciadaoin Wednesday
Di-Domhnaich Sunday *v* **Latha na**
  Sàbaid
Di-hAoine Friday
dìleas *(adj)* loyal
Di-Luain Monday
Di-Màirt Tuesday
dìnnear *(f)* dinner, **dìnnearan** *(pl)*
dìreach *(adj)* just, straight
Di-Sathairne Saturday
dithis *(f)* two people
do* *(ppn)* your
do* *(prp)* to, for
do-dhèante *(adj)* impossible
doirbh *(adj)* difficult
dòirt *(vb)* pour

dol *(vn)* going
Domhnall *(m)* Donald
dona *(adj)* bad
donn *(adj)* brown
doras *(m)* door, doorway, **dorais,
    dorsan** *(pl)*
dorcha *(adj)* dark
dòrtadh *(vn)* pouring
dragh *(m)* worry, **draghannan** *(pl)*
dotair *(m)* doctor, **dotairean** *(pl)*
draibh *(vb)* drive
draibheadh *(vn)* driving
dram(a) *(m)* dram (drink),
    dramaichean, dramannan *(pl)*
dràma *(m)* drama
dreuchd *(f)* post, job, office,
    dreuchdan *(pl)*
droch* *(adj)* bad (precedes noun)
duais *(f)* prize, reward, **duaisean** *(pl)*
dualchainnt *(f)* dialect,
    dualchainntean *(pl)*
dubh *(adj)* black
Dubhlachd *(f)* December,
    Dubhlachdan *(pl)*
duilich *(adj)* sorry; hard, difficult
duilleag *(f)* leaf, **duilleagan** *(pl)*
dùin *(vb)* close
duine *(m)* man, person, **daoine** *(pl)*
dùisg *(vb)* waken
Dùn Éideann *(m)* Edinburgh
dùnadh *(vn)* closing
dùsgadh *(vn)* wakening
dùthaich *(f)* country, district, land,
    dùthchannan *(pl)*

each *(m)* horse, **eich** *(pl)*
eachdraidh *(f)* history,
    eachdraidhean *(pl)*
eagal *(m)* fear
eaglais *(f)* church, **eaglaisean** *(pl)*
Earrach *(m)* Spring, **Earraich** *(pl)*
-eiginn some *v* **rud-eiginn,
    cuid-eiginn**
eile *(adj)* other, else
eilean *(m)* island, **eileanan** *(pl)*
Éirinn *(f)* Ireland

éist *(vb)* listen
éisteachd *(vn)* listening
esan *(pn)* he
eugh *(vb)* shout
eughachd *(vn)* shouting

fa leth particular, singly, separately
fada *(adj)* long
fàg *(vb)* leave
fàgail *(vn)* leaving
faic *(vb)* see
faicinn *(vn)* seeing
faigh *(vb)* get
faighinn *(vn)* getting
faighneachd *(vn)* asking
faighnich (de) *(vb)* ask
    (information of)
faireachdainn *(vn)* feeling
fairich *(vb)* feel
faisg (air) *(prp)* near, close (to)
falamh *(adj)* empty
falbh *(vb, vn)* go(ing) away
falt *(m)* hair
faod *(def vb)* may
Faoilteach *(m)* January, **Faoiltich** *(pl)*
far *(prp)* off (followed by G)
far an where, the place that
fàs *(vb, vn)* grow(ing)
feadh *(prp)* during, throughout
feadhain *(f)* some (people or things)
feannag *(f)* crow, **feannagan** *(pl)*
fear *(m)* man, **fir** *(pl)*
fear *(pn)* one, **feadhain** *(f, coll* used
    for *pl)*
fear-lagha *(m)* lawyer, **fir-lagha** *(pl)*
feasgar *(m)* evening, **feasgair** *(pl)*
feòil *(f)* meat
feuch (ri) *(vb)* see; make sure, try
feuchainn (ri) *(vn)* making sure,
    trying
feum *(def vb)* must
feur *(m)* grass
fhathast *(adv)* yet
fhéin self
fiadh *(m)* deer, **féidh** *(pl)*
fichead *(m)* twenty, **ficheadan** *(pl)*

fidheall *(f)* fiddle, fidhlean *(pl)*
fidhlear *(m)* fiddler, fidhlearan *(pl)*
fiodh *(m)* wood
fion *(m)* wine
fios *(m)* knowledge
fiosrachadh *(m)* information
firinn *(f)* truth
fliuch *(adj)* wet
fo* *(prp)* under
foghain *(vb)* suffice
Foghar *(m)* Autumn, Foghair *(pl)*
foghlaimte *(adj)* learned, educated
foghlam *(m)* education
foillseachadh *(vn)* publishing,
    revealing
foillsich *(vb)* publish, reveal
fón *(m)* phone
fón *(vb)* phone
fónadh *(vn)* phoning
fosgail *(vb)* open
fosgladh *(vn)* opening
Fraingeis *(f)* French
fraoch *(m)* heather
freagairt *(f)* reply, answer,
    freagairtean *(pl)*
freagarrach *(adj)* suitable
fuadaichean *(pl)* Clearances
fuaim *(m)* sound, fuaimean *(pl)*
fuar *(adj)* cold
fuil *(f)* blood
fuireach *(vn)* living (in), staying
fuireach ri *(vn)* waiting for
fuirich *(vb)* live (in), stay
fuirich ri *(vb)* wait for
furasta *(adj)* easy

gabh *(vb)* take; eat
    gabh *(vb)* mo lethsgeul
    excuse me
    gabh *(vb)* òran sing a song
gabhail *(vn)* taking; eating
gach every
Gàidheal *(m)* Gael, Gàidheil *(pl)*
Gàidhealdachd *(f)* Highlands
Gàidhlig *(f)* Gaelic
Gall *(m)* Lowlander, Goill *(pl)*

Galldachd *(f)* Lowlands
gaol *(m)* love
garaids *(f)* garage,
    garaidsean *(pl)*
geal *(adj)* white, bright
geama *(m)* game,
    geamaichean *(pl)*
geamair *(m)* gamekeeper,
    geamairean *(pl)*
Geamhradh *(m)* Winter,
    Geamhraidhean *(pl)*
(a') G(h)earmailt *(f)* Germany
Gearmailtis *(f)* German
geàrr *(adj)* short
geàrr *(vb)* cut
gearradh *(vn)* cutting
Gearran *(m)* February,
    Gearrain *(pl)*
geata *(m)* gate, geataichean *(pl)*
ged (a) *(cjn)* although
ged-ta however
geug *(f)* branch, twig, geugan *(pl)*
geur *(adj)* sharp
Giblean *(m)* April, Gibleanan *(pl)*
gille *(m)* boy, gillean *(pl)*
ginealach *(m)* generation,
    ginealaich(ean) *(pl)*
glan *(adj)* clean; fine, nice
glas *(adj)* grey, grey-green
glas *(vb)* lock
Glaschu *(f)* Glasgow
glasraich *(f)* vegetables
glé* very
gleusta *(adj)* canny, prudent
glic *(adj)* clever, wise
gloine *(f)* glass, gloineachan *(pl)*
gobha *(m)* smith, goibhnean *(pl)*
goid *(vb)* rob, steal
goirid *(adj)* short
goirt *(adj)* sore
gòrach *(adj)* silly, foolish
gorm *(adj)* blue
greas *(vb)* hurry up
    greas ort (you) hurry up!
grian *(f)* sun
grunn *(m)* a good deal, a lot

gu *(prp)* to, to the point of
   gu bràch *(adv)* ever
   gu bràch tuilleadh evermore
   gu dearbh *(adv)* indeed
   gu dòigheil *(adv)* fine
   gu dona *(adv)* badly
   gu léir *(adv)* completely
   gu leòr *(adv)* plenty
   gu luath *(adv)* quickly
   gu math *(adv)* well
   gu mì-fhortanach *(adv)*
     unfortunately
   gu snog *(adv)* nicely
   gu sonraichte *(adv)* especially
gun(*) *(prp)* without
gun *(cjn)* that
gu ruige *(prp)* to
gus *(prp)* until
guth *(m)* voice, **guthan** *(pl)*

i *(pn)* she
iad *(pn)* they
Iain *(m)* John
iarr *(vb)* ask, request, want
iarraidh *(vn)* asking, requesting,
   wanting
iasg *(m)* fish, **éisg** *(pl)*
iasgach *(m)* fishing
idir *(adv)* at all
ìm *(m)* butter
innis (do) *(vb)* tell (to)
innse *(vn)* telling
inntinneach *(adj)* interesting
ionnsachadh *(vn)* learning
ionnsaich *(vb)* learn
is *(def vb)* is
   is aithne do know
   (of person)
   is beag air dislike
   is caingeis le it doesn't matter to
   is caomh le likes
   is dòcha probably, perhaps
   is toil le likes
   is urrainn do can
ise *(pn)* she
ìseal *(adj)* low

ith *(vb)* eat
ithe *(vn)* eating
iuchair *(f)* key, **iuchraichean** *(pl)*
Iuchar *(m)* July, **Iuchair** *(pl)*

lag *(adj)* weak
lagaich *(vb)* weaken
lagachadh *(vn)* weakening
lagh *(m)* law, **laghannan** *(pl)*
làidir *(adj)* strong
laigh *(vb)* lie down
laighe *(vn)* lying down
làmh *(f)* hand, **làmhan** *(pl)*
làr *(m)* floor, **làir** *(pl)*
latha *(m)* day, **lathaichean** *(pl)*
Latha na Sàbaid Sunday *v* **Di-
   Dòmhnaich**
lathaichean saora *(pl)* holidays
le *(prp)* with
leabaidh *(f, irr)* bed, **leapannan** *(pl)*
leabhar *(m)* book, **leabhraichean** *(pl)*
leabharlann *(m)* library,
   leabharlannan *(pl)*
leag *(vb)* knock down, fell
leagail *(vn)* knocking down, felling
lean *(vb)* follow
leantainn, leantail *(vn)* following
leig *(vb)* let, allow
leigeil *(vn)* letting, allowing
léine *(f)* shirt, **léintean** *(pl)*
lethphinnt *(m)* half-pint,
   lethphinntean *(pl)*
lethsgeul *(m)* excuse, **lethsgeulan** *(pl)*
lethuair *(f)* half-hour, **lethuairean** *(pl)*
leudachadh *(vn)* expanding
leudaich *(vb)* expand
leugh *(vb)* read
leughadh *(vn)* reading
liath *(adj)* (light) blue, grey
lìon *(vb)* fill
lionn *(m)* beer, **lionntan** *(pl)*
litir *(f)* letter, **litrichean** *(pl)*
litreachas *(m)* literature
loch *(m)* lake, **lochan** *(pl)*
luath *(adj)* fast, swift
Lùnastal *(m)* August, **Lùnastail** *(pl)*

ma *(cjn)* if

mac *(m)* son, mic *(pl)*

madainn *(f)* morning, madainnean, maidnean *(pl)*

mair *(vb)* last, endure

Màiri *(f)* Mary

manaidsear *(m)* manager, manaidsearan *(pl)*

mar *(prp)* as, like

mar sin leibh goodbye to you *(pl or formal)*

Màrtainn *(m)* Martin

mar-tha *(adv)* already

Màrt *(m)* March, Màirt *(pl)*

mas e do thoil e please, *lit* if it is your wish

math *(adj)* good

ma-tha then!

màthair *(f)* mother, màthraichean *(pl)*

meadhan *(m)* middle, meadhanan *(pl)*

meadhanach *(adj)* middling

meàirleach *(m)* robber, meàirlich *(pl)*

meal *(vb)* enjoy

meal do naidheachd congratulations

mear *(adj)* merry

mì-fhortanach *(adj)* unfortunate

mi *(pn)* I

mìle *(m)* thousand, mìltean *(pl)*

milis *(adj)* sweet

mìn *(adj)* smooth

ministear *(m)* minister, ministearan *(pl)*

mionaid *(f)* minute, mionaidean *(pl)*

mìos *(m, f)* month, mìosan *(pl)*

miosail air fond of

mo* *(ppn)* my

modh cainnte *(m)* mode of speaking

modh *(m)* good manners, politeness

modhail *(adj)* well-behaved, polite

mol *(vb)* praise

moladh *(vn)* praising

mór *(adj)* big

Mórag *(f)* Morag

móran *(m)* much, many

mu *(prp)* about

mu dheidhinn *(prp)* about, concerning (followed by G)

mu dheireadh *(adv)* last

muillean *(m)* million, muilleanan *(pl)*

muir *(f)* sea, marannan *(pl)*

mura *(cjn)* if not

mus *(cjn)* before

na *(pn)* what, that which

nach *(interr prt neg etc.)*

naidheachd *(f)* news, naidheachdan *(pl)*

naoi *(num)* nine

naonar *(m)* nine people

neoini *(m)* nothing, zero

nigh *(vb)* wash

nighe *(vn)* washing

nighean *(f)* daughter, nigheanan *(pl)*

nis *(adv)* now

no *(cjn)* or

nochd *(vb)* appear

nochdadh *(vn)* appearing

nuair (a) *(cjn)* when, the time that

nurs *(f)* nurse, nursaichean *(pl)*

obair *(f)*, work, obraichean *(pl)*

(an t-) Òban *(m)* Oban

ochd *(num)* eight

ochdnar *(m)* eight people

òg *(adj)* young

Ògmhìos *(m)* June, Ògmhìosan *(pl)*

oidhche *(f)* night, oidhcheannan *(pl)*

Oidhche Challainn *(f)* Hogmanay, New Year's Eve

Oidhche Shamhna *(f)* Halloween

oifigeach *(m)* officer, official, oifigich *(pl)*

oifis *(f)* office, oifisean *(pl)*

oileanach *(m)* student, oileanaich *(pl)*

oilthigh *(m)* university, oilthighean *(pl)*

òl *(vb, vn)* drink(ing)

orains *(m)* orange-juice
orainsear *(m)* orange,
  orainsearan *(pl)*
òran *(m)* song, òrain *(pl)*
ospadal *(m)* hospital, ospadail *(pl)*

pailteas *(adv)* enough
pàipear *(m)* paper, pàipearan *(pl)*
pàipear-naidheachd *(m)* newspaper,
  pàipearan-naidheachd *(pl)*
pàirc *(f)* park, pàircean *(pl)*
Paras *(m)* Paris
pàrlamaid *(f)* parliament,
  pàrlamaidean *(pl)*
pàrtaidh *(m)* party, pàrtaidhean *(pl)*
pathadh *(m)* thirst
peann *(m)* pen, pinn *(pl)*
peant *(m)* paint, peantaichean *(pl)*
Peigi *(f)* Peggy
peitean *(m)* jumper, peiteanan *(pl)*
pinc *(adj)* pink
plèan *(m)* plane, plèanaichean *(pl)*
pinnt *(m)* pint, pinntean *(pl)*
pìob *(f)* pipe, pìoban *(pl)*
pìobaire *(m)* piper, pìobairean *(pl)*
pìos *(m)* piece
piuthar *(f, irr)* sister,
  peathraichean *(pl)*
pòg *(f)* kiss, pògan *(pl)*
poileas *(m)* police, poileis *(pl)*
port-adhair *(m)* airport,
  puirt-adhair *(pl)*
pòs *(vb)* marry
pòsadh *(vn)* marrying
post *(m)* postman, postaichean,
  puist *(pl)*
prìosanach *(m)* prisoner,
  prìosanaich *(pl)*
prògram *(m)* programme,
  prògraman *(pl)*

rach *(vb)* go
ràdh *(vn)* saying
Raghnall *(m)* Ronald
rannsachadh *(vn)* (re)searching
rannsaich *(vb)* (re)search

rathad *(m)* road, rathaidean,
  rothaidean *(pl)*
ré *(prp)* during (followed by G)
reòite *(adj)* frozen
reul *(m)* star, reultan *(pl)*
ri *(prp)* to, for etc.
riamh *(adv)* ever
ro, roimh *(prp)* before
ro* too
ruadh *(adj)* (darker) red
rud-eiginn *(m)* something
ruig *(vb)* reach, arrive at
ruigsinn, ruighinn *(vn)* reaching,
  arriving at
rùisg *(vb)* peel
ruith *(vb, vn)* run(ning)
rùsgadh *(vn)* peeling

sagart *(m)* priest, sagairt *(pl)*
salach *(adj)* dirty
salann *(m)* salt
sam bith any, at all
sàmhach *(adj)* quiet
Samhain *(f)* November,
  Samhainean *(pl)*
Samhradh *(m)* Summer,
  Samhraidhean *(pl)*
saoil *(vb)* wonder
saor *(adj)* free
Sasainn *(f)* England
seachd *(num)* seven
seachdain *(f)* week,
  seachdainean *(pl)*
seachdnar *(m)* seven people
seall *(vb)* look, show
sean *(adj)* old
seann* *(adj)* old (precedes noun)
seas *(vb)* stand
seasamh *(vn)* standing
seinn *(vb, vn)* sing(ing)
seinneadair *(m)* singer,
  seinneadairean *(pl)*
seòrsa *(m)* type, seòrsaichean *(pl)*
seòlta *(adj)* cunning, clever
seòmar *(m)* room, seòmraichean *(pl)*
Seumas *(m)* James

sgadan *(m)* herring, **sgadain** *(pl)*
sgeilp *(f)* shelf, **sgeilpichean** *(pl)*
sgeul *(m)* sign, news, story,
  sgeòil *(pl)*
sgeulachd *(f)* story,
  sgeulachdan *(pl)*
sgian *(f, irr)* knife, **sgeinean** *(pl)*
sgilling *(f)* penny, **sgillingean** *(pl)*
sgiobalta *(adj)* tidy, neat, deft
sgìos *(m)* tiredness
sgìth *(adj)* tired
sgoil *(f)* school, **sgoiltean** *(pl)*
sgrìob *(f)* trip, **sgrìoban** *(pl)*
sgrìobh *(vb)* write
sgrìobhadh *(vn)* writing
sguir *(vb, vn)* cease, stop
sia *(num)* six
sianar *(m)* six people
sibh *(pn)* you *(pl)*, you *(sg, formal)*
sìde *(m, f)* weather
sìn *(vb)* stretch (out)
sìneadh *(vn)* stretching (out)
sinn *(pn)* we
sìol *(m)* seed, **síl** *(pl)*
sìon *(m)* a particle, a small bit
  sìon *(m)* anything
  (in *interr* and *neg* sentences and in
  phrase **a h-uile sìon** everything)
shìos *(adv)* down (location)
shuas *(adv)* up (location)
sionnach *(m)* fox, **sionnaich** *(pl)*
sìos *(adv)* down, downwards
  (motion away from speaker)
siubhad *(def vb)* go on, continue
siùcar *(m)* sugar
siuga *(m)* jug, **siugaichean** *(pl)*
slàinte *(f)* health, **slàintean** *(pl)*
smaoineachadh, smaointinn *(vn)*
  thinking
smaoinich *(vb)* think
smoc *(vb)* smoke (of tobacco)
snàmh *(vb, vn)* swim
sneachd *(m)* snow, **sneachdannan** *(pl)*
snog *(adj)* nice
solas *(m)* light, **solais** *(pl)*
sonraichte *(adj)* especial

speal *(f)* scythe, **spealan** *(pl)*
sporan *(m)* purse, **sporain,**
  sporannan *(pl)*
spreadh *(vb)* burst
spreadhadh *(vn)* bursting
sràid *(f)* street, **sràidean** *(pl)*
sreap *(vb, vn)* climb(ing)
sròn *(f)* nose, **srònan** *(pl)*
staighre *(f)* stair, **staighrichean** *(pl)*
steidhichte *(adj)* established
stèisean *(m)* station, **stèiseanan** *(pl)*
stiall ort *(vb)* on you go, continue
suas *(adv)* up, upwards (motion
  away from speaker)
suidh *(vb)* sit down
suidhe *(vn)* sitting down
suidheachan *(m)* seat,
  suidheachain, suidheachanan *(pl)*
sùil *(f)* eye, **sùilean** *(pl)*
Sultain *(f)* September, **Sultainean** *(pl)*
suiteas *(m, coll)* or **suiteis** *(pl)* sweets
suitidh *(m)* sweet

tachair *(vb)* happen
tachair ri *(vb)* meet (with)
tachairt *(vn)* happening
tachairt ri *(vn)* meeting (with)
tadhail air *(vb)* visit (on)
tadhal air *(vn)* visiting (on)
tagh *(vb)* choose, elect, select
taghadh *(m)* election, electing
taghadh-pàrlamaid *(m)*
  parliamentary election
taigh *(m)* house, **taighean** *(pl)*
taigh-beag *(m)* toilet,
  taighean-beaga *(pl)*
taigh-òsta *(m)* hotel, pub,
  taighean-òsta *(pl)*
taigh-tasgaidh *(m)* museum,
  taighean-tasgaidh *(pl)*
taingeil thankful
taobh *(m)* side, **taobhan** *(pl)*
tapadh leat thank you *(informal)*
tapadh leibh *(pl or formal)*
tarraing *(vb, vn)* pull(ing)
tarsainn (air) *(prp)* across

té *(f, pn)* woman; one, **feadhain**
  (f, coll used for *pl* of 'one'*)*
teagaisg *(vb)* teach
teagamh *(m)* doubt, **teagamhan** *(pl)*
teagasg *(vn)* teaching
teaghlach *(m)* family,
  teaghlaichean *(pl)*
teanga *(f)* tongue, **teangannan** *(pl)*
teann *(adj)* tight
Teàrlach *(m)* Charles
teich *(vb)* escape, flee
teicheadh *(vn)* escaping, fleeing
teine *(m)* fire, **teintean** *(pl)*
telebhisean *(m)* television
teth *(adj)* hot
tha *(vb)* is
thall *(adv)* over there (location not
  at speaker)
thall thairis *(adv)* abroad (location)
theab *(def vb)* almost
thig *(vb)* come
thoir (do) *(vb)* give, bring (to)
thoir gaol do *(vb)* love
t(h)u *(pn)* you
tì *(f)* tea
tidsear *(m)* teacher, **tidsearan** *(pl)*
tighinn *(vn)* coming
tilg *(vb)* throw
tilgeil *(vn)* throwing
till *(vb)* return
tilleadh *(vn)* returning
timcheall air *(cd prp)* around
tinn *(adj)* sick
tiocaid *(f)* ticket, **tiocaidean** *(pl)*
tìr-mór *(m)* mainland
t(h)iugainn, thugainn *(def vb)*
  come along, let's go
tiugh *(adj)* thick
tog *(vb)* lift, build
togail *(vn)* lifting, building

toilichte *(adj)* happy
toirt (do) *(vn)* giving, bringing (to)
toll *(m)* hole, **tuill** *(pl)*
toll-iuchrach *(m)* keyhole,
  tuill-iuchrach *(pl)*
tòrr *(m)* a lot, **torran** *(pl)*
trèan *(f)* train, **trèanaichean** *(pl)*
trì *(num)* three
tric *(adv)* often
triùir *(m)* three people
tro, troimh *(prp)* through
trobhad *(def vb)* come along
trom *(adj)* heavy
truinnsear *(m)* plate,
  truinnsearan *(pl)*
tuig *(vb)* understand
tuigsinn *(vn)* understanding
tuil *(f)* flood, **tuiltean** *(pl)*
tuilleadh *(m)* more
tuit *(vb)* fall
tuiteam *(vn)* falling
turas *(m)* trip, journey, **turais**,
  tursan *(pl)*

uabhasach *(adj, adv)* terrible;
  terribly; very much (intensifier)
uaine *(adj)* green
uair one o'clock
uan *(m)* lamb, **uain** *(pl)*
uasal *(adj)* high, noble
ugh *(m)* egg, **uighean** *(pl)*
uile *(adj)* all
Uilleam *(m)* William
uinneag *(f)* window, **uinneagan** *(pl)*
uinnean *(m)* onion, **uinneanan** *(pl)*
uisge *(m)* water, **uisgeachan** *(pl)*
uisge-beatha *(m)* whisky
ur *(ppn)* your *(pl* and *sg, formal)*
ùr *(adj)* new
ùrlar *(m)* floor, **ùrlair** *(pl)*

Abbreviations used in Mini–dictionary

adj	adjective	*neg*	negative
adv	adverb	*num*	numeral
art	article	*pl*	plural
cd prp	compound preposition	*pn*	pronoun
cjn	conjunction	*pos*	positive
coll	collective	*ppn*	possessive pronoun
def	defective	*prp*	preposition
f	feminine	*prt*	particle
G	genitive	*rel*	relative
inf	infinitive	*sg*	singular
interj	interjection	*v*	vide, see
interr	interrogative	*vb*	verb
irr	irregular	*vn*	verbal noun
m	masculine	*	lenites following word

Picture Credits
Jacket: All special photography Joe Cornish, Paul Harris, Karl
Shone, Clive Streeter except CORBIS (UK): Neil Beer bottom left;
Paul Thompson centre right above; STILL MOVING PICTURE
COMPANY: Angus Johnston centre right below; Scottish Tourist
Board top left and centre below